Aftershocks

Aftershocks

*Economic Crisis
and
Institutional Choice*

Anton Hemerijck
Ben Knapen
Ellen van Doorne
(eds.)

Amsterdam University Press

Cover design: Maedium, Utrecht
Layout: Het Steen Typografie, Maarssen

ISBN   978 90 8964 192 2
e-ISBN   978 90 4851 185 3
NUR   754 / 781

Table of Contents

Preface

Is the current crisis simply too big to reflect upon? Do the sheer complexity and the dazzling dynamics of the financial and economic crisis impede the possibility of learning some lessons this early on? This book, I think, shows that the answer to these questions is negative. Indeed, some strategic lessons can and should be learned, even at this stage. Waiting until the crisis is over is simply not an option given ambition to prepare our societies for the world after the crisis.

Of course, as this book went to press, the severest economic crisis since the Great Depression was still underway. How to deal with the turmoil that it wrought, especially from a long-term perspective, remains an unanswered and highly debated question. Present and future economic stability is still highly uncertain. It is in this context that Anton Hemerijck, Ben Knapen (director and member of the Dutch Scientific Council for Government Policy, respectively) and Ellen van Doorne (member of the staff of the Prime Ministers' Office) set themselves a daunting task: to try to shed some light on the causes and ramifications of the crisis, even as the economic storm continued to rage.

The Scientific Council for Government Policy was not sure that it had a role to play at the front lines of combating the immediate consequences of that storm. Nor did it intend to publish a complete – let alone definitive – analysis of what went wrong and what exactly was going on. However, the council thought it would be important to encourage the editors of this special publication to seek expert opinions to explore the repertoire of policy choice and institutional design, on the basis of informed academic analysis and experiential observations and judgments of front line observers, as a first attempt to sketch the contours of a socio-economic order that could emerge out of the ruins of the crisis. If this crisis is also a chance for change, in what directions could that reconstructuring take us?

Twenty-four experts were selected from a broad range of fields and disciplines, on the basis of both their expertise in their given subject area as well as their institutional imagination and ability to think beyond the present circumstances. Aggregating their cumulative knowledge and insights, the editors have attempted to document the intellectual 'state of the art' in the midst of the crisis before hindsight can be given an opportunity to work its amnesiac magic. Interviewees were given time to consider the questions, and their responses are exceptionally well prepared and thought out. However, their final revisions to their contributions occurred in late September 2009. Thus, they were necessarily historically bound by the facts and information available to them at this time.

This book is therefore a special project, supported by the Dutch Scientific Council for Government Policy. The volume deviates from the kind of policy advice reports the council generally produces. The intellectual endeavour began as a series of workshops on the economic crisis, organised in conjunction with the network of the strategists of a number of Dutch ministries. At these events, it became apparent that there was a wide breadth of insight developing on this very new subject. As researching current events presents innumerable methodological and practical barriers, this somewhat unorthodox project of semi-structured interviews was proposed in order to explore and document the institutional features of these new debates. The volume covers a wide range of topics: from the need for a new European narrative that helps to position the European Union in a world order shaped by a new geopolitical and economic balance of power, to the need to reform the academic discipline of economics. All the topics invite further reflection with the intent to prepare a new agenda for the period following that of this current crisis. The volume clearly shows that we cannot and should not wish to return, either theoretically or institutionally, to the world that preceded the current crisis. There is a need for new paradigms, institutions, wisdom, and ideas. Political courage is imperative to pursue institutional change to prepare for a new age, in which, more than ever before, the social, ecological and economical agendas have to be discussed in a more integrated manner.

Since the onset of the crisis, the political and academic debates have begun to shift. Initially, the aftermath of the crisis was primarily concerned with immediate damage control and preventing a complete erosion of the economy's foundations. Recently, however, the debate has shifted, as people have begun to contextualise the crisis and wonder what this will mean for the future. More specifically, they wonder, what does this crisis mean for my pension? For my children? For my country? For the world's poor? For the structures of global institutions? To this end, this book is an attempt to illuminate – in real time – a cross-section of a vital debate.

The council is grateful to the editors who managed to involve some of the best brains of the world to come together in this book for what is, indeed, an interesting variety of some of the brightest economists, political scientists, historians and sociologists around today. On behalf of the Council, I would like to thank the editors (Anton Hemerijck, Ben Knapen and Ellen van Doorne) and the supporting editorial team for all the work they have done.

Wim van de Donk
Chairman of the Scientific Council for Government Policy

Acknowledgements

The aim of this volume is to explore the institutional impact, dimensions, and consequences of the global economic crisis of 2007. This volume is the result of a series of interviews held from May to September 2009 with various academics and experts across geographic, occupational, and disciplinary boundaries.

We asked our interviewees to think out loud, and the strength of this project is the result of their intellectual engagement, insightful ideas, comments, and constructive criticism offered throughout the entire process. Therefore, first and foremost we owe our thanks to these interviewees for being so generous, not only with their succinct and sharp analyses but also with their time. They were willing to look beyond their primary interests and sub-disciplines, to reflect on the causes, conditions, and consequences of the crisis, taking a dive into the unknown. Both individually and collectively, they expanded our understanding of the crisis and its possible aftershocks. We especially wish to thank them for their enthusiasm, their faith in this project and for their responsiveness to the demands of our speedy editorial process.

Meanwhile, it cannot be stressed enough how much an incredibly talented young team of research assistants contributed to this publication: Casper Thomas, Katherine Tennis, and Jessica Serraris. We are especially grateful to Casper Thomas, who operated in a dual capacity of co-interviewer and all-purpose editorial assistant. We also greatly appreciate the flawless editorial skills, writing assistance, and language improvements of Katherine Tennis and Jessica Serraris, turning all of our interviews into independent contributions, changing them from Q&A to essay format. With relentless vigour and sustained high quality, Casper, Katherine, and Jessica worked most of the summer of 2009 completing this project. We thank them most sincerely for their professionalism, commitment, and good spirits.

We would finally like to acknowledge the support of Wim van de Donk, Chairman of the WRR, whose encouragement was crucial to this venture. The many strengths of this volume are undoubtedly to the credit of our interviewees and our highly professional support and editorial team. Any remaining errors are our own.

Anton Hemerijck, Ben Knapen and Ellen van Doorne

The Institutional Legacy of the Crisis of Global Capitalism

Anton Hemerijck

1. GREEN SHOOTS OR FALSE HOPES

Two years into the first economic crisis of 21st-century capitalism, policymakers everywhere are anxiously awaiting signals of whether or not we have passed the nadir of the global downturn. Is the economy finally gaining traction after the worst economic crisis since the Great Depression? Will the 'green shoots' observed in global trade and US and EU equity markets, Chinese investments in public infrastructure, and Brazilian exports prove to be harbingers of a sustained economic recovery? As this book went to press in September 2009, economists from the Organisation for Economic Co-operation and Development, the World Bank, and the International Monetary Fund had come to endorse the view that the global economy was indeed stabilising (OECD, 2009).

The cascade into the greatest economic crisis since the 1930s began in 2006, with falling US house prices and rising defaults on US subprime and Alt-A mortgage loans. In February 2007, the Federal Home Mortgage Corporation, Freddy Mac, announced that it would no longer buy risky subprime mortgages and mortgage related securities. Next, the New Century Financial Corporation, a leading subprime mortgage lender, filed for bankruptcy in April 2007. By the end of July, investment bank Bear Stearns had liquidated two hedge funds heavily involved in mortgage-backed securities, and in August 2007, BNP Paribas, France's largest bank, halted redemptions on three investment funds. After a retail run in the fall of 2007, Northern Rock, a large UK mortgage bank, was eventually nationalised in February 2008. On 7 September, the two large semi-public mortgage banks, Fannie Mae and Freddie Mac, were placed in government conservatorship. On 15 September 2008, the American authorities let the 158-year-old investment bank Lehman Brothers fall, apparently without realising the consequence of triggering a worldwide credit freeze. Nobody knew which financial institutions (in the US or elsewhere) had bought into the dangerous subprime mortgages, and as a result, a severe crisis of confidence erupted in the fall of 2008. Because finance had become so globalised, when the housing and asset price bubble burst, the near collapse of the financial system spread rapidly across the entire world economy. The ensuing credit downgrade of AIG, the world's largest insurer, which had become involved in the Credit Default Swap (CDS) market, set the scene for a severe liquidity strain. This time, on September 16, however, the US government did come to AIG's rescue, with 85 billion dollars. In the midst of this predicament, a complete seizure of interbank money markets broke out, exposing the micro flaws of the internationally deregulated financial system. Morgan Stanley and Goldman Sachs ceased to exist as independent investment banks. Across the Atlantic Ocean, the Belgian-Dutch Fortis group was nationalised on September 28, and the next day the German Hypo Real Estate was saved, under government pressure, by a 35 billion euro life support injection from other financial institutions, while the Icelandic government nationalized the Glitner savings bank. A massive credit crunch subsequently threw the global economy into the worst financial crisis and recession since the 1930s.

While financial conditions may have started to ease, the jury is still out on whether 2010 will indeed bring a 'V-shaped' upturn, with its much hoped-for swift return to pre-crisis levels of growth. But given the severity of the crisis, we could also be heading for the beginning of a longer, more drawn out, slow and weak 'L-shaped' recovery. For the advanced economies, this would be akin to the experience of Japan's 'lost decade' of the 1990s. Worse still is the horrific scenario of a 'W-shaped' economic nightmare, whereby an apparently swift recovery, paid for by ballooning budget deficits, triggers runaway inflation which in turn can only be reined in with an aggressive hike in interest rates by central banks, setting the stage for a second deep recession in the aftermath of the present crisis. There is a fear that the unprecedented supply of cheap money from public authorities is setting the stage for another bubble. With such uncertainty, is talk of 'green shoots' premature? Perhaps it is only a mirage, a temporary fluke improvement in an otherwise severely battered and highly vulnerable global economy?

There is every reason to remain cautious about forecasting economic improvement. In the years ahead, various aftershocks, caused by the momentous economic contraction of the global downturn, will have to be reckoned with.

First, there is the aftershock of the looming crisis of unemployment. Unemployment usually lags behind general economic activity by roughly a two- to three-quarter delay, so labour market conditions in the advanced industrial world are expected to worsen in the coming years, even as stock markets improve across the globe. US unemployment is currently just below 10%, while in Europe unemployment has already reached double digits in many countries. Most worrisome is the surge in youth employment: in Latvia, Italy, Greece, Sweden, Estonia, Hungary, Lithuania, France, Ireland, and Belgium, youth unemployment has crossed the 20% threshold, and in Spain it is over 30%.

Even a tepid economic recovery will be insufficient to compensate for the job losses incurred during the crisis. Increasing unemployment will result in mortgage defaults and rising insolvencies, which will have an adverse feedback effect on the already weakened banking system. Their reduced appetite for lending could, subsequently, trigger another contraction in the financial sector with another round of disrupting effects for the real economy.

Second, there is the aftershock of the pension crisis. The sharp fall in equity markets has severely affected the value of pension fund assets, jeopardising pensioners' incomes in countries with large private pension provisions. In many western economies – especially the US and the UK – public pensions have been retrenched over the past two decades. Instead, people have been given incentives to choose their own private pension arrangements. Many have used real estate as investment for old age savings, feeding into the growth of the financial industry, which now has collapsed, bringing their savings down with it. For Europe, the dual challenges of the economic crisis, combined with the expenditure pressures of the ageing population, mark a real stress test for public finances.

Third, there is the aftershock of a fiscal crisis of the state. Costly bank bailouts, tax cuts, and other stimulus measures have drained the public purse. In Europe, the automatic stabilisers of comprehensive social insurance could result in a double bind of rising social benefit expenditures combined with declining government revenues. Declining population levels have already resulted in a shrinking work force, which significantly reduces tax revenues, even independently of the crisis.

Finally, there may be all kinds of political aftershocks. Once the recession subsides, elevated public debt-to-GDP ratios will make fiscal consolidation imperative. This will require tight fiscal control and painful cuts in Europe's cherished welfare programs. Yet retrenchment of social expenditures will certainly be met with strong public opposition, so it is politically unrealistic to count on rebalancing the budget solely through reductions in expenditures. In addition, taxes will have to be raised in the final stage of fiscal consolidation in order to pay down public debt even, though this could negatively affect growth prospects and leave little room for addressing newly emerging social needs.

Because of these likely economic, social and political aftershocks in the labour market, banking system, pension system, public finance, and social spheres, there is a real danger of the crisis persisting for more than just a few bad years. Japan's 'lost decade' following the crisis in the early 1990s provides a worrisome antecedent (Koo, 2008). Nevertheless, according to the OECD, we should count our blessings; a complete collapse of the world economy has been prevented. It appears that we are through the deepest waters of the economic contraction, and a nascent recovery is underway. However, caution is still warranted: a self-sustaining recovery in the real economy will only begin when private economic actors are again ready and willing to take over.

2. THE POLITICS OF ECONOMICS

The full political implications of the economic crisis are impossible to discern at present. Yet there has been one obvious shift: public authorities – especially governments and central banks – have taken an unprecedented hyperactive role in response to the credit freeze panic. Suddenly, in mid-2007, the state (re-)emerged as a key strategic economic actor. Faced with an exceptionally deep crisis, most advanced economy governments showed little inhibition in pursuing bold strategies of crisis management, on a scale truly unthinkable only a few years ago. This happened despite the standing hegemony of neo-liberal doctrine, which proclaimed unequivocally that government was the problem and markets the solution. Since the crisis, most observers would agree that the public authorities' activist crisis management strategies have succeeded in forestalling a much darker scenario – a rerun of the Great Depression. It is no exaggeration to claim that the state – or rather the taxpayer – has saved modern capitalism from meltdown.

The initial measures of crisis management concentrated on stabilising the financial system, often by bailing out overly indebted systemic banks. Meanwhile, central banks turned to reducing interest rates to close to zero percent, while simultaneously pumping hundreds of billions of euros and dollars into the world's weakened banking systems through quantitative easing. As the credit crunch started to affect the real economy, fiscal authorities turned to dazzlingly aggressive stimulus packages and tax cuts in the hope of further stimulating consumer demand. Many governments – especially China – invested heavily in public infrastructure projects. In Europe, numerous states have introduced wage subsidies, expanded short-term unemployment benefits in order to preserve existing jobs, and enacted new training programs and other active labour market measures. At the time of writing, governments on both sides of the Atlantic were considering tougher remuneration rules for bankers, regulatory caps on bank bonuses and golden handshakes, as well as a new regulatory regime for hedge funds. The EU is hoping to be able to enact more systemic and intrusive regulation of European financial markets, including credit agencies. In sum, public authorities have left no interventionist stone unturned in the face of the first economic crisis of 21st-century capitalism.

The powerful and unexpected resurgence of state intervention has reinforced the truism that without the state, market economies would not be able to thrive. Without public authorities capable of exercising legitimate coercion, capitalism would be impossible. This is what the economic anthropologist Karl Polanyi has called the 'embeddedness' of economics. Effective market allocation depends, first and foremost, on the political protection of property rights and contract laws. In his *The Great Transformation*, Polanyi shows that public intervention and regulation have historically played a decisive role in the institutional separation of society into an economic and political sphere by providing a supportive framework in which markets can prosper (Polanyi, 1944; 1985). The notion of embeddedness underlines the fact that economic activity is created and shaped by political decisions, social conventions, and shared norms and understandings. Although free markets are often misperceived as natural, sovereign, self-contained, and self-regulating, a market economy cannot exist independently of the society and rules in which it is located.

Embedding markets is essentially a political activity of institution-building. Institutions are enduring rules for making important (economic) decisions. The most important economic institutions are, of course, property rights. Property rights are assigned, restricted, qualified, and regulated by political decisions. Modern capitalism not only requires regulatory systems at the micro level, but also effective macro institutions, both monetary and fiscal. Although redistributive institutions such as unemployment benefits, public pensions, education, and health care are provided for through non-market arrangements, they are nevertheless intimately connected to the private market economy, through which they are financed and for which they perform stabilising and productive functions. Thus, social protection, despite not being market-generated, does serve to embed mature capitalist economies. All of the above institutional features of advanced market economies have a significant impact on production, resource allocation, regulation, economic growth, levels of productivity and employment, and the distribution of goods, services, incomes, and wealth (Granovetter, 1985; Swedberg, 1987; Maier, 1987).

As politics defines and qualifies property rights, it demarcates boundaries between the political and the economic realms of society. For advanced capitalism, it is imperative that the state allows the market to function relatively autonomously. Today, that very requirement commits the state to more rather than less activism, forcing it into expensive and radical measures of crisis management. Yet even during the neo-liberal globalisation period, it would be a mistake to think that the state withdrew from the management of advanced market economies. Admittedly, in most cases the dominant trend was toward privatisation and deregulation, but it should be emphasized that economic liberalisation is also a form of politically sanctioned state activism. There is also plenty of evidence of public interventions beyond liberalisation (Levy, 2006). Many European governments have been able to reconfigure labour markets and to re-orient social spending towards measures to promote employment through active labour market policies, while at the same time, for example, stepping up support for childcare in an attempt to encourage more women to enter the workforce (Hemerijck and Eichhorst, 2008).

In times of crisis, politics and economics become inseparably linked, and the precipitous return of the state to economic affairs is surely not the result of an unchallenged or widely shared political consensus. Severe economic turmoil always polarises political debate and economic analysis. Different economic and political actors disagree over what kind or how much intervention is called for in these unconventional times. In the op-ed pages of financial journals, a truly fierce intellectual dispute has emerged between the Nobel Laureate in economics Paul Krugman and the popular economic historian Niall Ferguson (2008). Krugman (2008) advocates a drastic Keynesian fiscal stimulus response to the crisis, whereas Ferguson – making a case for fiscal conservatism – critiques aggressive Keynesianism as a recipe for hyper-inflation, spiralling US fiscal deficits, and the ultimate demise of the dollar (Lynn, 2009).

In addition to these intellectual debates, governments have also come under fierce attack by their citizens. Mass unemployment, rising poverty and inequality, cuts in public sector pay and services, and reduced pensions and social benefits bring enormous pressure to bear on elected politicians. Moreover, governments have used tax revenues to bail out banks, whose CEOs continue to rally against more intrusive regulation. This confronts elected leaders with the daunting political challenge of communicating these 'pro-business' interventions (which arguably do avert further economic distress) to citizens in the real economy whose jobs, savings, and pensions are at risk. When banks receiving taxpayer support continue paying huge bonuses out to top executives and traders, such a political predicament can potentially become explosive.

Such pressures can even lead to the overthrow of ruling parties. The recent government turnovers in Iceland, Latvia, Hungary, the Czech Republic, and Greece are the first political repercussions of the crisis. The 2008 election of Barack Obama as President of the United States of America can also partially be attributed to the crisis. Similarly, the significant gains of the far right, populist, anti-EU, nationalist parties in Denmark, Austria, Hungary, the Netherlands, and the UK in the June 2009 elections for the European parliament reveal how the crisis and fears of unemployment can fuel xenophobia and protectionist sentiments. Finally, the landslide victory of the centre-left Democratic Party of Japan over the long-standing Liberal Democratic Party in the August 2009 general elections is the most recent example of such punctuated political change.

In addition, the crisis has led to a fundamental debate about the role of central banks. The goal of inflation targeting has, for at least two decades, been the neutral *modus operandi* of central bankers. However, with the crisis, this has become highly politicised. German chancellor Angela Merkel attacked the loose monetary policy of the European Central Bank (ECB), whereas Mervyn King, governor of the Bank of England, has been equally unconventional in his open critique of the huge fiscal deficits accumulated by the UK Labour Government.

Political strife over crisis management also features in the international arena. After the bankruptcies of Landesbanki and Icesave, which triggered the downfall of the Icelandic krona in the fall of 2008, Iceland has applied for membership of the European Union in hopes of joining the stable euro. The Netherlands and the UK, however, have made Icelandic EU membership contingent on a 4 billion euro reimbursement of British and Dutch savings lost in Landesbanki and Icesave.

On the European continent, moreover, most leaders prefer tougher, more intrusive, and systemic financial sector regulation. The Brits, on the other hand, fear that an overly ambitious European framework of financial market regulation will stifle the City of London's future room for manoeuvre in the global economy. An unresolved outstanding issue is the extent to which national rescues of ailing industries is in accordance with EU single market legislation.

Then there remains the fundamental disagreement between the US and the EU over the necessary aggressiveness of fiscal stimulus packages. European leaders, such as Angela Merkel and Nicolas Sarkozy, worry about the disturbing lack of attention paid to the medium- and long-term consequences of Obama's 800 billion dollar stimulus program. To the extent that the crisis is a crisis of excessive debt, which in the US is already three times gross domestic product, Europeans maintain that it cannot be solved by incurring further debt. What exit strategy does the Obama administration have in mind to restore fiscal responsibility and sustainable economic growth?

In short, the global financial crisis, together with its economic and social aftershocks, is very likely to fundamentally shape the narrative of politics and, as such, the outlook for social and economic policy reform in the decades ahead. Communicating and explaining policy measures, as well as finding effective and fair solutions of crisis management that citizens consider legitimate, form a key political precondition for a sustainable economic recovery. The political management of the social, fiscal, and emotive aftershocks of the crisis is surely a tall order.

3. FROM 'EMBEDDED LIBERALISM' TO THE 'WASHINGTON CONSENSUS'

Deep economic crises are moments of political truth. They expose both the strengths and weaknesses of existing policy repertoires and institutional structures. As a consequence, they encourage fresh thinking about the institutional arrangements embedding contemporary market economies. In the aftermath of both the Great Depression of the 1930s as well as the crisis of stagflation (low growth and high inflation) in the 1970s, economic and social policy regimes were transformed in quite fundamental ways.

The Great Depression and the Second World War have had a profound impact on the institutional architecture of North America and Western Europe after 1945. The experience of the deflation in the 1930s as well as the foolish adherence to the gold standard led post-war policymakers to embrace Keynesian economic management (Temin, 1989). The extent of market regulation and social protection differed from one country to the next, but governments in all advanced democracies took an active and strategic role in the stabilisation of the economy and the distribution of post-war prosperity. The lessons of mass unemployment and debt deflation from the Great Depression were taken to heart. Social protection came to be firmly anchored in an explicit normative commitment to granting social rights to citizens, protected by the nation-state. An impressive set of welfare programs was developed: an expanded education system improved the equality of opportunity; a comprehensive health insurance system spread the benefits of health care to the population as a whole; and a full range of income transfer programs – unemployment insurance, workers' compensation, disability benefits, old age pensions, survivors' benefits, children's allowances, and social assistance – were introduced to protect citizens from the economic risks associated with modern industrialism. The mixed social and market economy was based on the axial principle of full employment for male breadwinners and promoted a growth-oriented industrial policy to achieve this end. The dominant consensus among policymakers was that governments, collective bargaining, and the welfare state had key roles in 'taming' the capitalist economy through Keynesian demand management and market regulation. In trying to understand what went wrong in the Great Depression, Keynes introduced a completely new brand of economics focusing on the study of the behaviour of the economic system as whole, rather than the behaviour of individual actors. If the Great Depression gave rise to Keynesian economics, the 1950s and 1960s vindicated Keynesian demand management as a standard tool of economic policy. Keynesian macroeconomists in academia and public office proclaimed that enduring recessions would be a thing of the past.

The objectives of full employment and welfare protection were supported at the level of the international political economy by what John Ruggie later described as a regime of 'embedded liberalism'. On the one hand, governments encouraged the liberalisation of the economy through successive rounds of GATT negotiations that slowly broke down the regulatory regimes and trade barriers put in place during the Depression and the Second World War. On the other hand, the expansion of social programs compensated for the risks inherent to economic liberalisation. Western governments embraced the change and dislocation that comes with liberalisation in exchange for containing and socialising the costs of adjustment (Ruggie, 1982). As a consequence, the constraints imposed on national economic policies by the classical gold standard were relaxed, and the pursuit of 'free trade' was replaced by the goal of non-discrimination. Against the backdrop of the Cold War, the goal of price stability was sacrificed when this was deemed necessary to maintain an open international economy (Maier, 2009). The Bretton Woods monetary system of stable exchange rates laid the groundwork for the regime of embedded liberalism, allowing national policymakers freedom to pursue relatively independent social and employment policies without undermining international economic stability. It should be emphasised that the compromise of embedded liberalism was tailored to a world in which international competition remained limited and foreign investment was conspicuously based on a regime of capital controls.

The era of embedded liberalism was an era of institution building. The postwar domestic and international communities were resolved to contain the economic and political instabilities of the 1930s and 1940s. At the international level, the United Nations, the World Bank, the International Monetary Fund (IMF), and the European Community were established. Together, the Bretton Woods institutions, the national welfare state, and the European Community were all launched with an eye on avoiding the crises of the early 20th century. During the Golden Age of economic growth between 1945 and the early 1970s, each of the advanced industrial societies developed their own country-specific brands of mixed economy and welfare capitalism. What came out of the postwar era was therefore an international system of national capitalisms, not a global economic system (Berger/Dore, 1996; Berger, 2005; Rodrik, 2007).

Despite the historically unprecedented achievements of the post-war mixed economies in promoting civil liberty, economic prosperity, social solidarity, and public well-being, there is, of course, no such thing as an institutional regime for all seasons. In the late 1960s, the post-war celebration of unprecedented growth and social solidarity through democratic politics was already giving way to doubts. Rising inflation as a result of wage explosion and the resurgence of worker militancy and social protest confronted the sober and consensual political economies of the post-war era with a new political context, reflecting the new levels of economic prosperity and social expectations. The era of embedded liberalism came to end in the mid-1970s as the two oil shocks revealed contradictions in the mixed economy and welfare-friendly regime of embedded liberalism; specifically, its inability to contain inflation under conditions of near-full employment. Furthermore, increased international competition and de-industrialisation came to undermine the effectiveness of domestic Keynesian demand management. This led to a massive surge in unemployment, not seen since the 1930s. As Keynesian economists continued to analyse macro-economic performance in terms of a trade-off between employment and inflation, they lost their intellectual edge. After the second oil shock in 1979 led to tightened fiscal and monetary policies in the early 1980s, the world economy entered its severest slump yet. High inflation, mass unemployment, and sluggish growth provided an opportunity for an intellectual and political break with 'embedded liberalism'.

The crisis of stagflation thus set the stage for a political return to more unfettered market economies, away from public ownership, excessive regulation, and generous levels of social protection. The election of Margaret Thatcher and Ronald Reagan in 1979 and 1980 respectively, brought the belief in the primacy of self-regulating markets and a minimal state back into the limelight. The state was identified as the source of the problem of stagflation, as it was believed to distort the natural workings of the market. Beginning in the 1980s and gathering momentum in the 1990s, neo-liberal doctrines of fiscal discipline, low inflation, financial liberalisation, labour market deregulation, privatisation, and the marketisation of welfare provision from regulatory constraints gained precedence in the management of advanced market economies. However, it should be remembered that neo-liberalism did not spell the waning of state activism, but instead the redeployment of government initiatives to the new mission of liberalisation, deregulation and privatisation. State authorities shifted from a market-steering orientation to a market-supporting orientation.

Neo-liberalism lasted until the onslaught of the current crisis. What neo-liberalism stands for exactly is far from unanimously accepted. This is because neo-liberalism, unlike the academic concept of 'embedded liberalism', is most often used to denote an ideological political position. At a very general level, I associate neo-liberalism (based on the ideas of Wolfgang Streeck and Kathy Thelen) with the secular expansion of market relations inside and across the borders of national political economies. The key goal of neo-liberalism was to free up markets, institutions, rules, and regulations, which under the post-war settlement of embedded liberalism were reserved for collective political decision-making. With due caution, it would therefore seem justified to characterise neo-liberalism as a broadly based process of 'institutional liberalisation' of the fairly organised forms of capitalism that emerged out of the era of embedded liberalism. If the era of embedded liberalism was a time of institution building, then the era of neo-liberalism is best understood as a time of institutional disembedding. Important qualifications notwithstanding, the neo-liberal transformation in the 1980s and 1990s made modern capitalism more market-driven and market-accommodationist, releasing ever more economic transactions from public-political control, and turning them over to private actors and contracts. Throughout the advanced world, price stability rather than full employment became the principle objective of macro-economic policy.

As the global economy started to pick up in the second half of the 1980s, European economies were behind the curve compared to the stronger rebound in countries like the US and Japan. The European Commission, under Jacques Delors, rose to the occasion by introducing the concept of the Single Market, promoting privatisation and deregulation in an attempt to open up national markets. The Single European Market Act of 1986 was negotiated at a time when neo-liberalism was riding high. Neo-liberalism's view of the welfare state system was well summarised in the OECD Jobs Strategy, published in 1994, which launched a critical attack on the 'dark side' of double-digit unemployment of many of its European OECD members (OECD, 1994). Unemployment rates in France, Germany, and Italy were twice as high as in the US, and the 'prospect for survival' of the mixed economies of Western Europe was recognised as poor. The OECD economists singled out the accumulation of perverse labour-market rigidities that impeded flexible adjustment, blocked technological innovation, and hampered employment and economic growth. Downward wage rigidity was once again seen as the principle obstacle to full employment. Moreover, strong 'insider-outsider' cleavages with unfavourable employment chances for young people, women, the elderly, and the unskilled prevented the rigid European labour markets from replicating the higher employment rates of the US, the UK, or New Zealand. The fundamental European dilemma was conceived of in terms of a trade-off between economic efficiency and equality, growth and redistribution, competitiveness and solidarity. The policy recommendations that followed this analysis included retrenchment, deregulation, decentralisation, and privatisation. To its credit, in strengthening competition, neo-liberalism did help to lower prices and sober up public finances. It permitted higher rates of non-inflationary growth, and thus promoted prosperity in the US and the EU.

Because of neo-liberalism's emphasis on capital mobility, it is closely associated with the process of globalisation. Indeed, it was not until the 1980s that the world economy returned to the same level of capital mobility, foreign direct investment, and trade that it had achieved under the first wave of globalisation between 1870 and 1914. Globalisation is a catch-all phrase and a multifaceted concept. Broadly understood, it refers to the profound changes in the organisation of the world over the past quarter-century, especially with respect to the intensification of worldwide economic integration. Globalisation concerns the acceleration of the processes in the international economy and in domestic economies that operate toward unifying world markets (Berger, 2005). It describes the increasing cross-border flows of goods, services, and finance, the liberalisation of trade, geographically dispersed subcontracting and outsourcing of tasks, the increased propensity towards international migration, the spread of technological innovation, the increased role and weight of multinational companies, and the intensification of communication exemplified by the spread of internet use. A new wave of globalisation allowed for unprecedented levels of wealth, serving to lift millions out of poverty worldwide. Most economies around the world are in a much better position to respond effectively to external shocks than they were in the late 1970s.

During the 1980s, the Bretton Woods institutions of the IMF and the World Bank hopped on the bandwagon of neo-liberalism, to become the doctrine's most ardent advocates. Since the 1990s, neo-liberal structural adjustment programs engineered by the IMF and the World Bank have been implemented in almost every country across the globe, often by way of 'shock therapies'. In the 1990s, most Latin American countries firmly embraced the economic reform package that has come to be called the Washington Consensus (Kuczynski Godard/Williamson, 2003). These policies emphasised price stabilisation and structural adjustment measures such as fiscal discipline, privatisation, deregulation, trade liberalisation, reduction of tariffs, liberalisation of capital markets, and the opening of economies to foreign investment – all with the objective of making the economies more efficient and competitive, in the hope that resulting growth would trickle down. However, after more than a decade of such open-market reforms in Latin America and Sub-Saharan Africa, it should be noted that neoliberal adjustment failed to deliver much in the way of growth and social progress (Rodrik, 2007). As national controls over the movement of capital across borders disappeared, novel opportunities for both productive investment and speculation began to emerge. Once deregulation had taken place, however, national governments found it difficult to protect their economies when their currencies came under attack, as they did in crises like those in Western Europe (1992), Mexico (1994), Asia (1997), Russia (1998), and Argentina (2002).

In the final analysis, however, neo-liberalism did not completely undermine the institutions of embedded liberalism. Government ownership has been reduced through privatisation, and domestic and international market expansion has been encouraged through deregulation. However, neo-liberal politicians of various colours have been far less successful in retrenching the welfare state, especially in Europe. Notwithstanding the 'irresistible forces' urging for reform, the welfare state turned out to be a politically 'unmovable object' (Pierson, 1998; 2001). The distributive aspects of the welfare state have remained popular. In this respect, the neo-liberal program of institutional liberalisation and destruction was incomplete.

4. CONJECTURING REGIME CHANGE IN THE FACE OF PERSISTENT AFTERSHOCKS

In democratic systems, it is ultimately politics that decides over matters of social and economic governance. Economic crises create windows of opportunity for extraordinary politics to transform existing institutions. To paraphrase Rahm Immanuel, President Obama's chief of staff, they mark important political junctures 'not to be wasted'. Once again, the current economic crisis is fundamentally redrawing the boundaries between states and markets, calling into question many issues of economic policy, ranging from central banking, fiscal policy, financial regulation, global trade, welfare provision, economic governance and assumptions about human behaviour and rationality. Many observers, experts, and policymakers are seeking new answers, and looking for solutions to the new questions posed by the crisis. So are we. Thus far, intellectual and policy attention has focused on immediate crisis management, especially with respect to financial sector risk management. Little systematic thinking has been devoted to the question of whether or to what extent the crisis creates momentum for more fundamental structural institutional change. Will the political rules of the economic game be rewritten? Does the current crisis mark a new opportunity to reinvent 21st-century capitalism? Or is a return to the status ex ante of less fettered liberalisation and globalisation just as likely? To be sure, it is still too soon to draw conclusions about the future economic, social, cultural, and political consequences of this momentous economic shock. On the other hand, these questions are among the most pressing of our times. A tentative exploration of these questions is thus both intellectually and politically imperative.

For argument's sake, the intellectual starting point of the interviews we undertook with the contributors to this volume was the historical analogy that deep economic crises alter the modus operandi of our economies, politics, and societies in more fundamental ways than the immediate imperative of crisis management. To be sure, we should not fall into the intellectual trap of historicism, assuming historical parallels to re-appear in the wake of the recurring crises. If history can teach us anything, it is that the last crisis is never like the previous one. Our motivation for exploring the economic and political context of previous crises is our desire to understand and analyze the *differences* in historical context, more than to highlight historical *similarities* per se. Nevertheless, historical analogy will be our starting point, as it allows us to explore the timely questions of our age in a guided, semi-structured and, hopefully, productive manner.

With this historical framework in mind, we approached 24 leading experts in the worlds of finance, macro-economics, economic and political history, globalisation studies, development policy, international relations, social protection, sociology, political science, and strategic policy. We interviewed not only academic experts with a keen eye for the governance dimension of economic management but also practitioners from the financial industry. We interviewed public policy strategists and two respected politicians, towering figures in the advancement of European integration. We asked our expert colleagues to partake in an open dialogue and exchange opinions on the subject, in interviews conducted between April and early September 2009. Based on the transcripts of these interviews, and with feedback from our interviewees, our editorial team put together the essays presented in this volume.

The 24 experts we talked to all share a particular sensitivity to the interaction between political and economic forces in the context of economic turmoil. As such, they tend to analyse the crisis (and economic developments more generally) from the vantage point of the governance relations and institutional arrangements within which economic decisions and crisis management measures are played out. In addition to their focus on governance issues, the majority of these experts, either implicitly or explicitly, utilise a comparative perspective. Whether they make comparisons across time, between episodes of economic crisis versus stability, or across regions and countries, they largely follow a dual strategy: as well as analyzing different cases for similarities, they also search for unique differences. By thus highlighting the 'particular' as well as the 'varying' regime characteristics of different market economies across time and space, they are able to situate the current crisis in a much wider historical, social, and political context.

The viewpoints captured in this volume should be understood as work in progress, snapshots of opinion at a particular moment in time. They are not definitive conclusions. They should be viewed as first attempts to understand the social, economic, and political transformations as they are presently taking place, pursued by different economic, political, and social actors in diverse institutional contexts across the globe. The contributors to this volume made their final revisions to their texts in September 2009, and as such, these pieces are necessarily historically limited by the information available at that time. In this collection of interviews, we have strived to produce a proactive, creative, and timely intervention in this overwhelming debate. In so doing, we have tried to go beyond the more reactive commentaries on the merits of concrete measures in the financial sector that appear in newspapers on a daily basis.

We will certainly not assume to have the final word on the crisis. To the contrary, at this juncture, raising questions is perhaps more important than answering them. We explicitly aim to broaden, rather than conscribe, the policy debate and repertoire of institutional choice before us. Much to our surprise, many of the interviews in this volume display interconnected, mutually supportive, and complementary arguments. However, in various ways different perspectives and judgements continue to differ. We aspire to communicate this intellectual engagement to the reader.

The volume is organised into five main parts. Each one explores different dimensions and aspects of the institutional consequences of the crisis. It begins with 'Diagnosing the Crisis', which introduces the fundamental dynamics of the recent crisis in contributions by Barry Eichengreen, Charles Maier, Jean-Paul Fitoussi, and Paul de Grauwe. Part 2, 'Exploring Policy Space under Low Growth', contains contributions that explicitly reflect on the room for manoeuvre of national social and economic policy institutions, and outlines options for international coordination. The contributors to this section are Peter Hall, Suzanne Berger, Stephen Roach, Willem Buiter, and David Soskice. In Part 3, 'Coping with Paradise Lost', sociologists Mark Elchardus, Amitai Etzioni, and Richard Sennett suggest different interpretations of the changing moral and cultural support basis for the modern market economy, whereas Dominique Moïsi focuses on issues of social malaise in the EU specifically. Part 4, 'Embedding a New Global Contract', contains a diversity of opinions by André Sapir, Dani Rodrik, Nancy Birdsall, Anthony Giddens, Tony Atkinson, and Amy Chua on what possible forms a new architecture of global capitalism might take. Finally, Part 5, 'Realigning Europe', is devoted entirely to the future of the European Union. It includes contributions by Loukas Tsoukalis, Fritz Scharpf, Helmut Schmidt, Maria João Rodrigues, and Jacques Delors. The volume ends with a contribution by co-editor Ben Knapen. Given the nature of the volume, this piece should not be read as a synthesis or conclusion of the arguments presented in the interviews, but rather as an epilogue, highlighting relevant ideas and debates from the book in an attempt to bring them into the current policy debate.

5. FROM CRISIS DIAGNOSTICS TO CRISIS MANAGEMENT

How to diagnose the crisis? Does the current credit crunch bear any similarity to the Great Depression, or is it more similar to the 1980s crisis of stagflation? People make history by constructing and transforming institutions that both constrain and constitute their social action. New institutions are hardly ever designed from a *tabula rasa*. Just as institutions shape the conduct of human actions, human conduct, in turn, reshapes institutions. Crisis management today may be critically informed by previous crisis experiences. Just as neo-liberalism did not lead to a return to the Roaring Twenties of unfettered capitalism, the current crisis is equally unlikely to bring about a restoration of the post-war regime of the embedded liberalism of national political economies.

The current downturn was triggered by a financial crisis not by a 'real' economy crisis, and in this regard, it is more similar to the Great Depression than to the 1970s crisis of stagflation. Barry Eichengreen and Kevin H. O'Rourke have concluded that today's crisis is surely as bad as the Great Depression. In 2008, industrial production, trade, and stock markets plummeted even faster than in 1929-30 (Eichengreen/O'Rourke, 2009). However, whereas after the 1929 crash, the world economy continued to shrink for three successive years, in the wake of the 2007 crisis, policy responses were much better, and led to a swift upswing in trade and stock markets in the first half of 2009. This suggests that the biggest difference between this crisis and the one in the 1930s was timely, effective, and coordinated crisis management to arrest economic collapse. Monetary expansion has been more rapid, and the willingness to run deficits is considerably greater. In short, policymakers were able to avoid the deflationary, protectionist, and nationalistic policy responses that aggravated the decline in the 1930s. There are two overlapping theories of why this has been the case. Dani Rodrik attributes it to the fact that policymakers in developed countries learned from the mistakes of the 1930s and are now firmly committed to open economies, whereas Fritz Scharpf notes that international economic interdependence has progressed so far (especially in the EU) that protectionism is simply no longer a viable option.

The crisis indeed revealed how much the world economy has fundamentally transformed over the past three decades, and this makes the crisis different from any historical precedent. The swift global fallout after the US sub-prime mortgage crisis demonstrates the stark reality of 21st-century global economic interdependence – hardly any country in the world has remained unaffected. The rapid response of public authorities, national governments and central banks attests to effective crisis management, which was sorely lacking in the 1930s.

In his inaugural speech, Barack Obama (2009) claimed that the economic crisis was "a consequence of greed and irresponsibility", a view which is shared in this volume by Amitai Etzioni and Amy Chua, who both allude to the soulless consumerism and decadence of credit-dependent Americans (Etzioni, 2004). For Etzioni, possessive individualist greed triggers demise in social capital and the erosion of trust in government. According to Charles Maier, the history of the current crisis is perhaps less a tale of improvident borrowing than it is a tale of profligate lending. Examining the *supply* of credit provides a far more telling analysis than looking at its *demand* by ordinary consumers. Maier claims that while governments adopted the imperatives of balanced budgets, inflation targeting, deregulation, and privatisation (thus constraining the money supply), the private financial sector was allowed to use financial innovation to create as much money as it saw fit. This led to massive – though fictitious – wealth creation throughout the 1990s. Indeed, Richard Sennett notes that the combination of this overly abundant supply of credit with the income stagnation of the middle classes meant that the dominant share of US consumer credit card purchases were spent on health care by Americans without insurance. It was not greed, but rather the necessity and availability of credit that led to the overwhelming indebtedness of American citizens. For Sennett, the culture of the market economy has lost its moral force for the foot soldiers of the new capitalism (Sennett, 2006; 2008).

Conspicuous consumption and greed are not new. As such, they cannot explain the speed or the depth of the global crisis after 2007. What then are the deeper, more structural and systemic causes of the crisis? Why did academic economists fail to anticipate the coming crisis? The full-blown crisis after the downfall of Lehman Brothers surprised everybody – policymakers, academic economists, and economic commentators alike. However, it had been building up for years, and preventing the collapse of Lehman would not have prevented a global crisis. In retrospect, three factors can be identified that began to merge in the early years of the 21st century, and eventually created an unforeseen but lethal combination: (1) loose monetary policy; (2) the global trade imbalance between the US and China; and (3) lax financial regulation as a result of the liberalisation of capital markets in the 1980. In addition to these, a fourth contributing factor was the theoretical bias that developed in the academic profession towards the economics of market efficiency and human rationality.

Loose monetary policy

The origins of the crisis date back to the aftermath of the 'dotcom' bubble in 2000. When the Fed realised that US aggregate demand was falling sharply and had the potential to throw the entire economy into a full-blown recession, it responded by radically lowering interest rates to one percent. Initially, the US housing sector remained stable, and there were no signs of overheating. However, after another interest rate cut by the Fed, a housing bubble began to expand. With lower interest rates, people could afford much larger home mortgages. Greenspan's loose monetary policy worked well in the beginning: The US economy remained strong – although this was largely thanks to the housing bubble – and companies diligently repaired their balance sheets. This cheap money created a very competitive environment for financial institutions, which could only get high returns if they made ever-riskier investments.

It would, however, be a mistake to single out American or British capitalism as the sole culprit of the crisis. Loukas Tsoukalis reminds us that although continental European economies may have been sceptical about American growth initially, they eventually allowed their banks to dance to the lucrative tune set by American and British capitalist structures. Many European banks invested in large quantities of securitised US mortgages and other innovative financial instruments, such as credit default swaps and collateralised debt obligations. In the end, European financial institutions ended up being more leveraged than their American counterparts. In addition, European monetary unification brought interest rates down dramatically in the previously high-interest Southern tier of EU countries and in Ireland, which, according to Barry Eichengreen, provided cheap funding to financial speculators. The result was an enormous housing and lending boom, which, combined with the lack of a pan-European system of financial governance, at least partially explains why the instabilities in American financial markets contaminated Europe so easily and quickly. Moreover, many contributors to this volume have argued that even the EU's Lisbon Agenda aimed to mimic a (grossly misperceived) US growth scenario.

In addition, the compression of incomes in the US throughout the neo-liberal period was compensated by a reduction in household savings and mounting private indebtedness, which allowed spending patterns to be kept virtually unchanged. At the same time, limited social safety nets forced the government to pursue active macro-economic policies to fight unemployment, which increased government indebtedness as well. Thus, growth was maintained at the price of increasing public and private indebtedness, adding to the already existing macro imbalance. In this respect, Jean-Paul Fitoussi points to the problem of competitive social deflation. In the era of neo-liberalism, structural inequalities were allowed to persist and widen further, both within and between countries. Indeed, Tony Atkinson finds that while many developed countries saw their GDP increase by up to 25% over the past fifteen years, median incomes barely rose at all (and in some countries even declined), revealing a highly skewed distribution of growth. In macro-economic parlance, increased inequality implies weak domestic demand: the skewed wealth distribution and high unemployment rates were bad for consumer demand and therefore for the economy as a whole. In addition, global demand contracted even further in the wake of the Asian financial crisis, when Asian emerging economies started to hoard reserves so as not to become dependent on IMF loans in hard economic times.

Global imbalances

This brings us to the second factor that contributed to the crisis: the macro imbalance in trade. This imbalance has accelerated dramatically over the past ten to fifteen years, partly as a result of loose US monetary policy. Asian emerging economies and the oil-exporting countries accumulated large current account surpluses, and these were matched by large current account deficits in the US, as well as the UK, Ireland, and Spain. A key driver of these imbalances was the high savings rates in countries like China, and Suzanne Berger believes that the run-up to the crisis should actually be traced back to the 1997 Asian financial market crash. Following this disaster, Asian governments (and citizens) felt increasingly insecure and ramped up their reserves – primarily in US dollars – in order to avoid becoming vulnerable to such a scenario in the future. This exacerbated the US debt burden, further perpetuating the trade imbalance.

Lax financial regulation

Loose monetary policy and the international trade imbalance were compounded by a third factor: the deregulation of the financial sector. With the liberalisation of capital markets, finance became global, but regulation remained national. In addition, throughout the neo-liberal epoch, even domestic financial markets were systematically deregulated, allowing financial innovations to evolve unchecked. As the financial sector grew and became truly global, insufficient latitude was reserved for domestic government regulation and international supervision (Posner, 2009).

Willem Buiter commented on this, noting that allowing the scope of the market and the domain of the mobility of financial institutions to exceed the span of regulatory control is a recipe for disaster. Financial sector deregulation allowed the macro imbalances in savings rates to stimulate a massive wave of financial innovation, focused on the origination, packaging, trading and distribution of derivatives, credit default swaps, and other securitised credit instruments. Since the mid-1990s there has been huge growth in the value of credit securities, an explosion in the complexity of the securities sold, and a related explosion of the volume of credit derivatives, enabling investors and traders to hedge underlying credit exposures. As securitisation grew in importance from the 1980s on, this development was lauded as a means to reduce banking system risks and to cut the total cost of credit intermediation. Securitised credit intermediation would be less likely to produce banking system failures. When the crisis broke, it became apparent that this diversification of risk holding had not been achieved. The deregulation movement had been aimed at the regulated industries in general, and encompassed the banking system only because it was highly regulated. The economists and politicians who pressed for deregulation were evidently not sensitive to the fact that deregulating banking has a macro-economic significance that deregulating railroads or telecommunications does not.

In retrospect, Stephen Roach wonders whether some of these new breakthroughs in financial innovation were in fact more destructive than constructive. Eichengreen explains how the politics of international deregulation, together with computer-based finance mathematics, finally extricated the capacity to produce money by credit from public control – which to some extent at least had tied it to the production and consumption capacities of the real economy. The financial industry thus acquired the capacity and the licence to make money out of money, and to generate claims to resources at a rate so rapid that the real economy could not possibly follow. It could even be argued that money ceased to a public institution directing economic activities into productive endeavors. Instead, it was reduced to being a commercial commodity itself, decoupled from its previous function for the real economy, no longer bounded by any national base, interest, regulation, or other direct or indirect requirement to commit itself to productive function beyond itself (Streeck, 2009). For the past two decades, increases in US debt came from financial innovation, rather than the real economy. Once upon a time, a home owner took out a mortgage, and household debt increased. But since the late 1990s, mortgages could be used to secure mortgage-backed securities, and those securities could in turn be used to secure a collateralised debt obligation. The end result was more borrowing, but no increase in real economy activity. Moreover, when assets, driven by cheap money, came to be bought not because of the rate of return on investment but in anticipation that such assets and securities could be sold at a higher price, the stage was set for an asset bubble of overvalued stocks in relation to real economy fundamentals. Privatized money production on a hitherto unknown scale, according to Fitoussi, should be understood as a response to the general stagnation of growth and profitability after the 1970s. The inevitable result was a rapidly growing debt pyramid vastly in excess of the real economy's ability to pay. The above three features of loose monetary policy, the savings and trade imbalance, and lax regulation ultimately exacerbated the pro-cyclical and self-reinforcing nature of the downturn.

Academic failure

Judged by Milton Friedman's method of positive economics, which holds that economists should be judged by the predictive powers of their theories and not by the validity of the assumptions they make in the construction of their economic models, the failure to anticipate the first major economic crisis of 21st-century global capitalism should be viewed as an utter failure (Friedman, 1962). Why were so many economists so blind? To be sure, a small minority of eminent members of the economics profession, notably Robert Shiller (2003; 2008), Raghuram Rajan (2005), and Nuriel Roubini (2006), did point to the great risks of an unchecked housing bubble. Dani Rodrik (2007) and Barry Eichengreen (2007b) warned against the negative fallout potential of the global imbalances. Yet the majority of mainstream economists failed to recognise what was going on. Or rather, what Chuck Prince of Citi Group said of the financial industry, that "… as long as the music is playing, you've got to get up and dance", also applied to the academic economists' profession.

Paul de Grauwe intimates that perhaps the root cause of this academic oversight was the error of modern mainstream economics in believing that the economy is simply the sum of micro-economic decisions of rational agents. The profession of economics was so caught up in this rational actor and market efficiency paradigm that it completely forgot some of the most elementary dynamics of economic crises: animal spirits. Fundamental to Keynesian economics is the idea that instead of rational actors, much economic activity is governed by animal spirits, best understood as waves of optimism and pessimism (see also Akerlof/Shiller, 2009). Animal spirits grip investors and consumers and thus, endogenously, generate self-fulfilling prophecies by influencing output and investment (Grauwe, 2008). Left to their own devices, capitalist economies will experience manias, followed by panics. It is the function of the modern state to sail into the wind of these excesses: when the population overspends, they should over-save, and vice versa.

If Keynesian economics was the intellectual product of the 1930s, the 1970s crisis of stagflation brought Keynesian paradigmatic hegemony (Hall, 1989) to an end. In its wake, anti-Keynesian monetarism gained respectability by being better able to explain the predicament of stagflation as the result of stop-and-go fiscal demand stimulus measures by governments and, following the 'new classical' macro-economics of rational expectations, wage hikes adapted to inflationary expectation. In the evolution of this paradigm shift from Keynesianism to monetarism and rational expectation macro-economics, the study of animal spirits has almost completely disappeared from mainstream macro-economics and the economics of finance. When expectations are assumed to be rational, intellectual models leave no room for waves of pessimism and optimism to exert an independent influence on economic activity. In rational models of macro-economics, it is the combination of exogenous shocks and slow transmission that creates cyclical movements in the economy. In this vein, Blanchard and Summers (1987) suggested a reason why wages did not fall when unemployment was high in Europe in the 1980s. They argued that 'hysteresis' in wage setting can prevent the real wage from falling enough to restore full employment, if wages are set to preserve the jobs of those people already employed, rather than to move others out of unemployment. In these mainstream models there is no place for endogenously generated business cycles. Likewise, the preoccupation of business-cycle macroeconomists had been to prevent inflation by keeping interest rates up, just below the level that would risk precipitating a recession. Modern macro-economics, especially within central banks, became excessively fixated on taming inflation and much too benign about housing price and asset bubbles.

Paul de Grauwe argues that even if prices and wages become more flexible, this will not necessarily reduce the business cycle movement in output. As a result, society's desire to stabilise output will not be reduced. Central banks that respond to these desires will face the need to stabilise output at the risk of reducing price stability. The efficient-markets hypothesis, which argues that deviations from equilibrium values cannot last for long, also fuelled the idea that free markets are self-regulating and self-legitimising, and that financial innovation is always beneficial to everyone.

As time went on, more and more professional economists were drawn onto the bandwagon of passive acceptance of the dominant intellectual paradigm. Barry Eichengreen observes that most academic economists shied away from probing the underlying vulnerabilities of loose macro-economics, financial deregulation, mortgage and pension markets, and distorted incentives and bonus schemes in the big financial institutions that exacerbated economic instabilities. Moreover, the high level of sub-disciplinary specialisation in the field of economics made it difficult for any single academic to put all the pieces together. This intellectual inertia and sub-specialisation blinded academic economists to the underlying causes of the crisis. In this respect, the current crisis is a wakeup call, re-introducing the concepts of animal spirits, imperfect information, cognitive limitation, and heterogeneity in the use of information back into macro-economic and financial market modelling and analysis.

To some extent this lesson also applies to the more heterodox field of comparative institutional political analysis. In retrospect, Suzanne Berger pleads guilty to imagining that financial markets played a mere auxiliary function in her understanding of globalisation. The Varieties of Capitalism school, founded by Peter Hall and David Soskice, also failed to adequately conceptualise the institutional links between the real economy and the financial economy. Loukas Tsoukalis adds a political factor: as deregulation brought concentrated wealth to sectors that benefited from even further deregulation, accumulated wealth was efficiently translated into a strong financial lobby in London, New York, and Washington. The financial sector effectively bought political power. Therefore, the failure of politics lies in part in its inability to resist being hijacked by financial interests. Blaming neo-liberal ideology and intellectual inertia is insufficient.

6. THE POLITICAL CONTOURS OF THE NEW EMBEDDEDNESS

The fundamental insight that emerged from most of the interviews is that economic markets are not self-creating, self-regulating, self-stabilising, and self-legitimising. While this important lesson is certainly not new, in the past decades of neo-liberalism, policymakers do seem to have forgotten the fundamental truth that the benefits of global economic interdependence rely heavily on robust social and political institutions, reminiscent of the era of embedded liberalism. Domestic and supranational institutions must be able to bind, bond, and bridge advanced polities, economies, and societies. However, despite the temptation to think of the future of global capitalism as a global version of post-war embedded liberalism, this surely is not feasible, efficient, nor practical. Today, the process of globalisation is too far advanced to be able to go back to national economic management of the era of 'embedded liberalism'. As a consequence, some policy recipes that were successful before (including currency devaluations and trade protectionism) are no longer available to national policymakers, in part due to European and WTO economic integration. In this respect, concerted coordinated action at the international level is essential to effectively govern the global economy.

Unfortunately, once the genie is out of the bottle, it is far more difficult to re-regulate an economy than to deregulate it. The neo-liberal era may have come to an end, but whether the crisis indeed marks the ascendance of a new regime is an open question. Some of the rules of economic regulation and policymaking will be rewritten, as Charles Maier believes. The economic crisis has brought the world to a new policy crossroads, but it also needs to be acknowledged that the room for manoeuvre and institutional innovation may be fairly restricted, not only because of the likelihood of low economic growth, but also because of domestic and international political constraints and barriers. The question of institutional choice and regime change, for present purposes, encompasses two key dimensions. Internationally, the task will be to devise a stable and sustainable system for international cooperation and regulation, which addresses the diverse needs of advanced, developing, and the least-developed economies; domestically, institutional change requires recalibrating the role of the state in shaping a stable economy by combining economic dynamism with a more equitable distribution of life chances. Walking the fine line between protectionism and protecting domestic policy space will be difficult.

Effective solutions to the current global crisis require international cooperation, but no government is able to go ahead with an internationally coordinated plan without taking into account issues of domestic legitimacy. Nowhere is this double bind between international coordination and national allegiance more salient than in Europe. Any solution to the crisis has to be both effective and legitimate at the level of the global market as well as at the level of the nation-state. In his contribution, Peter Hall underlines the extent to which political shifts play a key independent role in the selection of policy responses and institutional adjustments. Previous crisis episodes have revealed how hard times exacerbate existing tensions, invariably decreasing satisfaction with existing governments. If the crisis results in an extended period of high unemployment, the voting public may grow disenchanted with the prevailing policy regime, which they identify as economic liberalisation. Facing the likelihood of relatively low growth, the key challenge that political leaders will face is therefore not so much how to manage growth, but how to manage expectations, Tony Atkinson contends. Suzanne Berger rightly underscores that even before the economic crisis there was no evidence that citizens were shifting allegiances away from the nation-state. In Europe, the 2005 referenda on ratification of the European constitution demonstrated the strength of nationalism. Various public opinion polls overwhelmingly reaffirmed that citizens held their national governments accountable for their security and wellbeing, and felt betrayed by the globalising ambitions of the EU. The economic crisis intensified these sentiments, thus bringing the centrality of the role of the nation-state back into the limelight. The European welfare state, following this line of reasoning, was introduced as a way of re-establishing this legitimacy and rebuilding the capacities of the state. Looking back, Suzanne Berger argues that the nation-state remained vital throughout the globalisation period. Whereas in good times the hand of the state may have been hidden, in hard times it re-emerged visibly and powerfully. Berger's central observation implies a fundamental re-thinking of the role of the state in the economy.

The crisis has affected different economies differently, as a result of their relative vulnerability to endogenous and external economic shocks and also because of the differing institutional capacities they were able to mobilise to address the economic duress. The smaller economies of Western Europe, which have been unable or unwilling to muster fiscal stimulus packages on par with those of Germany and France – for example Belgium, the Netherlands, and Sweden – are behind the curve of recovery. Ballooning budget deficits in Ireland, Greece, and Spain raise severe doubts about recovery. In August 2009, the Bank of England surprised everybody with another round of quantitative easing of 50 billion British pounds, admitting that the recession appears to have been deeper than previously thought. The economic crisis has hurt the new EU member states of Eastern and Central Europe the most. Hungary, Romania, and Latvia are surviving primarily on emergency aid from the IMF. The Baltic states, which predicted GDP declines between 13 and 17 per cent in 2009, have already been forced to introduce tough retrenchment programs in public finances. Other countries, like the Czech Republic, Slovenia, Slovakia, and Poland, are doing relatively well. The temptation to focus on the incipient recovery of the more advanced OECD countries, as well as on the so-called emerging BRICs – Brazil, Russia, India, China – runs the risk of glossing over the far more devastating effects the crisis has had on developing countries, which cannot muster the resources for a counter-cyclical fiscal stimulus. Even gas- and resource-rich Russia is likely to suffer a steep fall in GDP.

At the moment, there are a variety of competing models of capitalism: Anglo-Saxon, Rhineland social market economies, and new statist Chinese capitalism. However, as much as we can anticipate the policy debate about competing models to reach new levels of intensity in the near future, it is our contention that it is useless to couch policy responses to the current crisis in terms of a battle between warring alternatives. Triggering ideological strife and polarising advocacy coalitions do nothing to move the policy discussion towards better understanding or more effective policy solutions and economic governance. Moreover, models come and go. There is no 'one best way': institutional designs that underpin market economies will differ according to domestic and regional preferences and needs.

The 'Varieties of Capitalism' approach to analyzing the different domestic strengths and weaknesses of the advanced political economies can help us in understanding how different economies and economic regions will adapt to the post-crisis environment (Hall and Soskice, 2001). Compared to the US, European countries were slow in recognising the severity of the crisis. As a consequence, monetary easing and fiscal stimulus measures were implemented less aggressively than in the US. One reason why fiscal stimulus programs were less expansive in Europe is due to the fact that the EU is made up of many small, open economies. This creates free-rider problems, with the benefits of fiscal stimulus spilling over into neighbouring economies. While the US is more indebted, it has the advantage of being an immigrant economy with flexible labour markets, which will make it relatively easier to mobilise labour and other resources than in the ageing European and Japanese economies.

Under conditions of low growth, China as well as European export-oriented economies will no longer be able to rely primarily on industrial exports to drive their economies. In Europe, this means that domestic employment will need to be shifted towards services that are locally produced and locally consumed. Specifically, Fritz Scharpf suggests focusing on the potential growth industries of health care, childcare, care for the aged, and above all education and training.

Across Europe, many of the new member states of Eastern and Central Europe have been disproportionately damaged by the crisis. Peter Hall cites Wade

Jacoby (2002), who argued that former communist countries made the transition to the market economy at the height of the neo-liberal era and were sold the most radical version of the market model, particularly by the IMF and World Bank. Now they are suffering more than other countries as a result of this irrational exuberance. Emerging economies, specifically Brazil and India, are expected to do much better in the post-crisis period. According to Nancy Birdsall, this is partly due to the extent to which they were able to decouple themselves from financial globalisation. By contrast, lower-income developing countries, which traditionally have relied heavily on trade, will suffer severely from the crisis. Sub-Saharan countries sorely lack the economic resources and institutional capacities to implement counter-cyclical fiscal policies.

Dani Rodrik defends countries' rights to protect their own social arrangements and institutions. The objective of international economic arrangements must be to attain the maximum 'thickness' in economic transactions (in trade and investment flows) that is consistent with maintaining space for diversity in national and regional institutional arrangements. As a consequence, Rodrik concurs that markets must remain primarily embedded at the level of the nation-state, as long as democratic governance and political identities remain nationally embedded. Economic relations between states should be structured with the aim of opening up trade and investment flows subject to the proviso of maintaining heterogeneous national arrangements. Where national models conflict, what Dani Rodrik calls 'traffic rules' must be designed to manage the interface between domestic arrangements. Protected policy space would allow rich countries to provide social insurance, address concerns about labour, the environment, health, and safety consequences of trade, and also shorten the 'chain' of delegation. Meanwhile, poor nations should be enabled to position themselves to benefit from globalisation through economic restructuring. All nations must be given the space to create financial systems and regulatory structures attuned to their own conditions and needs. To this effect, substantive policy concerns would be brought to the table of international economic negotiations. Surely, this goes beyond the neo-liberal zeal to establish 'level playing fields'.

The global crisis has laid bare important changes in the global distribution of wealth and power. The power of the US is on the wane, and emerging economies such India and China have meanwhile become key global economic players. However, their economic prowess is not yet reflected by their representation in international bodies. At the same time, the EU is faced with a plethora of internal problems in the wake of Eastern enlargement. Quite surprisingly, the international community is already adjusting to this new multilateral reality. Whereas existing institutions usually continue to reflect the international distribution of power of the status quo ex ante, the IMF and the World Bank have recently allowed for far more domestic heterodoxy than ever before. The crisis has changed these institutions practically overnight. In terms of substance, the Washington Consensus rules no longer govern, and Dominique Strauss-Kahn, director of the IMF, realised that without change, China and other emerging economies would not stay engaged and therefore demonstrated flexibility in reform.

Since the economic crisis, the supranational Bretton Woods organisations that converted to the Washington Consensus, such as the IMF, the World Bank, and the WTO, have faced a crisis of legitimacy. In order for these global organisations to recover, they must reform by, firstly, fully integrating the emerging countries and, secondly, promoting equitable and sustainable models of globalisation. By 2009, in institutional terms, the elite club of rich industrial nations, known as the G7 – Britain, Canada, France, Germany, Italy, Japan and the United States, has been permanently replaced by the Group of 20, including China, Brazil, India and other fast growing developing countries, as the global forum for economic policy. The rise of the G20 marks an instance of profound institutional change. However, despite its successes, the G20, according to Barry Eichengreen, has problems. It is not clear why these 20 specific countries were appointed to represent the world. From a social justice perspective as well, the G20 insufficiently represents the poorest countries. One way of rationalising these arrangements would be by moving to a Group of 24, based on the representation in the International Monetary and Financial Committee of the IMF. Of the 24 representatives in this committee, five represent individual countries, whereas the others represent groups of countries. All this makes it a far more effective structure to supersede the G20. Another shortcoming of the G20 is Europe's inability to speak with one voice. The EU should come to recognise that two seats – one for the euro area and one for the rest of the EU – is sufficient, a view which is shared by André Sapir. This would streamline decision-making, both within the G20 and the IMF, while freeing up seats at the table for currently underrepresented developing economies and regions, as Nancy Birdsall points out.

A final political challenge is that this economic crisis coincides with a major environmental crisis, whose solution requires a complete transformation of our modes of production and ways of living. Anthony Giddens reminds us that regardless of the institutional changes following the crisis, the imperative to act on issues such as climate change, energy insecurity, and water scarcity will remain paramount (Giddens, 2009). He also notes that climate change policies can play an important role in revitalising economic growth. Averting climate change should be an important policy goal when prioritising stimulus spending. Investments should go towards clean energy, and the adaptation of green technologies should be given prominence, a view that is shared by Nancy Birdsall and Tony Atkinson. Thanks to the crisis, substantive global issues, such as climate control, water management, renewable energy, and other long-term concerns of sustainable development are now high on the world political agenda. This is a welcome correction.

7. EUROPE AT A CROSSROADS

Over the past two decades, ridiculing the so-called 'European Social Model' has been a favourite pastime of business leaders, political elites, and economic experts – especially at Davos. In 2009, this is no longer the case. A number of political leaders, chief executives, and top economists even seized the moment at the World Economic Forum by cautiously pointing out the relative merits of the European welfare states and the Rhineland coordinated political economies. As unbridled Anglo-Saxon capitalism was blamed for the financial crash, German Chancellor Angela Merkel openly endorsed the European "social market economy" – a free market tempered by a generous welfare state, consensus-building politics and industrial relations – as a model for the future. Only a few years ago, policy pundits could not have imagined such a future for Europe's social market economies. These regimes, which are known for reining in free markets with capital regulation, providing generous insurance benefits paired with high quality social services, maintaining stable industrial relations, and supporting comprehensive vocational training and education systems, seem to have been able to mitigate the hardship of the economic crisis. In the United States, where the stock market collapse has wiped out retirement savings and rising unemployment is leaving ever more people without health insurance, officials in President Barack Obama's administration are looking towards recent pension and health care reforms in the Netherlands, Sweden, and Switzerland for inspiration. In China, where the American economic demise has brought the perils of excessive domestic saving to the fore, the government announced a Keynesian stimulus program to deepen and strengthen social safety nets in the areas of pensions, health care, active labour market policy, vocational training, unemployment insurance, and close supervision of finance. Do these developments indicate a shift towards holding the much-maligned European welfare system up as a model for the new 21st-century global capitalism (Begg et al, 2008)?

How robust is the renewed conversion to the European social model really, even within the European Union itself? Can the European Union stay unified in the face of the crisis? Will the Euro grow stronger or weaker? Can Europe's problems be resolved without the creation of some form of economic governance alongside the European Central Bank? Does the crisis offer an opportunity for the European Union to become a stronger political force in world economic affairs? Or, on the contrary, will the Union continue to be jeopardised by joint-decision traps as the crisis polarises the ideological debate between different 'socio-economic models'? Moreover, since the crisis, anti-globalisation feelings have increased the support for right- and left-wing populist parties in national elections, and this is undermining the popular legitimacy of the European project. What kind of social Europe is effective and legitimate in the aftermath of the current crisis? European economic integration, to be sure, has been highly implicated by the neo-liberal consensus of the 1980s and 1990s (Dyson/Featherstone, 1999). As the current technocratic elite in Brussels have come to ascendance during the neo-liberal era, they may be unlikely to take the lead in promoting a new and embedded governance framework for the European political economy. Many of our Europe-based interviewees believe that the EU is increasingly becoming part of the problem rather than the solution to the crisis. Interestingly, our North American colleagues have a more sanguine perspective on the future of Europe.

From the European perspective, Peter Hall underscores the extent to which Europe's predicament is more political and institutional in nature than programmatic. Both Dominique Moïsi and Mark Elchardus believe that the all-pervasive cultural narrative of the European welfare state, in the light of the crisis, has bred media-triggered political disenchantment, demise in social capital, and fuelled the expansion of left- and right-wing populism, eroding confidence in the European project (Echardus, 2002; 2004; Moïsi, 2008). Many observers fear serious nationalist backlashes across the EU member states, which will make it ever more difficult to reach a political consensus over effective and legitimate domestic and European social and economic policy. Fritz Scharpf laments the neo-liberal judicial bias in the single-market policy repertoire, while Helmut Schmidt deplores the lack of political leadership (see also Schmidt, 2008). Jacques Delors laments the demise of the spirit of cooperation in the wake of eastward enlargement. Loukas Tsoukalis views intergovernmentalism and the unanimity requirement of the European Union as its most serious political setbacks, because of its tendancy toward institutional deadlock. Fritz Scharpf connects the inability of the EU to the vulnerability of a regime of completely liberalised markets. EU macro-economic, fiscal, and monetary policy repertoire is asymmetrically designed to serve only the purposes of price stability and fiscal sustainability, and has therefore served to undermine Europe's popular national welfare systems (Scharpf, 1999; 2004). It was designed to guard against the inflationary pressures of the 1970s and early 1980s, but the problems of a deflationary crisis were ignored. Moreover, Tony Atkinson observes that under the rhetoric of the Lisbon Agenda, structural inequalities were allowed to persist, by narrowly focusing on employment as the cure for all economic ailments (see also Atkinson et al, 2002). In the original vision of Lisbon, economic and social policy goals were placed on an equal footing (Rodrigues, 2009). Yet this was abandoned with the 2005 refocusing of Lisbon on growth and jobs. Nine years after the social accord of Lisbon, the conclusion is that the 'trickle-down' effect has not worked. Overall poverty rates have not decreased, and child and old age poverty have actually increased in some EU countries, notably in Germany, Poland, Italy, Latvia, Romania and Bulgaria.

Jacques Delors infers that as a result of the timely imperative of the enlargement of 2004, the programmatic deepening of the EU took a back seat (see also Delors, 2006). As a consequence, the EU now lacks the necessary unity to put forward a coherent package of supranational social and economic crisis management. According to Delors and Helmut Schmidt, this is also due to the overall weakness of the Commission. In hard times, national politics trump the European common good, as national leaders move to protect their own industries, workers, and voters.

However, looking at Europe from the other side of the Atlantic, the perspective is rosier. Peter Hall believes that European welfare states will weather the storm, noting that even a mere 2% per year of GDP growth will enable them to sustain their welfare systems in the long run. Nancy Birdsall and Suzanne Berger even conjecture that ultimately a transition towards a more European welfare system in the US is not unlikely, in spite of the American emphasis on low taxes and government expenditures (Birdsall, 2008). Amy Chua deviates from this perspective, however, by noting that American small-government values make a transition to a European welfare system highly unlikely (see also Chua, 2007).

Barry Eichengreen was positively surprised by the unanticipated flexibility of Europe's regime of macro-economic management. Prior to the crisis, there were worries that the rigidity of the Stability and Growth Pact and European monetary union would prevent the EU from responding swiftly to the financial crisis (Eichengreen, 2007a). In fact, despite the initial delay in cutting interest rates, the ECB responded very quickly, by providing essentially unlimited amounts of liquidity to the euro-area financial systems. At the same time, the Stability and Growth Pact was relaxed in order to increase governments' capacities to borrow in the interests of recapitalising their banks. These EU measures may have helped to offset the relative weakness of national stimulus plans.

What is perhaps most revealing is that the euro has become more attractive as a result of the crisis, by virtue of its stability and security (Eichengreen, 2007b; 2009). Despite mounting social problems, countries like Spain, Ireland, and other smaller European economies show no signs of wanting to abandon the euro-area. A fair number of traditionally euro-sceptical EU member states, such as Denmark and Sweden, now view the prospects of joining the euro-area far more favourably in the wake of the crisis. Hungary and Poland have both indicated that they want to speed up their transition to the euro as a result of the crisis. Iceland has already applied.

Dani Rodrik believes that the demise of the Washington Consensus will benefit the EU, with some of the EU's larger member-states possibly becoming significant international players. Throughout the second half of the 20th century, the EU has been a guinea pig for multilateral governance and has an unparalleled understanding of domestic social complements to the single-market process. This has created a healthy balance between domestic policy space and international trade efficiency. In the process, the EU developed an institutional knowledge base for successful international governance which knows no equal. To maintain its international legitimacy, it must, according to André Sapir, now use this knowledge and become a true advocate of multilateral reform in global governance (Sapir, 2007). Just as economic internal integration was the prevailing European narrative for the past 50 years, Europe must now develop a new narrative based on multilateralism and globalisation for the coming half-century. However, for the EU as a whole, its role as a credible advocate of multilateral reform can only come at the expense of renouncing some of its antiquated institutional privileges in global governance institutions. In order to benefit from the unity the EU has nurtured, it will be necessary that Europe learn to 'speak with one voice' internationally and thus give up outdated voting privileges in the IMF and the World Bank.

Although many of our experts highlighted the necessity of further European economic integration in the wake of the crisis, at the level of domestic European politics, the crisis has prompted a shift towards nationalism, undermining popular legitimacy for further European integration. In this respect, Peter Hall may be right in contending that ultimately, the biggest barrier to achieving an effective European response to the crisis is political. Already in the 2005 referenda on ratification of the European constitution, the rising strength of nationalism was clearly demonstrated. Citizens felt betrayed by the liberalising and globalising ambitions of the EU. The economic crisis heightened such sentiments and brought nationalism back into the limelight of European politics. In the past, national political leaders often misused EU regulation as a scapegoat for unpopular reforms. Popular support for the European project suffered as a result, but so did the credibility of political elites. Anti-EU, anti-immigrant, populist, radical right-wing, and anti-capitalist left-wing groups have gained influence in recent years. Their growing support puts pressure on existing governments and centrist parties to proclaim nationalist responses to the crisis and play down their commitments to European integration. As a result, it comes as little surprise that EU political legitimacy suffered tremendously in the wake of the crisis; it was discredited by its earlier role as champion of market liberalisation.

Loukas Tsoukalis claims that the old division of labour between EU and national institutions (the former generally concentrated on market liberalisation measures, while the latter retained a near monopoly over redistribution and welfare) has become politically unsustainable. Europe needs a new moral vision, a social narrative capable of restoring its legitimacy in difficult times. This is rendered more difficult by the absence of EU officials elected by Europe as a whole, as Peter Hall observes. Over the past decades, the EU has constantly reinvented itself, showing the creativity and dynamism needed to overcome the myriad of challenges it has faced since its inception. However, currently, in order for Europe to be an effective agent of reform, it must become a reliable political defender of collective interests and values with a stronger caring dimension. In short, the European Union, in the words of Loukas Tsoukalis, needs a breath of fresh political air.

8. REGIME CHANGE WITHOUT THE PUNCTUATED PENDULUM SWING

Will the gravity of the economic crisis trigger a moment of extraordinary politics and institutional reconstruction? Can we expect the crisis to usher in a more active economic role for government intervention, market regulation, and international coordination? Will there be a pendulum swing back to a stronger appreciation of market embeddedness?

Although most of our interviewees expect to see some degree of institutional change in the wake of the crisis, several of the authors have doubts about the likelihood of a swift and punctuated regime change occurring. Peter Hall notes that although market optimism took a severe beating, a new era of state intervention and optimism will not necessarily follow. Today, citizens have as little faith in the state as they have in the market, and because they are presiding over recession, whatever governments do during an economic crisis is usually seen as a failure. Therefore, states should expect some popular backlash. In addition, Barry Eichengreen believes that if the crisis created a moment for extraordinary politics, that moment is quickly passing. However, if in upcoming years, the resulting sense of insecurity is exacerbated by persistently high levels of unemployment and a perpetually unstable stock market, pressure may slowly grow for the American government to step in to undertake fundamental reforms. This would undermine the old adage that "government is the problem, markets the solution."

Just as the current crisis is unlikely to trigger a swift pendulum swing of institutional design, it should be noted that neo-liberalism also did not attain institutional hegemony overnight. While the elections of Margaret Thatcher and Ronald Reagan may retrospectively have marked the beginning of the neo-liberal era, it was only with the fall of the Berlin Wall that this doctrine achieved global influence. The neo-liberal rise to dominance was largely evolutionary; it emerged gradually through a series of institutional transformations and policy changes over a long period of time. In contrast to the traditional belief that institutional shifts are always marked by rapid changes at critical junctures, it can be expected that future institutional shifts are likely to follow the logic of incremental transformative change through institutional evolution. By comparison, the rise of embedded liberalism indeed represented a far more punctuated process of institution building.

With this in mind, it is interesting to speculate about how the observed policy changes in the wake of the crisis will contribute to such a scenario of gradual institutional evolution. Specifically, five key policy changes warrant such an examination: (1) changes in central banks' mandates and modes of operation, (2) the resurgence of international policy coordination, (3) the reappraisal of welfare policies, (4) taking climate change seriously, and (5) the search for new economic indicators that go beyond traditional measures of GDP.

The crisis has pushed central banks into a broad range of new interventions, aimed at safeguarding financial stability. One intellectual lesson that has emerged from this crisis is that economists have to redefine what global and domestic financial macro-economic stability means. Macro-economic and financial stability is a much wider concept than price stability, and sometimes the two even conflict. Stephen Roach advocates a new mandate for the Federal Reserve; it should lean against the winds of financial excess and asset bubbles. Similarly, Willem Buiter, Paul De Grauwe, and Barry Eichengreen all argue that the ECB will in the near future be required to perform a variety of new functions, including undertaking liquidity- and credit-enhancing measures, becoming a lender of last resort, and maintaining general financial stability. In order to achieve financial stability, the ECB must be allowed to deploy new instruments, such as counter-cyclical adjustment of capital ratios for banks and minimum reserve requirements, which should be used to limit excessive credit creation by banks. However, if the ECB is to play a significant financial stability role, it cannot retain the degree of operational independence it was granted in the Treaty over monetary policy in the pursuit of price stability. Changing this will be difficult, because the ECB is based on the European Treaty, which is extraordinarily tough to amend (all 27 member countries must agree to any changes). As the crisis lengthens and deepens, the absence of close cooperation between the European fiscal authorities on the one hand, and the ECB bankers on the other, will make both groups progressively less effective. This comes in addition to the problems the ECB encounters as a result of the absence of even a minimal 'fiscal Europe'.

The ultimate litmus test of effective macro-economic regime change lies in the establishment of a new systemic risk regulator, an issue up for discussion at the G20 summit to be held in late September in Pittsburgh. Both the Turner report of the British FSA (2009) and the De Larosiere Commission (2009), reporting to the European Commission, have suggested the creation of a new European body for regulation and oversight of supervision, staffed by full-time independent professionals. They argue that these independent professionals would not come under pressure from the financial sector and other special interests to moderate efforts to coordinate the application of existing supervisory standards and would encourage cooperation among supervisors. Banking should be subject to a capital regime entailing more and higher capital requirements, more capital against trading book risk-taking, and a counter-cyclical framework with capital buffers built up in periods of strong economic growth that would be available in downturns. Already, powerful financial interests have rallied against the proposals of Lord Turner and De Larosiere, especially their proposals to curb pro-cyclical policies, bonuses, and remuneration packages in the financial sector. Given sufficient prudence and regulation, De Grauwe thinks there is no reason to fear that quantitative easing will lead to inflation, as extra liquidity will not promote inflation when liquidity is sorely lacking. Willem Buiter contends that if Europe truly wants to establish a single market for financial product services, it will need to delegate regulation to the supra-national domain of the EU. Ultimately, Europe must establish a powerful EU-level authority to which national supervisors report and whose instructions they carry out, in a manner analogous to the relations between the ECB and national euro area central banks (Buiter, 2008). Nonetheless, at the Pittsburgh summit of the G20 on September 25, some agreement was reached on a timetable for regulatory reform, serving to reign in executive compensation, to raise capital requirements and leverage ratios for financial institutions, and to reduce the imbalances between consuming countries like the US and export-dependent China, Germany, and Japan. Moreover, the G20 came together on new IMF voting rules with the added power and authority of the developing economies.

In many advanced economies, welfare policies are being re-assessed and re-calibrated. In Europe, the crisis has been, in many ways, a stress test for the welfare state. Although the crisis may put a strain on many redistributive institutions, this can also have positive consequences, as Tony Atkinson acknowledges. For one, social policy has resurfaced at the centre of the political debate. The crisis has reminded many Europeans of the importance of social programs to support the unemployed, the disabled, and the others most negatively affected by the crisis. In this respect, the economic crisis may reinforce, rather than undermine, the legitimacy of the welfare state. In China, the government has recently realised that internal consumption could be a new driver of growth, but they have yet to make the necessary investments in health-care and welfare to support such a development. In the US, on the other hand, the social debate since the onset of the crisis has focused almost exclusively on health-care reform. There are significant political hurdles to achieving such reform, as the bitter and even violent debates on the issue in the US demonstrate. Obama is cautious about taxes, but according to Nancy Birdsall, a shift towards a more European social model and a retreat from the 'cowboy' model of capitalism seems inevitable, in spite of the American emphasis on low taxes and low government expenditures.

Future productivity growth is likely to come from sources like green energy and low carbon path investments. However, the challenge, according to Nancy Birdsall, will be to find funding, from either the market or the government, to finance the R&D that forms the backbone of these new sectors of the low-carbon economy.

Going beyond welfare state recalibration and sustainable development as separate phenomena, Jacques Delors, Tony Atkinson, and Jean-Paul Fitoussi underscore the need for a different set of indicators of social and economic progress exceeding the traditional measure of GDP growth. In fact, the crisis is partially the result of the exclusive focus on economic growth. The formulation of a new portfolio of social and economic indicators (including, for example, various dimensions of adult numeracy and literacy, access to public services, poverty, environmental health, climate control) is especially politically opportune in the face of a period of lethargic and drawn-out recovery. GDP growth may no longer be an adequate proxy for 'doing well'. To address this issue, in early 2008, Nicolas Sarkozy put together a committee of leading economists, chaired by Joseph Stiglitz, Amartya Sen, and Jean Paul Fitoussi, to rethink GDP as an indicator of economic performance and to consider alternative indicators of social progress. The unifying theme of the report that came out in September 2009 is that the time is ripe for shifting measurement from indicators of economic production to one reflecting people's income, consumption, and wealth, with an emphasis on the household perspective. In other words, the Commission renders more prominence to the distribution of income, consumption, and wealth, in correspondence with sustainability indicators (Stiglitz et al, 2009). What is interesting to note here is that economic progress and international coordination, in the views presented by Delors, Fitoussi, Atkinson, Birdsall, and Rodrik, are made contingent upon substantive policy choices, such as poverty reduction and climate management, in much the same way as the regime of 'embedded liberalism' hinged on (male) full employment and adequate social protection. What these observers thus seem to advocate is perhaps best described as a form of 'embedded globalization'.

Periods of unsettled beliefs can thus inspire new politics. We have learnt this from the experience of the Great Depression in the 1930s, as well as the crisis of stagflation in the 1970s and 1980s. After two decades of neo-liberalism, a critical re-imagining of economy and society, including the role of public authority and political sovereignty, is underway. In addition, there is a fundamental need to offer a better understanding of the international constraints and possibilities for substantive concerted action in a new world order of 'embedded globalization' where national governments remain in charge for regulating a global economy. Even in the realm of international coordination, any sustainable solution to the global crisis continues to rely heavily on domestic legitimacy. Nowhere is this political challenge more apparent than in Europe.

Bibliography

Akerlof, G.A. and Shiller, R.J. (2009), Animal Spirits. How Human Psychology Drives the Economy and Why It Matters for Global Capitalism. Princeton: Princeton University Press.

Atkinson, T. et al. (2002), Social Indicators: The EU and social inclusion. Oxford: Oxford University Press.

Begg, I. et al. (2008), Is Social Europe Fit for Globalisation? A study of the social impact of globalisation in the European Union. Brussels: CEPS, European Commission.

Berger, S. (2005), How We Compete: What Companies Around the World Are Doing to Make It in Today's Global Economy.

Berger, S. and R. Dore (1996), National Diversity and Global Capitalism. Ithaca: Cornell University Press.

Birdsall, N. (2008), 'The Development Agenda as a Global Social Contract; or, We Are All in This Development Boat Together.' WRR Lecture, Saving Globalisation from its Cheerleaders.

Blanchard, O. and Summers, L. (1987), 'Hysteresis in Unemployment', *European Economic Review* 31, 1/2: 288-295.

Buiter, W. (2008), 'Lessons from the Global Crisis for Social Democrats', Den Uyl Lezing, 22 December 2008.

Chua, A. (2007), Day of Empire: How hyperpowers rise to global dominance – and why they fall. New York: Doubleday.

Delors, J. (2006), L'Europe tragique et magnifique. Les grands enjeux européens. Paris: Éditions Saint-Simon.

Eichengreen, B. (2007a), The European Economy since 1945: Coordinated capitalism and beyond. Princeton: Princeton University Press.

Eichengreen, B. (2007b), The Breakup of the Euro Area. NBER Working Paper no. 13393.

Eichengreen, B. (2009), 'Viewpoint: Stress Test for the Euro,' Finance and Development, IMF.org.

Eichengreen, B. and O'Rourke, K.H. 'A Tale of Two Depressions', VOX. www.voxeu.org/index.php?q=node/3421 (last visited: 10 September 2009).

Eichhorst, W. and Hemerijck, A. (2008), 'Welfare and Employment: A European Dilemma.' IZA Discussion Paper 3870.

Elchardus, M. (2002), De dramademocratie. Tielt: Lannoo.

Elchardus, M. (2004), 'De Schizofrenie van Populaire Politiek of: Hoe Ernstig te Zijn in een Dramademocratie?' WRR Lecture, Democratie: Retoriek, Realiteit en Toekomst: Over de Rol van Overheid, Burgers en Media.

Etzioni, A. (2004), The Common Good. Cambridge: Polity Press.

Featherstone, K. and Dyson, K. (1999) The Road to Maastricht: Negotiating economic and monetary union. Oxford: Oxford University Press.

Ferguson, N. (2008), The Ascent of Money. A Financial History of the World. Penguin.

Friedman, M. (1962), Capitalism and Freedom. Chicago: University of Chicago Press.

FSA (2009), Turner Review: A Regulatory Response to the Global Banking Crisis. 2009. www.fsa.gov.uk/pubs/other/turner_review.pdf (Last visited: 10 September 2009).

Giddens, A. (2009), The Politics of Climate Change. Cambridge: Polity Press.

Granovetter, M. (1985), 'Economic Action and Social Structure: the Problem of Embeddedness', *American Journal of Sociology*, 91:3, 481-510.

Grauwe P. de (2008), 'Animal Spirits and Monetary Policy'. CESifo working paper; no. 2418. Category 7: Monetary Policy and International Finance, München: CESifo, Center for Economic Studies & Institute for Economic Research.

Hall, Peter A. (ed.) (1989), The Political Power of Economic Ideas: Keynesianism Across Nations. Princeton: Princeton University Press.

Hall, P. and D. Soskice (eds.) (2001), Varieties of Capitalism: The institutional foundations of comparative advantage. Oxford: Oxford University Press.

Jacoby, W. (2002), 'Talking the Talk and Walking the Walk: The Cultural and Institutional Effects of Western Models', in: Frank Bönker, Klaus Müller and Andreas Pickel (eds), Postcommunist Transformation and the Social Sciences: Cross-Disciplinary Approaches. Boulder: Rowman & Littlefield.

Koo, R.C. (2008), The Holy Grail Of Macro-economics: Lessons From Japan's Great Recession. John Wiley & Sons Inc.

Kuczynski Godard, P. and Williamson, J. (2003), After the Washington Consensus: Restarting Growth and Reform in Latin America. Peterson Institute.

Krugman, P. (2008), The Return of Depression Economics and the Crisis of 2008.

Larosiere Commission (2009), Financial Supervision in the European Union. http://ec.europa.eu/commission_barroso/president/pdf/statement_200902 25_en.pdf (last visited: 10 September 2009).

Levy, J.D. (2006), The State after Statism: New State Activities in the Age of Liberalisation. Boston: Harvard University Press.

Lynn, M. (2009), 'Professor Paul Krugman at War with Niall Ferguson over Inflation.' *Sunday Times*. August 2009.

Maier, C.S. (1987), In Search of Stability: Explorations in historical political economy. New York: Cambridge University Press.

Maier, C.S. (2009), 'The World Economy and the Cold War in the Middle of the Twentieth Century,' in: Leffler, M. and Westad, O.A. (eds.) (2009), The Cambridge History of the Cold War, Vol.1. Cambridge: Cambridge University Press, 44-66.

Moïsi, D. (2008), The Geopolitics of Emotion: How cultures of fear, humiliation and hope are reshaping the world. London: Bodley Head.

Obama, B. (2009), Inaugural Address, 21 January 2009. www.whitehouse.gov/blog/inaugural-address/ (last visited: 10 September 2009).

OECD (1994), Employment Outlook 1994. www.oecd.org/dataoecd/59/18/2485457.pdf (last visited 10 September 2009).

OECD (2009), What is the Economic Outlook for OECD Countries? An Interim Assessment. 2009. www.oecd.org/dataoecd/10/32/43615812.pdf.

Pierson, P. (1998), 'Irresistible Forces, Immovable Objects: Post-industrial Welfare States Confront Permanent Austerity', Journal of European Public Policy, 5 (4): 539-60.

Pierson, P. (ed.) (2001), The New Politics of the Welfare State. Oxford: Oxford University Press.

Polanyi, K. (1944; 1985), The Great Transformation. Boston: Beacon Press.

Posner, R. (2009), A Failure of Capitalism. The Crisis of '08 and the Descent into Depression. Cambridge: Harvard University Press.

Rajan, R. (2005), 'Has Financial Development Made the World Riskier?' NBER Working Paper, no. W11728.

Rodrigues M.J. (ed.) (2009), Europe, Globalisation and the Lisbon Agenda. Cheltenham: Edward Elgar.

Rodrik, D. (2007), One Economics, Many Recipes: Globalisation, institutions, and economic growth. Princeton: Princeton University Press.

Roubini, N. (2006), 'Why Central Banks Should Burst Bubbles'. International Finance 9:1, 87-107.

Ruggie, J.G. (1982), 'International Regimes, Transactions, and Change: Embedded Liberalism in the Postwar Economic Order', International Organisation 36 (Spring 1982).

Sapir, A. (ed.) (2007), Fragmented Power: Europe and the global economy. Brussels: Bruegel.

Scharpf, F.W. (1999), Governing in Europe: Effective and Democratic? Oxford: Oxford University Press.

Scharpf, F.W. (2003), 'The Vitality of the Nation-state in 21st Century Europe.' WRR Lecture, De Vitaliteit van de Nationale Staat in het Europa van de 21e Eeuw.

Schmidt, H. (2008), Außer Dienst: Eine Bilanz. Munich: Siedler.

Shiller, R.J. (2003), The New Financial Order: Risk in the 21st Century. Princeton: Princeton University Press.

Shiller, R.J. (2008), The Subprime Solutions: How Today's Financial Crisis Happened, and What to Do About It. Princeton: Princeton University Press.

Sennett, R. (2008), The Craftsman. New Haven: Yale University Press.

Sennett, R. (2006), The Culture of the New Capitalism. New Haven: Yale University Press.

Streeck, W. (2009), 'Four books on capitalism: review essay', *Socio-Economic Review*, 741-754.

Streeck, W. & Thelen, K. (2005), Beyond Continuity: Institutional Change in Advanced Political Economies. Oxford: Oxford University Press.

Stiglitz, J., Sen, A. and Fitoussi, J.-P. (2009), Report by the Commission on the Measurement of Economic Performance and Social Progress, Paris.

Swedburg, R. (1987), Principles of Economic Sociology. Princeton: Princeton University Press.

Temin, P. (1989), Lesson from the Great Depression. Cambridge: MIT Press.

PART I

DIAGNOSING THE CRISIS

For many, the crisis was a double surprise. Not only did the collapse of the financial sector happen overnight, the spread of the crisis to the real economy took shape at an amazing speed. Now that the dust of the first shock is starting to settle, it is time to trace the roots and origins of the crisis in an attempt to determine its causes. That is the purpose of this part of the volume. Diagnosing the crisis will proceed along various lines of enquiry, addressing global macro-economic instabilities, the role of financial institutions, the absence of regulation, and dominant intellectual trends in the economics profession.

An analysis encompassing practically all of these issues is provided by Barry Eichengreen, the first contributor to this volume. His narration provides a broad frame of reference for the following contributions. Eichengreen's account illustrates the extent to which the current crisis both resembles and differs from the Great Depression of the 1930s.

The next contribution, by historian Charles Maier, tempers the expectations of lessons learned from the past. Of course, earlier crises may offer interesting analogies, but the present circumstances are radically different to previous crisis situations. In addition to historiographical wisdom, Charles Maier offers an alternative history of the crisis: a narrative based not on excessive borrowing but on profligate lending.

Jean-Paul Fitoussi, drawing on his extensive collaboration with Joseph Stiglitz and Amartya Sen, highlights an often overlooked structural instability in the past twenty years of global capitalism. Fitoussi argues that the crisis is rooted in the problem of reverse income distribution, both in the United States and Europe, which fatally depressed global demand. Looking beyond the aftermath of the crisis, he proposes new indicators of social and economic progress and prosperity, considerably expanding the narrow focus on GDP as the foremost indicator of economic vitality.

Paul de Grauwe closes by drawing attention to the intellectual hegemony of rational expectations and macro-economic modelling over the past decades. In his view, intellectual inertia and mathematical sophistication have adversely affected both academia and economic institutions, as this led to significant blind spots for deeper structural economic problems in the run-up to the crisis.

A Tale of Two Crises

Barry Eichengreen

PROFESSOR OF ECONOMIC AND POLITICAL SCIENCE,

UNIVERSITY OF CALIFORNIA, BERKELEY

"I remember the weekend preceding the Bear Stearns deal. I was pulling weeds in the garden and thinking that Monday could be a frighteningly historic day – not unlike what happened when the Credit Anstalt failed in 1931. For the duration of that weekend I feared that Monday morning would bring an economic catastrophe of the same scale as the 1931 financial collapse.

"When the Treasury and Fed stepped in and brokered the rescue of Bear Stearns, it was possible to breathe a sigh of relief. Maybe I was too relieved – just like US policymakers were too relieved. During the run-up to the Lehman Brothers bankruptcy in the fall of 2008, I was less alarmed than I had been in March when the Bear Stearns problem erupted. If the authorities had dealt successfully with Bear Stearns, I thought, there was no reason why they shouldn't deal successfully with Lehman Bros. It was not as if Lehman Bros' problems were a surprise to the markets. Financial market participants had had time to arrange their affairs and square their positions. Surely they understood that Lehman Bros. might collapse.

"As it turned out, everyone was caught off guard by the severity of the market reaction. I was surprised, but more importantly our leaders were surprised and the markets were surprised. No one anticipated the full implications of the Lehman bankruptcy for AIG or for the market in credit default swaps. We didn't appreciate the importance of counterparty risk. We didn't understand the extent of leverage and the impact on the market for distress sales. The bottom line is that there were important respects in which our knowledge of financial markets was incomplete."

A HISTORICAL PERSPECTIVE

With the failure of Lehman Brothers, the financial system was brought to the verge of collapse. As economic activity imploded in the 2008 Q4 and 2009 Q1, analogies with the Great Depression no longer seemed exaggerated. If anything, focusing exclusively on the figures for the United States, as many observers did, caused one to understate the severity of the contraction. The drop in output was even severer in 2009 Q1 in Germany and Japan than in the United States. Looking globally, the downturn in the year starting in April of 2008, where Kevin O'Rourke and I put the business cycle peak, was every bit as severe as the twelve months following August 1929, the month that marked the onset of the Great Depression.

But what made the Great Depression 'great' was its duration – the fact that it was allowed to persist. Globally it was allowed to continue for four years. In some countries, including the Netherlands, it lasted even longer. The current downturn only went global around April 2008. We have seen only one year of global recession with some signs now that the world economy is beginning to pull out of its nosedive.

The current crisis relates to the 1930s depression via its historical development as well. The story of the 2008 crisis is one of ongoing financial deregulation and intensifying competition in the financial sector. In the immediate aftermath of the Great Depression, policymakers scrambled to regulate financial systems, impose limits like the Glass Steagall Act on the types of business in which banks could engage, and limit the amount of risk that banks could take.

Deregulation gained momentum as memories of the financial instabilities of the 1930s faded. With time, in the US and elsewhere, the belief that government intervention breeds inefficiency began to trump these memories of financial instability. Deposit interest rates were freed, forcing banks to compete for their funding. Brokers' commissions were deregulated, enticing big brokers like Bear Stearns that had previously lived comfortably off of commissions on stock trades into new lines of business. Investment and commercial banks were allowed to compete with one another, forcing both to ratchet up their bets in the scramble to survive. Franchise value was eroded by this competition, encouraging financial institutions to take ever greater risks in the struggle to stay afloat. Adding fuel to the fire were the abundant supplies of liquidity, not least the flow of financial capital from Asia to the United States. Excessively loose monetary policy in the United States also provided liquidity in great quantities. Distorted incentive schemes and skewed compensation practices in the big financial institutions exacerbated these instabilities.

In Europe a similarly combustible mix emerged, albeit for different reasons. Risk-taking was again at the heart of the problem, although its origins were different. The single market intensified competition among national financial systems and markets. Facing more cross-border competition, European financial institutions made use of more leverage in the scramble to remain competitive. European monetary unification brought interest rates down dramatically in the previously high-interest southern tier of EU countries and in Ireland, providing cheap funding to financial speculators and frothy housing markets.

Yet these changes had been underway for decades prior to the economic crisis. It is therefore important to ask: Why were their destabilising effects not better anticipated? Officials, academics, and policymakers alike all failed to identify the gravity of the risks. To be sure, some of us warned of a disorderly correction of global imbalances, while others like Bob Shiller warned of a bubble in the housing market. But no one put all of the pieces together and forecast a crisis of the magnitude of the one that broke out in 2007-8.

I see three explanations for this failure. First, an economy is a highly complex non-linear system. This makes predicting the precise way that events may unfold impossible. It is always possible to shout 'fire' in a crowded theatre – to continuously warn that a crisis is coming. But what use is that? There is a 'type 2' as well as a 'type 1' error – economists don't want to be accused of regularly predicting 11 out of the last 7 crises.

Globally, the downturn was every bit as severe as the twelve months following August 1929.

Second, few of us were versed in the details of the new financial instruments developed in the course of the last decade – credit default swaps and collateralised debt obligations, for example. This kind of nuts-and-bolts financial engineering was not taught in the top economics Ph.D. programs. Officials were no more knowledgeable or better briefed. The only people familiar with the intricacies of credit default swaps prior to 2007 were a few specialists in the financial markets more concerned with their own bottom lines than with the financial system as a whole.

Third, to paraphrase Chuck Prince, no one wanted to stop dancing as long as the music kept playing. This was true of academics and officials and not just financial market participants. When things were going well, people preferred to believe that they were going well for a good reason. As more officials and academics bought into the ideology of market fundamentalism, they focused more on rationales for the success of recent policies than on probing for vulnerabilities and weaknesses. Nonconformity was uncomfortable when so many people were making so much money, and so many academic colleagues were being invited to lavish investment bank conferences. Theories pointing to potential problems were there for the taking, but people failed to reach out and grab them. It was not the underdevelopment of economic theory, in other words, that caused the crisis. Instead, academics and regulators chose to cherry-pick those theories that provided justification for why things had been going smoothly and for why this should continue. They neglected work on asymmetric information, agency theory, and behavioural finance, among other topics, that might have pointed out existing problems, opting instead for work that reassured them of the stability of an unstable system.

History is the alternative to theory. Contrary to what some people say, lack of appreciation of history has not been a problem in the crisis. But history is a double-edged sword. It provides a lens through which to view the present, but this lens can also result in short-sightedness. The policy-making community had learned valuable lessons from the 1930s crisis and depression. Those lessons led it to react forcefully when parallels with the Great Depression became apparent. In contrast to the 1930s, policymakers implemented counter-cyclical monetary and fiscal policies. So far, so good. However, this perspective, informed by the history of the 1930s, caused some oversights. Regulators failed to recognise the importance of the shadow banking system because there had been no shadow banking system in the 1930s. They missed the importance of collateralised debt obligations and credit default swaps because there had been no analogous instruments in the 1930s.

AN ANALYSIS OF POST-CRISIS RECOVERIES

Different countries will fare differently in their recoveries from the crisis. The US recovery will be slow and lethargic by the standard of past economic recoveries. The country will emerge from its crisis with a heavy debt burden, a mix of loose monetary and tight fiscal policies unfavourable to investment, and an undercapitalised banking system that will be reluctant to start lending vigorously again. At the same time, the US has an advantage as a result of its flexible labour markets, which will make it easier than in Europe and Japan to move labour and other resources out of finance and residential construction and into other activities.

History is the alternative to theory.

How would I grade the US authorities overall? I would give them an 'A-' for monetary policy: very good except for failing to take adequate account of derivatives, credit default swaps and the shadow banking system, as well as being too close to the Troubled Asset Relief Program (TARP) in the autumn of 2008. The US authorities get a 'B' for fiscal policy. Relying half on tax cuts and half on increases in public spending, as the Obama Administration did, was broadly appropriate; tax cuts get into people's pockets faster, but there is no guarantee that they will spend them, especially when uncertainty is high. Infrastructure spending takes more time, but the increase in spending is guaranteed. In other words, it made sense to rely roughly half and half on each.

With the benefit of hindsight (that is, knowing then what we know now), the $ 787 billion fiscal package was probably undersized. Unemployment rose even faster than the incoming administration anticipated when it put the package together at the end of 2008. But this is not something that could be known at the time; we had to wait for the July 2009 revision of the 2008 Q4 GDP figures to know how quickly the economy was contracting at the time when the fiscal package was being designed.

For housing policy, I would give the US authorities another 'B'. Most of the provisions of the Administration's program were intended to reduce the interest payments homeowners were required to make, but few addressed the need for principal reduction. If mortgages are still worth far more than the homes to which they are attached (if mortgagees are 'under water'), then no interest rate, no matter how low, provides sufficient incentive for homeowners to keep paying down this debt (especially in a system like ours where mortgages are non-recourse). In these circumstances, foreclosures will remain widespread, and the housing market depressed.

I give the US authorities a failing grade for banking policy. The stress tests and the conclusion that the 19 biggest banks would be required to raise only $ 75 billion in new capital amounted to moving the goal posts, to use an expression from American football. Adequately recapitalising the banks so that they had a sufficient cushion to begin lending vigorously again was politically impossible. US policymakers therefore changed the definition of what it meant to be 'adequately recapitalised' to mean raising just enough new capital to survive in a reasonably adverse scenario. But there is no way that, with only this amount of capital, the banks could resume the vigorous lending typical of a recovery period. Lack of adequate bank lending will be a chronic problem in the coming recovery. Since the AIG bonus scandal, the American public has been disenchanted with taxpayer-funded bailouts, and understandably so. So while there was no technical obstacle to adequately recapitalising the banks, there was a political obstacle. The way the TARP was done (Secretary Paulson said, "Trust us to do the right thing and exempt us from all legal liability") made the further use of taxpayer funds to recapitalise the banks politically unacceptable to the public. Under both the Bush and the Obama administrations, the Treasury has opted not to push this issue, knowing that Congress would simply refuse to appropriate more funds. Instead, in order to avoid scaring the public, US policymakers announced that $ 75 billion of additional funds would render the banks adequately capitalised, the facts notwithstanding to the contrary. They prayed that, with time, the problem would resolve itself.

Turning to other recovery experiences, China has fared relatively well despite suffering a 20 % collapse in exports. The Chinese authorities applied the largest fiscal stimulus of any country scaled by the size of GDP. They also applied that stimulus earlier than any other country. If you add to the increase in direct public spending the increase in bank lending directed by the authorities, much of which went into investment by public enterprises and others, the effective fiscal stimulus is larger still. Despite some undesirable buy-Chinese provisions, their stimulus package was on the whole quite admirable. It was an exemplar to the rest of the world.

The changing structure of the global economy, as well as China's recognition of its citizens' demands for higher living standards and increased consumption, will eventually force Chinese policymakers to move away from their current savings-based growth model. This will require constructing a stronger social safety net to break citizens' incentive to engage in excessive saving. The authorities have already taken a number of steps to build up the social infrastructure, improve health care, and expand access to education. These programs are designed to re-assure residents that the state will help them in the event of a proverbial rainy day. Hence they need to save less. Still, the reality is that the transition will take time to complete.

In Europe, major exporting countries, above all Germany, will find that their export markets in Central and Eastern Europe are growing more slowly than in 2005-7. They will feel growing competition in sectors like machine-tool and other capital-goods production from China and, eventually, India. Germany has maybe a decade to implement a new economic strategy before China pushes the country out of its existing export markets. This new strategy should involve moving resources out of the production of manufactures and into the still-underdeveloped service sector.

As a result of Europe's slow recognition of the severity of the crisis, fiscal stimulus was implemented more slowly and less aggressively than elsewhere. The result will be a more lethargic and drawn-out recovery. The European Central Bank for its part did a good job in responding to the crisis. Despite the initial delay in cutting rates, it responded more quickly and aggressively than many expected in light of the large size of its Executive Board, which can make quick decision-making difficult, and the heterogeneity of the euro area, which means that different countries would prefer different policy responses. The response of the ECB may have helped to offset the relative weakness of national stimulus plans.

The other reason that fiscal stimulus programs were less aggressive in Europe is that European economies are very open, as a result of which much of the benefit of fiscal stimulus spills over to a country's neighbours. This creates free-rider problems. Europe needs better fiscal policy coordination to prevent their recurrence. The Stability and Growth Pact as written will not provide a solution. Fiscal discipline must be achieved at the national level – by building political institutions and public consensus around the principle that countries will run surpluses in good times so that they can run deficits in bad times. Nor will simply targeting a specific date by which budget balance will be achieved – as both the US and German governments have done – really solve anything. Germany has set a target to eliminate the deficit by 2016. However, as soon as such targets become uncomfortable, they tend to be scrapped. The only reliable way of achieving budget balance is by building a domestic political consensus around the need for fiscal prudence.

Europe faces further challenges as a result of the deep integration of its national financial markets. You can't have national regulators of an integrated pan-European financial market. Turning the clock back to the time when Europe had banks and financial markets that were national is unrealistic; the internationalisation of banks must be accepted and matched by the creation of a true pan-European bank regulatory agency.

The crisis has also increased the appeal of euro area membership. When the crisis broke, it became apparent that the euro area provided a safe harbour. Membership was the only guarantee of access to the emergency credit facilities of the ECB. However, the crisis also resuscitated the question of whether the euro had been a good idea in the first place. Euro adoption bears some of the responsibility of the susceptibility to the crisis of countries like Ireland and Spain. When they joined, interest rates came down dramatically. The result was an enormous housing and lending boom that has contributed directly to the difficulties that followed. Now Ireland, for example, faces double-digit unemployment and a 10% collapse in GDP. The question is whether the benefits in good times justify the costs borne in bad times. Was there a way that countries like Ireland could have obtained the advantages of the common currency – and advantages there surely were – without also setting itself up for a painful fall? Would more fiscal discipline have been possible? Would tighter regulation of the Irish banking system have helped? Would this have been enough to avert an unsustainable boom and strengthen the resilience of financial systems?

THE NEED FOR NEW COOPERATION AND NEW VISION

Since the crisis, there have been worries of protectionist policies, not least because protectionism was such a problem in the 1930s. In the last couple of years, these have been ushered in on the backs of stimulus packages and crisis recovery plans. Protectionist measures in the advanced countries have reflected the concern that the costs of stimulus packages are national – they impose a heavier burden on future domestic taxpayers – but the benefits are global as the stimulus to demand spills out to other countries. Similarly, lack of coordination of monetary policies may lead to sharp currency movements that again elicit protectionist reactions. If some countries continue with loose monetary policies after other countries exit from such policies, the exchange rates of the first set of countries will depreciate, which will look like currency manipulation to the second group of countries, which will be tempted to retaliate.

This means that a priority for the international community should be to coordinate its response to the crisis. Governments have been reasonably successful at doing so by the standards of the 1930s. The G20 was very significant in this regard: as a venue for cooperation, it allowed policy coordination to encompass both the advanced and developing economies. It would have been folly to think that the G7 could serve as a steering committee for the 21st century world economy and make consequential decisions about these issues without China and other emerging economies at the table. The crisis gave the G20 visibility and purpose. It considerably enhanced the stature of the new group.

Countries have shown a willingness to come together and discuss multilateral responses, but there has been little clarity on the exact shape that those responses should take.

Despite its successes, the G20 has problems. It is not clear why these 20 specific countries were appointed to represent the world. Why for example is Argentina in, while Columbia and Venezuela are out? One way of rationalising these arrangements would be by moving to a Group of 24 based on representation in the International Monetary and Financial Committee (IMFC) of the International Monetary Fund (IMF). Of the 24 representatives in this committee, five represent individual countries, whereas the others represent groups of countries. The IMFC exists by virtue of the Articles of Agreement of the IMF, a fact that lends it legitimacy. All this makes it a suitable structure to supersede the G20.

Another problem with the G20 and another obstacle to international policy coordination generally is Europe's inability to speak with one voice. Twenty, much less 24, is an uncomfortably large number of participants to meet and take quick action. The problem is that the EU has as many as ten seats at a table (counting the European Commission, Spain – which attended the recent G20 meeting at European insistence even though it is not one of the designated countries – and the other European members). The EU should reorganise its representation into two seats – one for the euro area and one for the rest of the EU. This would streamline decision-making, both within the G20 and the IMF – while freeing up seats at the table for currently unrepresented states and regions.

The biggest challenge, however, is not decision-making structures but a lack of common vision. Countries have shown a willingness to come together and discuss multilateral responses, but there has been little clarity on the exact shape that those responses should take. Despite their increased voice in the institutions of international economic governance, emerging economies have failed to articulate a decisive vision of exactly what they want organisations like the IMF and the World Bank to do. Emerging economies want more voice and representation, but having more voice and representation in an organisation that follows the same policies and makes the same mistakes hardly constitutes an improvement. Now that their own money is on the line – now that they are providing more of the funding for the IMF – emerging markets will probably not want to move towards an IMF that lends without conditions – clearly they will attach priority to having their money repaid. But they have given little indication as to how they would like to alter these conditions or lending rules.

The same 'vision problem' is apparent in discussions of the dollar-based international reserve system. China and Russia have proposed using the Special Drawing Rights (SDR) of the IMF as the main form of international reserves. Yet they have not yet provided concrete ideas about how to manage this transition and make an SDR-based system a reality. Their calls for an enhanced role for the SDR have been of largely symbolic value; they have been a way of signalling dissatisfaction with the prevailing dollar-based reserve system.

Making the SDR a true reserve currency would require a very extensive effort in building new markets. For the SDR to be an attractive form for central banks to hold reserves in, it would have to be possible for them to buy and sell SDRs freely without moving prices; there would have to exist liquid markets in SDR claims. For liquid markets to exist, the SDR would have to be an attractive instrument in which to do other business. It would have to be possible to use it for financing trade, undertaking international investment and making transactions in foreign exchange markets. Currently, to exchange Thai baht for Korean won, a trader must sell his baht for dollars and then use those dollars to buy won. Foreign exchange markets would have to be restructured so that currency traders went through the SDR rather than the dollar; again, this assumes the existence of deep and liquid markets that do not, at present, exist. Someone – the IMF? – would have to act as market maker, buying and selling SDRs for other currencies at narrow big-ask spreads. All this is not going to happen overnight.

Even the euro, now ten years old, is not an attractive alternative to the dollar as a reserve currency, precisely because markets in euro area government bonds are not as liquid as markets in US government bonds. The implication is that moving from a dollar- to an SDR-based reserve system would take decades, not just years. In any case, the fact of the matter is that the Chinese are probably more interested in making the Chinese renminbi a reserve currency – a process that will probably take as long to complete as the SDR project.

New mechanisms are also needed for preventing the re-emergence of global imbalances. One idea would be to mechanise the process of determining whether or not a country has a chronically undervalued currency that is working to destabilise the international balance. It is simply not feasible for the IMF or, for that matter, anyone else to determine the 'fundamental equilibrium exchange rate' between, for example, the renminbi and the dollar. It would be easier to monitor the economic relationships that those exchange rates affect, like China's current account balance. Imagine that China ran a current account surplus of, say, 10% of GDP for several consecutive years. By amending the Articles of Agreement of the IMF, it could then be made subject to a tax on its reserves, and that liability would give it an incentive to adjust. The resulting tax revenues could be used to provide funding for the IMF. They could be used to provide resources for development lending and grants through the World Bank. They could pay for the peace-keeping operations of the United Nations. In addition, they would give a surplus country an incentive to adjust. To be sure, a country that wished to continue running surpluses – that found it difficult to adjust their saving and investment – would be able to do so, but it would pay a price. So it would feel additional adjustment pressure.

A TIME FOR EXTRAORDINARY POLITICS?

In the US, the gravity of the economic crisis led many to proclaim that this was a moment of extraordinary politics. The crisis had opened people's eyes to the flaws in the US economic system. It was claimed that this was an opportunity for profound reforms which would produce radical new state structures and transform state/market relations.

If there ever existed such a moment of extraordinary politics, it is quickly passing. Recall the aftermath of Hurricane Katrina. The public was horrified by graphic images of inequality, where the divisions ran along racial lines, and by the inadequacy of the government's response. People wrote that those images would change American society forever – that such pronounced racial and economic inequalities simply could not be allowed to persist and that radical changes in government programs would follow. But after a few months, those pictures fell off the front pages of the newspapers. The sense of urgency passed. There was a return to business as usual.

Similarly, with the financial crisis, it is not clear that the resolve created by immediate events will be enduring enough to support true social and political reform. To be sure, American households have lost, on average, a quarter of their retirement wealth. If, in the upcoming years, the resulting sense of insecurity is exacerbated by continued and persistently rising unemployment and a perpetually unstable stock market, then indeed pressure will grow for the state to step in and undertake fundamental reforms. Americans may, once and for all, discard the old adage that "government is the problem, markets the solution."

If there ever existed a moment of extraordinary politics, it is quickly passing.

However, I suspect that the period of extraordinary politics is already over. The US has too many vested interests and is too wedded to free-market ideology for radical change to occur easily. The medical-industrial complex made up of insurance companies and hospitals is as strong as ever, and big banks will continue to push against strengthened regulation. Real change will require government to convince the public that it can build mechanisms that prevent the state from being captured by these special interests. Medical and insurance companies are important financial contributors to the key senators in the health care debate. Financial interests are similarly powerful in the current debate over financial re-regulation. Given this, how can we be sure that a new systemic financial regulator will act in the interest of the public and the stability of the system rather than in the interest of the industry?

It is true that the crisis has already brought about profound changes in the operation of some public institutions, but these may return to the status quo before long. The Fed is one example. The crisis pushed the Fed into a broad range of new interventions and thus into a more politicised role, from which it will try to escape as soon as possible. The crisis debunked the idea that setting interest rates had been perfected to the point of a science rather than an art. No longer were generic rules and mechanical inflation targeting systems seen as acceptable. The idea that the Fed should not lean its weight against growing bubbles or financial excesses in the economy was similarly discredited. The central bank is now engaged in a wide array of new operations in many different financial markets, and this makes new mechanisms of accountability necessary: setting interest rates can remain politically insulated, but intervening in markets that profoundly affect people's pension portfolios cannot. For this reason, the Fed is likely to try to retreat from these new lines of work, returning to its old role of regulating monetary policy, albeit this time with a closer eye to avoiding bubbles and promoting financial stability.

Health care reform in the US, with a public option ensuring universal coverage, would be a positive development, but it will not solve all of the country's problems. Most importantly, contrary to expectations, it will cut rather than create jobs. The US currently spends twice the OECD average on health care, and the primary ambition of the current reform is to dramatically reduce this figure. As a result, a variety of middle-level jobs in insurance companies are likely to be cut.

All of these issues bring the US's capacity for extraordinary political change into question. However, there is one development that has largely gone unnoticed that the US should be quite pleased about: unlike in the 1930s, there has been little populist backlash or rise in anti-immigrant politics as a result of the crisis. While the reason for this is unclear, one possible explanation is that, unlike in the 1930s, the US now has a welfare state system, which – although nowhere near as elaborate as Europe's system – at least grants citizens recourse to unemployment benefits in the hard times that they are currently facing.

Overall there is room for optimism. In response to the crisis, the international community has come together in ways unimaginable seven decades ago. Nevertheless, there is still a lot to be done, and there is still plenty of room for creative policymakers to leave their mark on the post-crisis period.

A History of Profligate Lending

Charles Maier

PROFESSOR OF HISTORY,

HARVARD UNIVERSITY

CONTOURS OF THE CRISIS

The current crisis was triggered by the rapid realisation that the vast amount of debt which banks and securities dealers had taken on, sliced, diced and repackaged as derivatives, and sold to other financial intermediaries was probably hugely overvalued. Paper claims amounting to hundreds of billions, perhaps trillions of dollars or euros, confidently marketed as assets now appeared to be mere liabilities. The credit default swaps or insurance policies that might supposedly hedge against these risks also threatened to collapse. The sense of panic naturally enough impacted the equities markets, as it appeared that consumer demand for real products must wither as well. Thus, the first economic crisis of the 21st century has consisted of two components: a dramatic collapse of asset values, which has perhaps been staunched by massive stimuli packages, and a downturn in real activity. Even if this may be ending in the final quarter of 2009, the crisis will leave a long-term residue of high unemployment levels. Emerging from the crisis, societies will therefore require a profound redistribution of people and jobs.

> ## Just as the landscape of employment is in a state of upheaval, so too is the global distribution of power.

Just as the landscape of employment is in a state of upheaval, so too is the global distribution of power. The era in which Europe and the United States held the greatest percentage share of global economic transactions is coming to an end. This does not necessarily imply that the West will become poorer, but it is clear that the hegemony of the two great Western economic powers will come to an end. It should be noted that although the crisis dramatically intensified this transition, this shift would have taken place anyway. A crisis of the sort we are experiencing now has merely made these facts clear.

In times of crisis, the past is often scanned for beacons of orientation. Previous crises may offer interesting analogies, but it should be realised that differences in historical context hamper direct comparisons. The crisis of the 1930s, for example, certainly did teach us lessons on fighting the immediate fire of recession, but its historical context was completely different. For one thing, the sequencing was different. The equities crash of 1929 preceded the great deflationary contraction of 1931, whereas in 2008-2009 they threatened to strike together. Neither do the poisoned political atmosphere and the legacy of nationalism following World War I find ready parallels in the current political climate. Admittedly, nationalism is flaring up again in various guises, but much less strongly than in the 1930s. To a large extent, the European Union can be thanked for this, as it precludes much nationalist exuberance. The willingness of the EU, the United States, the IMF, and other agencies to extend lifelines also has mitigated aggravated nationalist reactions.

PROFLIGATE LENDING

Since the outbreak of the global recession, commentators have issued a myriad of explanations of how such a crisis could occur. Strikingly, virtually everybody agrees that the crisis must be traced to instabilities in the subprime mortgage market in the US. Households were talked into improvident mortgages they could not support, and cunning financial experts repackaged and resold these mortgages as unsound derivatives. Without a doubt, the crisis partly stems from the fact that there was –and still is – no clarity as to the value of these 'toxic' assets. Should they be 'marked to market' or radically written down as almost worthless, or should they be deemed to have a come-back value if only they can be held without pressure to liquidate? In addition to focusing on the subprime mortgage problem, some commentators (specifically the defenders of the financial community) have liked to present the collapse of Lehman Brothers as the catalyst that caused the unstable economic structures to collapse, but this is in fact an exculpatory explanation that serves to shift the blame from reckless financial behaviour to a supposedly inept public authority. Preventing the collapse of Lehman Brothers would not have prevented the crisis. Nevertheless, this narrative has become the conventional history of the economic crisis, and there seems to be little interest in pursuing different lines of inquiry. Although problems in the mortgage market and the collapse of Lehman Brothers certainly played an important role, these explanations of the crisis suffer from historical myopia: the more structural causes of the crisis date back further. Most importantly, this narrative neglects the fact that for over-borrowing to be possible, there needs to be a willing lender that is capable of supplying this abundance of credit. The history of the economic crisis is less a tale of improvident borrowing than it is a tale of profligate lending.

Such an alternative historical narrative of the economic crisis would take the *supply* of credit as the starting point, rather than its *demand*. The core of such a narrative runs as follows. The sustained inflationary trends of the 1970s exhausted public patience with neo-Keynesian political wage bargaining and welfare expenditures. To the surprise of many observers, the Western public voted in leaders who abandoned the neo-corporatist efforts of the 1970s and sought to return to market discipline and to bring their money supplies under control. The result (or at least the intended result) in the early 1980s was a significant monetary tightening: Central banks were made more independent of national finance ministries, and both the monetary and fiscal policies of the Western economies were characterised by restraint. Of course, there were exceptions to this rule – Ronald Reagan essentially spent his way out of the 1980s recession – but in general such was the type of political economy dominant in the Western economies. This regime of restraint and deregulation was a new departure from the previous political economy of the post-war era. Until the 1980s, national governments had held themselves responsible for increasing societal affluence. This policy paradigm was expressed through a variety of welfare institutions and elements of non-market regulation. Many of these institutions and arrangements were dismantled in the 1980s, a process spearheaded by the United States in partnership with Britain, whose ideological support was an important legitimating factor.

An alternative historical narrative of the economic crisis would take the supply of credit as the starting point, rather than its demand.

But while publicly adopting the imperatives of contraction and deregulation, national governments struck an implicit deal with the private sector. Although governments accepted the staunching of public monetary expansion, in effect they allowed the private financial sector instead to create all the money and monetary equivalents it wanted. This transfer of capacities was crucial to usher in the era of neo-liberalism; it provided an incentive to develop a variety of ways to create new money, whether via credit cards, derivatives, or any of the other new financial products the market has spawned over the past 25 years. This transfer of monetary power from one sector to another may have been largely unintended, and indeed never really understood; but economics is a study of revealed preferences, and to an extent, so is the history of political economy. In retrospect, what was revealed by the economic policies of the 1980s, especially in the United States and the United Kingdom, was a preference for the private sector taking up the task of ensuring continued economic growth.

The financial sector happily accepted this new responsibility. The amount of money in circulation has exploded since the 1980s, and this was not driven by consumer demand. Credit was actively pushed on people and businesses, at home and abroad. Indeed, even today as the crisis continues, most Americans receive frequent offers for new credit cards. The great puzzle is why this growth of privately emitted purchasing power did not just rekindle inflation. An important explanation is that citizens were protected from potentially disastrous consequences of this profligate lending in two ways. First, the economic recovery in the late 1980s effectively absorbed a large portion of this credit money. Subsequently, during the 1990s, the economic crisis was exported to South American and Southeast Asian countries. These countries borrowed huge sums, and the whole gamut of new financial products, credit cards included, was pushed on them as well. In this way, lending appeared to be endlessly profitable.

This massive, though fictitious, wealth creation through profligate lending by the private sector should be understood against the backdrop of dominant trends in the world economy during the second half of the twentieth century. Although the implicit deal between the public and private sectors may have been a significant shift, the premise on which their respective economic behaviour was based remained constant: economic growth as the symbol of national prowess. This mentality was a remnant of the Cold War, a time characterised by competitive pressure to outperform the rival political block. This legacy has proven exceptionally sticky; to date, the collective social imagination has been unable to replace this symbol.

The emphasis on economic growth had regained impetus with the end of World War II, which had left Europe and other parts of the world in physical, social, and economic ruin. For both the Eastern and Western Bloc, the need for economic reconstruction defined the immediate post-war years. Reconstructing their economies reinforced the trade-off between present and future, which is always at the heart of economic progress. Countries imposed an economic regime in which immediate gains were deferred in the hope of securing a more affluent tomorrow. This amazing psychosocial discipline that peaked in the 1950s cannot be entirely explained by the necessity of reconstruction. The adversarial contest between East and West further fostered a mentality that could forestall immediate gratification; Cold War victory, so it was perceived, also depended on economic growth. Likewise, the success of the European welfare state also in part depended on the Cold War. It was a symbol of national pride signifying the social sensitivity of the world of free market capitalism. In these ways, the Cold War exerted a profound behavioural impact on economic habits.

The years of restraint lasted until the mid-1960s, when the demands of the present, of consumption and social welfare, of youth culture and expressivity reclaimed the present at the expense of the future. Although this was a period of Cold War détente, the imperative of economic growth left a lasting imprint on the politics of national economies, and it remained the yardstick with which to measure national success. Therefore, by the early 1970s, some of the foundations of profligate lending had already been laid: a strong demand for consumption and welfare, and the continued expectation of growth that held a firm grasp on national economies.

Nothing in the course of human history had to happen.

The move towards to profligate lending depended on one further political-economic factor – the dwindling importance of labour as an economic force. Starting in the 1960s, the balance of power in the workplace had begun to erode, as labour markets tightened and traditional industries such as coal and steel entered a period of overproduction and decline. This period marked the transition to a post-industrial society that no longer put as great an emphasis on labour and production. It ended a period that would, in the words of the Italian sociologist Aris Accornero, be remembered as 'the century of work'. New lifestyles, the expansion of consumption, and new migrants all dissolved the once heroic austerity of labour. Over the course of half a century, Western mass prosperity, which had originally been based on mass-production industry, fragmented into a kaleidoscopic society shaped by migration, job evolution, ideological reassessment, and insecurity. In short, the premises of the Western political economy were fundamentally altered. The traditional European proletariat dissolved, as industrial labour lost its salience for Western economic progress.

These historical transformations had two consequences: first, labour and heavy industry could no longer account for the bulk of economic growth. In addition, the free market economy started losing its countervailing power. Traditionally, labour had to be pacified to offset what was offered to the financial sector, but when the financial sector was given its expanded license to issue credit in the 1980s, such tradeoffs no longer had to be made. This especially applied to the UK and the US, where Thatcher and Reagan effectively destroyed labour's remaining power. These transformations in the landscape of the political economy, combined with a continued emphasis on economic growth, proved to be fertile soil for the recent quarter-century of profligate lending.

Although tracing the historical contingencies that preceded the current economic crisis aid in interpreting it, such analysis sheds little light on what the consequences of the crisis are likely to be. Much will depend on the political choices that will be made in its aftermath. Unfortunately, the elbow room for politics is limited. Germany and France have already adopted a relatively conservative political agenda. Obama, similarly, has to manoeuvre around conservative criticism that the US is heading for huge inflation. Policy space is further restricted by the conflict between current and future recovery needs; the instruments you need today are the same instruments that will get economies into trouble tomorrow.

That said, the crisis is certainly not inconsequential. Some of the rules of the economic game will be rewritten. The erratic behaviour of hedge funds may be restrained, and complicated financial products will face demands of greater transparency. But whether the crisis indeed marks the beginning of the new era is an open question. Intriguingly, the crisis could result in a reassessment of the most vital political-economical imperative inherited from the Cold War period: economic growth. There is now an opportunity to ask the question, what if we do not grow? Japan, for example, is a country that has not grown for ten years but has remained a rich society. The emphasis on growth arose in the context of reconstruction and East-West adversarial relations. From there, it grew to become a generally embraced and virtually unquestioned maxim. Under today's circumstances, and with the political imperatives that underpinned profligate lending having taken a severe blow, there is a window of opportunity for rethinking the goals of both the national and international political economy.

A similar point can be made on the subject of employment. During the 19th century, much employment was seasonal. In contrast to the second half of the 20th century, full, year-round employment was not a policy objective. In other words, it is not a historical given that every individual is always equally needed in the workforce. There is no economic reason why labour could not return to being the slack resource in programming optimal economic performance. Only the value we place in work and the shame of unemployment drive aspirations of full employment, but such values of political economy are, as we have seen, historically contingent.

Finally, the conclusion is certainly warranted that the crisis has served as a reality check. After having been able to postpone the inflationary consequences of two decades of profligate lending, reality has finally caught up. People simply did not have the wealth they thought they did. This, however, does not mean the crisis could have been foreseen. In retrospect, one can always identify signals that warned of the impeding collapse, but such omens are only meaningful after the fact. More important than searching for the omens of the crisis, or trying to ascribe to it a certain inevitability, is reconstructing a causal narrative that is plausible rather than determinist; a story that makes sense of today's outcomes but without precluding other outcomes. Nothing in the course of human history *had* to happen.

The Problem of Social Deflation

Jean-Paul Fitoussi

PROFESSOR OF ECONOMICS,

INSTITUT D'ETUDES POLITIQUES

"The idea of a separation between the financial system and all other systems underpinning globalisation, such as the social system, the real economy, and global trade, is worrying. This separation is in fact an intellectual curiosum. The fact that it was fashionable and dominant – as the great influence of Real Business Cycles theories since the beginning of the 1980s attests to – is not a proof of the theory in itself, but is instead just an illustration of the non-linear evolution of economic theory. In Keynes's General Theory, the system was indecomposable, meaning that the fate of various sectors was jointly determined. Later, we suffered a backward evolution in thought, though it was hidden by great mathematical sophistication.

"However, in actuality, financial issues, trade issues, social issues, and economic issues are all deeply intertwined. Considering the financial sector as separate from its entanglements precluded asking how developments in this sector influenced income inequality and economic disequilibria; this was essentially a forbidden debate. The dichotomy was an integral part of the Washington Consensus, which has dominated the international political economy since the 1980s.

"With the current crisis, the intellectual underpinnings of this model are finally being called into question by an audience that extends beyond a few radical critics. This crisis also offers an opportunity to redefine the stakes of monetary policy. In the last twenty-five years, price stability seemed to be the sole objective of monetary policy. And indeed, central banks all over the world ought to be commended for having successfully fought against inflation. At the same time, successful price stabilisation was neither a necessary nor a sufficient condition for economic stability. Macro economic stability is a multidimensional concept that includes price stability, but extends far beyond this indicator. To achieve economic stability, monetary policy needs a multiplicity of instruments to be used alongside interest rates: targeting asset prices, regulatory measures and quantitative easing (or restricting). To pursue multiple objectives requires, above all, a strong coordination with other policies, in particular fiscal and social policies."

INEQUALITY AS THE ROOT OF THE CRISIS

The crisis has structural roots. The potential aggregate demand deficiency actually preceded the financial crisis - the crisis simply made it apparent. This lack of demand was due to structural changes in income distribution. Since 1980, the median wage in most advanced countries has stagnated and in some cases even declined. Inequalities have grown as, at the same time, high levels of unemployment were tolerated, above all in Europe. This situation has no historical equivalent in times of peace. These trends have a variety of causes, including asymmetric globalisation (with greater liberalisation of capital than of labour markets), deficiencies in corporate governance, and a breakdown of the more egalitarian social conventions that had emerged after World War II.

Most importantly, these trends are the result of the political-economic dogmas of the last quarter-century. The Washington Consensus not only favoured the liberalisation of the financial system, it also was a doctrine that allowed little room for political governance, especially in financial and economic affairs. To ensure the freedom of financial flows, the Washington Consensus prescribed structural reforms aimed at increased flexibility and minimal state intervention. This was paired with a misperception of what globalisation meant. Under the Washington Consensus, globalisation was perceived as a process that occurred between nation-states. In reality, the nation-state has always had a clear function of putting strict limits on the manoeuvring room of free markets, protecting its population and ensuring some degree of equality. This function has been neglected as a consequence of the belittling of the state under the Washington Consensus.

By itself, increased inequality implies weak global demand; only the top income tiers increased their spending. Much of their excess income was invested in various new assets promising high returns. In such a context, it is no surprise that aggregate demand within countries shows little growth. Global demand encountered further problems because of the way the 1997 Asian crisis was managed. The international financial institutions imposed structural adjustment programs on countries in need that prescribed very restrictive macro-economic policies. These countries had no choice but to conduct pro-cyclical policies. Most countries learnt during this episode that to avoid such tutelage, they needed to self-insure against macro-economic instabilities. The only way of doing so was to accumulate reserves. This depressed global demand even further. Those countries which could not hoard reserves – mostly developing economies – are now forced to appeal to the IMF, which continues to issue loans under the same stringent conditions. This may further aggravate the global imbalances that underpin the crisis.

These structural weaknesses in demand would have translated into weak demand growth if expansionary monetary policies had not been used to avoid the consequences of insufficient aggregate demand. In the United States, inequalities increased and many people were forced to decrease savings and indebt themselves to maintain their spending power – a process facilitated by lax monetary policy. But this does not apply to the US alone; almost everywhere, private indebtedness grew as median wages stagnated. At the same time, limited social security provisions forced the US government to pursue macro-economic policies to fight unemployment, increasing government debt.

The crisis is the story of increasing inequalities.

In Europe, the redistribution of wealth towards higher incomes resulted in an increase in national savings and depressed growth. In the past 15 years, Europe's institutional setting, notably the deficit constraints embedded in the Maastricht criteria and the Stability and Growth Pact, resulted in a low reactivity of fiscal policy and a monetary policy that was far more restrictive than necessary. This led to a regime of 'soft' growth, which in turn implied mounting public debt.

In short, the crisis is the story of increasing inequalities which depressed aggregate demand and prompted a monetary policy characterised by low interest rates. As a consequence, private debt was allowed to increase beyond sustainable levels. At the same time, the search for high-return investments by those who benefited from the increase in inequalities led to a vast overvaluation of asset prices. This bubble has now burst. So although the crisis may have emerged in the financial sector, its roots are much deeper and lie in a structural change in income distribution that had been going on for 25 years. From this perspective, the causes of the crisis were endogenous to the financial system.

The financial sector itself also suffered from a troubled dynamic. Much of its erratic behaviour can be explained by the fact that it had to perform during a period of very low interest rates. To maintain their profitability, banks found it useful to develop new financial products and to increase their risk exposure. But financial innovation and risk-taking do not increase the average returns of the world economy, hence much of the increase in wealth generated in this manner was illusory. The promises of the financial sector were even an arithmetic impossibility, as each institution promised to deliver a rate of return higher than the average. Of course, such a system was not sustainable.

The most astounding part of this history is that the central banks all over the world did not recognise these instabilities. Even a layman could have recognised that on the basis of the level of asset prices and price-earning ratios, the financial system was fraught with problems. This can be attributed to human irrationality and myopia, but in fact there was very little that could have been done. Increasing the interest rate, for example, would have only precipitated the crisis. Those instruments that could have worked to avert it were not part of the dominant neo-liberal doctrine. Under this doctrine, deregulation and increased competition were the preferred tools to control the economy. Quantitative control to limit leverage for instance was not even considered a possibility, and running up public debt was considered out of bounds. In this way, the system held itself captive. As the huge quantitative easing of the last year indicates, a crisis is sometimes needed in order for such instruments to be dusted off again.

The consequences of the crisis will be exceptionally damaging, especially in the areas of employment and poverty. Already, it appears that the International Labour Organisation's worst case scenario of 50 million unemployed worldwide is optimistic and will more likely soar to 60 million. In addition, over 200 million workers are likely to be pushed into extreme poverty, mostly in developing and emerging economies where there are no social safety nets, meaning that the number of working poor – earning below 2 USD per family member – could rise to 1.4 billion. These problems strike women in particular, which in turn has grave consequences for the life expectancy of their children.

The consequences of the crisis are unlikely to be alleviated quickly, as the gap in global demand continues to haunt the world economy. This problem is particularly worrying as the US will no longer exercise its role as the global consumer of last resort. The collapse of international trade is in fact one of the most dramatic consequences of the crisis, hitting the developing economies in particular. This strongly calls for additional development financing, especially for low income countries, in order to increase investment.

DOWNWARD SOCIAL COMPETITION

The crisis calls for a coordinated response at the world level, as free-riding must be avoided at all costs. Economists often jokingly assert that the world is a closed economy, and this does make clear the need for a truly global response. Any free-riding reduces the multiplier effects of a stimulus packages. Strikingly, it is Europe, the world biggest economy, which is currently free-riding on the global scene. When measured as percent of GDP, the stimulus package in Europe is in fact much lower than for example in China, Japan, or the US. Europe is also the least willing to let the crisis result in increased deficits. Even taking automatic stabilisers into account, the burden the crisis places on public debt is small in Europe. Europe's attitude seems to be one of passivity; it is, once again, waiting for the others to recover first. This is a highly risky strategy, since exchange rate movements may prevent the European economy from benefitting from a recovery in the rest of the world.

Europe's response to the crisis should be understood against the backdrop of its institutional architecture. At the moment, Europe is something of a hybrid: it is not quite a federation, nor is it purely a collection of individual nation-states. As a consequence, Europe has a vacuum of sovereignty and lacks a capacity for actual governance when an event such as the crisis occurs. It cannot respond in a timely fashion because fiscal policies remain under national discretion. Coordinating fiscal policy at the European level is difficult since members do not share the same philosophies. Although monetary policy is a federal matter, the mandate of the ECB is constrained by the various European treaties; the ECB is bound by the criterion of price stability. The only reason Jean-Claude Trichet could flood the market with liquidity was that price stability was not under pressure. It was, in this sense, a case of circumstantial luck. These shortcomings in European economic governance are easy to explain. The absence of reactivity in Europe is not contingent, but structural. It stems from the dissociation between power and legitimacy. The European government is unable to act in a discretionary way, because that would go beyond its mandate. National governments with the legitimacy to act lack the instruments, as their fiscal policy is constrained by the stability pact, and monetary and exchange rate policies are federal. The European contradiction thus lies in the fact that there is no federal policy to sustain internal demand, which means that growth can only be export-led.

The consequences of the crisis will be exceptionally damaging, especially in the areas of employment and poverty.

Also, in terms of fiscal policy, European governance lacks teeth. This problem manifests itself at the national level: The only workable instruments member states have at their disposal are fiscal and social competition, and European countries are not afraid to use them. Europe presents itself as a collection of small economies competing with each other, whereas it is, and should act as, a large competitive economy fostering cohesion. This has triggered what one could call competitive social deflation, trying to attract business by decreasing taxes and social regulation, and trying to increase exports by lowering wages and labour costs. This gradually turns the EMU into a zero-sum game: the export market share won by one country is always lost by another. Each European nation sees itself more and more as a small country, the reference space being a globalised environment rather than just Europe, and thus enters into institutional competition with its neighbours using its social compact. In this system of impoverishing competition, European citizens are the primary victims, suffering through a quasi-stagnation of GDP per capita, strong wage moderation, an increase in inequalities, and a progressive dismantling of collective protections.

GLOBAL INEQUALITIES AND RECALIBRATION

The problems confronting Europe find their equivalent at the global level, but whereas the European game is zero-sum, globally it is in fact a negative-sum game. The crisis has made this absolutely clear, as the competition to be the lowest tax bidder has led to fundamental imbalances. By offering low tax rates and few social requirements, emerging and developing economies were attractive to multinationals. This problem of delocalisation is augmented by the crisis; for many firms, moving is the only means of survival. The two most crucial sectors, the automotive and the banking industries, have their own dynamic in this respect. In those sectors, firms are too big to fail, or their bankruptcy would entail systemic effects. With firms in these two sectors running into problems as result of the crisis, governments were more or less forced to bail them out. There were no other solutions in the banking sector, and letting firms go bankrupt in the automobile sector would have been too costly in terms of employment. But these bailouts remained purely national affairs. When France, for example, offers to help the automobile industry, it bails out Peugeot and Renault because such firms have national roots. But one of the requirements conditioning the financial aid was that if cutbacks were needed, it should be the foreign branches that suffered.

These bailouts could be labelled unfair competition because emerging and developing economies typically do not have either the means or the credibility to bail out their national firms, regardless of whether they are banks or big firms in the real economy. These consequences may have been unintentional, but they are nevertheless important. The problem is augmented by international agreements such as those under the WTO, as they typically imply that if a government bails out an industry, the aid should be given to all firms in the industry regardless of their national origin. To sustain a national firm, an emerging economy should also help the (usually bigger) foreign firms installed in its territory. The seemingly symmetric rules are thus applied to an asymmetric playing field. The world economy cannot recover if developing and emerging economies are structurally disadvantaged. The world community should devise compensation to help these countries recover and conduct counter-cyclical policy. This would be a very effective investment because the propensity to consume in these countries is very high.

The global policy response should be based on the idea of protection without protectionism. Specifically, this means helping the developing world to set up a decent social protection system. Secondly, the destructive social and fiscal competition should be halted, both within Europe and on a global scale. This downward spiral was the prime cause of the reverse redistribution of income that led to the inequalities which, in the end, caused the crisis. Stopping this would be a major leap forward. This would require some form of cooperation among countries to end what is essentially the modern equivalent of the beggar-thy-neighbour policies common in the 1930s: tax competition, wage deflation and social dumping.

These new policy imperatives should be complemented by a strategy to boost global demand. This means investment in the most productive real economy public goods, such as green technology. Decreasing energy consumption is a highly rewarding investment because the results it yields are permanent. Contrary to what was commonly professed during recent decades, investment in social protection also yields high results. Unemployment, for example, is very costly because it results in decreased opportunities for subsequent generations who suffer from poor education and become unemployed themselves. The potential returns on investments that break this cycle are enormous. A similar point holds for investments in health care – a healthy worker will have a higher disposable income. Put simply, saving a person for society yields long-term gains.

It is timely to reintroduce some 'socialist' elements into our capitalist system.

As the crisis unfolds, the complaint that there is no budgetary manoeuvring room for such measures is often heard. Both public and private debt are indeed already very high, but doing nothing will mean these debts will be even higher in the future. The only way to alleviate debt in the long run is to find new growth engines. These new engines have to be found quickly. If nothing is done, deflation is the most likely outcome. This means governments have to also rapidly consider investments in shovel-ready projects such as transportation and construction. Of course, inflation will alleviate debt as well, but this is not a very attractive option. This said, Western economies may have stuck rigidly to the idea of fighting inflation, as price stability was thought to be a necessary and almost sufficient condition for overall macro-economic stability. Rethinking the objectives of political economy could imply a new balance between price stability and other objectives.

The biggest obstacle to tackling the current economic predicaments is, however, intellectual, not real. We suffer from a stubborn legacy of ideas from the past. This concerns, in particular, the issue of public debt. The general attitude towards public debt has been very hostile over the past 25 years. But this hostility is grounded in an arithmetic misperception. Most politicians (and, curiously, many economists) claim that public debt comes at the expense of future generations, but this is not true. Public debt is an intra-generational problem rather than an intergenerational one. In all cases, future generations inherit both the debt and the public bonds. Moreover, loans can be invested in real assets yielding long-term gains. Future generations will inherit these assets, which more than offset the inherited debt.

This is a rather straightforward point, but nevertheless politically unpopular; old doctrines die hard. The crisis does offer a window of opportunity, however. The crisis of the 1970s resulted in a radical shift, and the decades that followed were characterised by a gradual loss of faith in the capacity of government action. The current crisis could result in a shift to the other side of the debate, with people again realising that government is fundamental to maintaining economic stability. Judging by the current hyperactivity of the state, it is not unlikely that the state will indeed make a comeback. The crisis has made it clear that markets are simply not self-regulating, and are prone to failure if not embedded in politics.

It should also be remembered that societies are always run by two conflicting principles of organisation. The first is the principle of the market: one euro, one vote, which may lead to an unsustainable level of inequality. The second is the principle of democracy: one person, one vote, which emphasises the fundamental equality of citizens. On the one hand, we have the market and inequalities; on the other, democracy and equality. The system has to search for a structural compromise between these two principles, otherwise one of them will disappear. Besides, the crisis demonstrates that giving too much priority to the first principle – markets and inequalities – is economically inefficient. Over the last quarter of a century, the need to constantly compromise between these two principles has been forgotten. We are now rediscovering this need rather abruptly. Indeed, it is democracy which is saving the capitalist system. All over the world it is the taxpayer who is asked to contribute to the salvation of the financial system. It is therefore timely to reintroduce some 'socialist' elements into our capitalistic system.

The Crisis as a Paradigm Shift

Paul de Grauwe

PROFESSOR OF INTERNATIONAL ECONOMICS,

UNIVERSITY OF LOUVAIN

"I cannot pinpoint a single event that made me realise that an economic crisis was imminent, but I had been worried about the artificiality of US growth long before the collapse of Lehman Brothers or Northern Rock. Popular fiction reassured people that the US's extraordinary growth rates were the result of increased productivity, but this story was a farce: US growth was based primarily on a consumption boom. Such a boom can partially contribute to increased productivity because it increases industrial capacity and provides access to the latest technologies. Yet at its core, it is driven only by irrationally increased consumption.

"Because people failed to understand the instability and artificiality of this growth model, other countries began to emulate it. In Europe, the Lisbon agenda sought to mimic American growth mechanisms, and in so doing, it institutionalised many of the flaws of the US's system in Europe. In this way, the crisis spread even before it began.

"Of course, even those of us who recognised these symptoms could never have predicted the gravity of the coming crisis. I expected an eventual slowdown of US growth, but certainly not an economic crisis that would spread internationally, pulling the entire global economy under water. In hindsight, some form of financial crisis may have been inevitable, but its severity came as a surprise to everybody."

A CRISIS OF ACADEMIA

When Lehman Brothers and Northern Rock collapsed, citizens were shocked by the risk-taking in the financial industry. They should not have been. Popular surprise was a consequence of silence from an indoctrinated academic community, whose role should have been to question and critique the actions of businesses and the state. Instead, since the 1980s, the intellectual community had dogmatically paid tribute to the infallibility of financial markets. They trusted that prices reflected fundamental values, and that markets were efficient self-regulating machines. Throughout this period, markets were systematically deregulated, and financial innovations evolved unchecked; insufficient institutional space was reserved for government regulation and supervision.

It is understandable that actors in the financial sector should promote such an intellectual paradigm given the enormous benefits they reaped from deregulation. What is less forgivable is that regulators and academics were drawn – largely unquestioningly – down the same ideological path. Based on academic advice, regulators assumed that markets were self-stabilising and used only market-based regulatory tools. Unfortunately, capitalist markets are subject to regular boom and bust cycles, and allowing banks and financial services unrestricted access to these markets left investors vulnerable to extreme shocks and insecurity.

New financial innovations – especially in the US and the UK – created new ways to quantify, repackage and then sell risks, and this was marketed as 'technological innovation' within the industry. Additionally, risk could be increased, as there were growing numbers of stakeholders globally to share it. Through this excessive risk-taking, the financial sector was able to create many new products - marvels of sophistication that brought unprecedented growth rates. These growth rates captured the popular imagination, convincing people that the ticket to unrestrained growth was a high-risk financial sector. Anybody who dared to question this was ostracised, and the dogma became ingrained. In retrospect, there were plenty of warning signs that the models underlying these systems were flawed, but academics, at the time, were unwilling to listen to contradictory voices.

The economic crisis has prompted a paradigm shift: financial markets are no longer seen as unquestionably efficient.

For example, in 2005, Raghuram G. Rajan, former chief economist of the International Monetary Fund, warned of the mounting and increasingly globalised risks that financial markets had taken on because of technological change, deregulation, and industry changes. He warned specifically of the housing-market price bubble, and noted that although the economy appeared very healthy at the moment and deregulated finances had brought fantastic growth, there was cause for concern about economic vulnerability. He called for measured but vigilant monetary policy and prudential supervision, extending beyond commercial and investment banks to also include hedge funds. As time went on and the disasters that he and like-minded thinkers predicted failed to materialise, more and more people were drawn onto the bandwagon of passive acceptance of the dominant intellectual paradigm. Eventually, nearly the entire academic community was forced to concede that, indeed, this must be a new world with new rules and new rhythms, where deregulated markets were, after all, the best way to achieve growth.

This is a tangible example of a societal shift, where an entire society moves in a new intellectual direction, completely forgetting the lessons of the past. This may be driven by euphoric optimism or even religion; in this case it was driven by efficient markets. Alan Greenspan, then head of the Federal Reserve, summed up this intellectual short-sightedness when, in response to proposals to increase regulation and oversight, he rhetorically answered, "Why should we wish to inhibit the pollinating bees of Wall Street?"

Yet the current crisis has reaffirmed that the models that economists were using were incomplete at best. After the financial crises in the late 1980s, the powerful assumption of human rationality gained predominance, overshadowing behavioural models. Dynamic Stochastic General Equilibrium (DSGE) models became the norm, which assume that all actors act rationally and are capable of obtaining and processing full information. They assume that all fluctuations in investment or output are the result of exogenous shocks that actors respond to automatically to bring the system back into equilibrium.

We need a new science of macro-economics. This science must be based on the assumption that individuals have severe cognitive limitations, and that they do not understand much about the complexities of the world in which they live. This lack of understanding creates biased beliefs and collective movements of euphoria when agents underestimate risk, followed by collective depressions in which perceptions of risk are dramatically increased. These collective movements turn uncorrelated risks into highly correlative ones. What Keynes called 'animal spirits' are fundamental forces driving macro-economic fluctuations. The basic error of modern macro-economics is the belief that the economy is simply the sum of micro-economic decisions of rational agents. But the economy is more than that. The interactions of these decisions create collective movements that are not visible at the micro level.

It will remain difficult to model these collective movements. There is much resistance. Too many macro-economists are attached to their models because they prefer to live in the comfort of what they understand, namely the behaviour of rational and superbly informed individuals.

REVISITING KEYNES

The current economic crisis began in the US and the UK – the countries that had been at the forefront of high-risk innovation in the financial sector. The combination of intellectual short-sightedness, excess faith in markets, and new technological innovations in finance allowed banks to take on excessive risks. Bubbles developed in real estate, the stock exchange, and commodity markets. Banks became too deeply absorbed in these expanding sectors, and when the bubbles burst, the banks took the hit.

Luckily, however, the economic crisis has prompted a paradigm shift: financial markets are no longer seen as unquestionably efficient and outside of the realm of regulation. The crisis brought to light the fact that bubbles and crashes are endemic to capitalist systems, yet these cycles undermine a fundamental principle of market efficiency: that prices reflect underlying value. With the new paradigm shift, people are beginning to remove the blinders of free market indoctrination and are beginning to see that prices are also affected by non-market forces, and that prudent government intervention in the economy is sometimes necessary and desirable.

One of the biggest problems that Europe faces in the recovery process is a lack of coordination.

In this new climate, both Keynes's paradox of thrift, and Fisher's analysis of debt deflation should be dusted off and revisited. Keynes's paradox of thrift says that whereas an individual's attempts to save more will generally be successful, an entire society's attempts to save more - because of an 'animal spirit' of pessimism about the economy - will be self-defeating. If everyone as a collective whole attempts to save more during a period of recession, they will create decreased aggregate demand, which will lead to declining revenues for companies, sparking salary cutbacks and layoffs. In aggregate, increased collective attempts to save more will lead to decreased possibility for savings, further worsening the recession.

Similarly, Fisher's analysis of debt deflation says that whereas an individual's attempt to reduce debt will generally be successful, a society's attempt to do so – because of an 'animal spirit' of economic pessimism – will be self-defeating. If all people attempt to sell their assets at the same time, all of their assets will lose value. This will erode everybody's solvency and will further aggravate the need for people to deflate their debts and sell assets.

Both of these paradoxes expose fundamental market failures, illustrating situations where markets fail to coordinate private actions towards an ideal outcome. Instead of reasoning past these problems in the spirit of free-market orthodoxy, the intellectual community must face up to them and organise policies to prevent them. In both of these situations, the government is the only actor capable of overcoming the coordination failure and restoring equilibrium to the market.

Specifically, governments must stabilise the banking sector. In addition, in order to counter the Keynesian *savings* paradox, governments must *spend*; to counter Fisher's debt *deflation* paradox, governments must *issue* public debt.

Unfortunately, this may be difficult. Many national governments have been too co-opted by the financial sector to create meaningful regulatory mechanisms. In addition, much of the financial industry operates at an international level that cannot be regulated nationally. As a result, there may need to be moves towards international coordination of policies, even moving in the direction of creating world governance to deal with financial regulation.

THE EUROPEAN REACTION TO THE CRISIS

Banking

Europe has been less willing than the US to intervene and re-regulate the financial sector. Initially, the European Central Bank (ECB) was able to respond to the crisis as rapidly as the American Federal Reserve Bank. However, over time Europe lost the political will to reform its banking sector. Unfortunately, the urgent need to clean up banks' balance sheets came into conflict with the immediate political interests of governments that depended on financial sector support.

However, if banks are not reformed, the crisis will linger on. Remnants of bad assets will continue to re-emerge over time, haunting the economy in the long run, instead of being dealt with all at once. To avoid this, governments must intervene, separating good loans from bad ones, and managing the bad loans separately. It may even be necessary for governments to nationalise the reformed banks temporarily. If they do not, banks may be hesitant to begin lending again, and taxpayers will be forced to pay the burden of the bad loans without earning back any funds for the public purse.

Despite Europe's general tendency to shy away from bank reform, there have been some exceptions. In the 1990s, for example, Sweden was able to completely nationalise banks and reform heavily from within. The Swedish government did not hesitate to fire top managers and allow shareholders to lose their investments. While politically difficult in the short term, this approach is preferable in the long term to the approach taken by countries such as Belgium and the Netherlands, where governments pump money into banks and provide shareholders with guarantees in case of bank failures, but stop short of any fundamental reforms that will resolve the systemic problems.

The European Central Bank

In order to allow for more aggressive measures to be taken against banks, the ECB must be given more autonomy and power. As a single monetary union, the

EU must be willing to put national interests aside in favour of the goals of the entire union. Member states should not interfere with the post-crisis recovery measures that the ECB undertakes, and they should allow it an increased mandate beyond mere inflation targeting.

Member states must put more faith in the recovery measures implemented by the ECB. Recently, German Chancellor Angela Merkel criticised it for using aggressive non-standard methods to tackle the economic crisis, and accused them of caving to pressures from the Bank of England and the Federal Reserve Bank to take steps that would prompt inflation. Regardless of the special historical fear that Germans have of inflation, such criticisms are uncalled for.

Tactics such as quantitative easing are necessary in a post-crisis period. The yield spread on government bonds in the euro-zone has widened, and many countries, including Ireland, Greece, and Italy, have seen their government bond markets declining. In such a situation, the ECB has the power to use quantitative easing to buy these government bonds and return the bond market to equilibrium. They could also do this in the corporate bond market, helping ailing companies in the short term, and making profit by reselling them in the long term.

Given sufficient prudence and regulation, there is no reason to fear that quantitative easing will lead to inflation; extra liquidity will not promote inflation when liquidity is sorely lacking. Nevertheless, it will be critical that the ECB continues to monitor the economy closely and halt these policies the moment the economy begins to recover again, otherwise the excess reserve holdings of banks could be activated and cause inflation in the future. Simply suspending quantitative easing as the economy recovers should prevent these dangers, yet if the ECB still fears inflation, it can also increase the minimum required reserves in banks to neutralise excess liquidity. Given these technical capacities to reverse inflationary pressures, inflation must not be used as a pretext for preventing sorely needed recovery policies.

In addition to putting more faith in the ECB's current capacities, the EU should consider broadening its mandate of operations. Currently, the ECB is focused almost exclusively on inflation targeting, taking the view that low inflation is the key prerequisite to macro-economic stability and high potential growth. Although low inflation is a necessary condition to economic and financial stability, it is certainly not sufficient in and of itself. The ECB should not limit its objectives to keeping inflation low, but it should also aim at maintaining financial stability. In order to achieve this objective of financial stability, the ECB must also use additional instruments, such as counter-cyclical adjustment of capital ratios for banks and minimum reserve requirements. These instruments should be used to limit excessive credit creation by banks.

Coordination and trust

One of the biggest problems that Europe faces in the recovery process is a lack of coordination. No member state is willing to implement significant stimulus packages unilaterally because of the fear of spill-over into neighbouring countries. This leads to an inefficient situation, caused by a lack of coordination. If all states invested in stimulus plans in a coordinated way, then spill-over effects would work both for and against each country, neutralising negative outcomes. Sadly, governments do not trust each other enough to make this work, resulting in sub-optimal levels of stimulus funding.

The economic crisis brought to light academic failures in the field of macro-economics.

In addition to this problem of trust, the EU has a fundamental imbalance between national-level and EU-level capacities. Although the European Union has successfully achieved full monetary integration, spending and taxation remain primarily the prerogatives of national governments. Thus, the national level is the only one equipped with the economic influence to create and back up bonds on the international market. They are the only level of governance able to recapitalise bonds, take over institutions' debt, and bail out companies. Unfortunately, in a globalising world, many companies transcend national boundaries. For example, when the Belgian and Dutch government needed to save the international bank Fortis, they first had to split the company into national sub-companies.

This imbalance clearly highlights the need for continued EU integration. The EU still does not have a full government, since one of the most basic powers of government is having the power to tax and spend in a given territory. Although the EU has an elected Parliament and executive institutions (the Council and the Commission), it lacks the power of national governments to restore the stability in the banking sector and to stimulate the economy.

One limited step towards a European approach to stimulating the economy would be the issuance of euro-bonds. The revenue from these bonds could be used to finance investments in the EU. Globally, many countries – especially China – have focused on accumulating safe assets, buying primarily US government bonds. The post-crisis period is a ripe moment for Europe to exploit the euro-zone that it has created – which is comparable in the size of its money markets and bond markets to the US – by promoting euro-bonds, guaranteed by the collection of governments and financial institutions in the EU.

However, the biggest barrier to achieving these reforms may be the political shifts prompted by the economic crisis. Ironically, although the crisis highlighted the necessity of further economic integration, at the popular political level it prompted a shift towards nationalism and an accompanying decline in enthusiasm for European integration.

CONCLUDING THOUGHTS

The economic crisis brought to light academic failures in the field of macro-economics: rational actor models do not reflect human realities, and the market is not an infallible self-regulating mechanism. The intellectual community must go back to the drawing board to imagine new ways of regulating increasingly globalised markets. There must be a move towards increased government intervention to regulate and supervise the financial industry and to minimise market failures resulting from coordination problems.

In post-crisis Europe, there needs to be increased integration, with more power granted to the EU's supranational institutions. In order for the EU as a whole to recover from traumas such as the current crisis, it must be given more power to tax and spend as one unified government, in part by issuing euro-bonds. The economic crisis has had profound repercussions for European economies. Hopefully, it will trigger institutional changes that will make Europe better equipped to face such economic and financial upheavals in the future.

PART 2

EXPLORING DOMESTIC POLICTY SPACE UNDER LOW GROWTH

Although the crisis is a global phenomenon, policy responses to the crisis are largely structured by domestic institutional arrangements. The contributions to this part of the volume explore the margin of national institutional capacities for the post-crisis era. The economic and political context of the future is, however, dramatically different than before the crisis, as growth is likely to be slow and protracted.

Both Suzanne Berger and David Soskice underscore the extent to which national institutional arrangements remain the locus for economic and social reform, as well as market regulation under low-growth conditions. Stephen Roach focuses more on the essential role that national central banks can play, by regulating systemic risk in order to mitigate and solve underlying macro-level economic problems. However, he also highlights the need for an international regulator of systemic risk able to harmonise regulatory objectives across borders.

Willem Buiter urges us not to squander the unique and essential opportunities for re-regulation posed by the crisis. If domestic and supranational policy-makers do not act now, there is a huge risk that pre-crisis instabilities will recur. He further draws attention to the problem of mounting public and private debt as systematic debt, and the inescapable tall order of reducing this liability. Peter Hall makes the timely observation that new institutional arrangements need to be developed in a political context which might oppose the resurgence of state interventionism.

The free market economy may have lost much of its legitimacy, but this does not necessarily entail a new era of embedded global liberalism. More than ever, governments face the task of finding new legitimising narratives to gain the support of their currently dubious publics.

Finding these new narratives is contingent on new growth drivers. As David Soskice points out, neither businesses nor the financial sector is well placed to restore consumer demand and economic growth. He recommends using fiscal policy to either provide public sector employment for women, or improved education and training programs. Suzanne Berger similarly suggests that, especially in the US, redistributive reform in health care and improving basic education systems would bring wealth to segments of the population which have thus far been unable to contribute much toward economic demands. In addition, she identifies a silver lining: the crisis unsettled deeply ingrained beliefs and is therefore also an opportunity for new generations with alternative strategies to enter the political realm.

The Significance of Politics

Peter A. Hall
HARVARD UNIVERSITY

"My first indication of the risks of potential crisis came when the financial press began to speak openly about the 'bets' that international financial institutions were making, whether on the direction of the markets, on takeovers, or the like. Banks were no longer making investments; they were making bets. It was commonly understood that the character of banking had changed over the past 15 years, as financial institutions dramatically increased their leverage using new derivatives. But the level of risk taking described by Susan Strange as 'Casino Capitalism' was a new phenomenon. A few years prior to the crisis, respected financial publications began explicitly using the word 'bet' to describe the investments institutions were making. That was when I began to worry, realising that this had become a fundamentally different banking sector than the one I grew up with."

THE POLITICAL FACE OF THE CRISIS

In order to understand what the economic crisis will mean for the future, some analysis of history is in order. Although the crisis is economic in nature, the significance of economic developments cannot be understood separately from the political context that brackets them. Historically, the post-war period can be subdivided into three distinct periods: an era of embedded liberalism, the transitions of the 1970s, and a period of neo-liberalism. Only by understanding each period as one marked by distinctive formulae designed to respond to the economic and political challenges of the period can one fully appreciate how political economies change.

The period of embedded liberalism, to use John Ruggie's felicitous phrase, spanned roughly 30 years, beginning with the close of World War II and ending around 1975. These years have been described as *les trente glorieuses*. Throughout the 1950s and 1960s, Western countries were still highly industrial economies, and Fordist modes of mass industrial production were prominent. The biggest economic challenges the developed economies faced were ones of sustaining demand and securing efficiency under this mode of production. The political challenges of this era were rooted in concerns about class conflict, specifically, finding ways to secure compromise between capital and labour. Class conflict is, to this day, rooted in memories of the political conflicts of the 1920s and 1930s, and over time its pertinence has eroded. However, in the period of embedded liberalism, the prospect of such conflict was still the foremost political challenge in the minds of policymakers both in Europe and the United States, where electoral politics was visibly organised along a class cleavage.

In response to these economic and political challenges, the dominant policy formula created by the Western economies can be described as the Keynesian welfare state. It was marked by the regularisation of collective bargaining, Keynesian macro-economic policies, and the gradual development of extensive systems of social support. In broad terms, those policies were implemented in both Europe and, to a lesser extent, the US. They addressed the political challenge by fostering class compromise, and the economic challenge by sustaining demand. Keynesian demand management helped to generate the macro-economic stability required by mass production systems, and collective bargaining distributed the gains from the rapid productivity increases available in such systems, so as to sustain consumer demand for the products the system manufactured.

The second period, which can be interpreted as one of transition, is a difficult time-span to delineate, but lasted roughly from 1968-1983. Economically, the biggest challenge of this period was stagflation: price inflation accompanied by rising unemployment and general economic stagnation. Politically, the reorganisation of class boundaries posed a significant challenge, as the potential for class conflict gradually waned. Thus, the old formula for political and economic cohesion broke down in this period, and few strategies were immediately available to replace it. Stagflation was itself the result of intensified distributive conflict. By this time, the service sector was becoming more important, opening up new cleavages in labour and offering lower rates of productivity growth that called into question the post-war economic formula.

This period of transition set the stage for the third post-war period: the neoliberal era. This era began in the early 1980s and lasted until the current economic crisis began. The economic challenge of this new period was defined by the sharply lower rates of growth that began in the 1970s: how could societies create new jobs in the service sector under low-growth conditions? As good jobs in the core manufacturing sector became scarcer, an insider/outsider dichotomy emerged, with workers in the core economy having relatively secure positions, but those on the margins, including the young and many women, finding few such employment opportunities. Increasing competition in more open international markets intensified these challenges.

Politically, the neo-liberal period saw the completion of a shift dating back to the 1970s, namely the declining political salience of class conflict. This shift was reflected in weakening political affiliations, a phenomenon that elections experts describe as "de-alignment", as ordinary citizens no longer voted so frequently along class lines, and there was growing cultural fragmentation in the electorate. To borrow the typology of Herbert Kitschelt, overlaid on the traditional left/right cleavage was a left-libertarian/right-authoritarian cleavage. The latter was reflected in the growing political salience of post-materialist values – in many ways a legacy of the 1960s counterculture – which became a prominent theme in the new 'culture wars' characterising the 1980s. Thus, over the past three decades, social-democratic parties have secured much of their support from the middle classes and left-leaning libertarians. Centre-right parties, their traditional counterparts, have been increasingly challenged by factions or parties on the radical right, who appeal to right-authoritarian and anti-immigrant sentiments as well as to anti-EU voters in Europe. This shift in the character of political cleavages helped move the entire political spectrum towards the right in the US and Europe.

We should not neglect the role that politics will play in the development of new economic policies.

The policy formula concocted to cope with these challenges can be described as a move away from state intervention toward the allocation of resources through markets, which was writ large in Europe by the project to create a single European market with the Single Europe Act of 1986. At the domestic level, the objective was to render markets more competitive through privatisation and deregulation. At the international level, it was to open up global markets to more intense competition. The European policy response was marked by a shift away from the use of active demand management toward the use of supply-side policies to address employment issues. On the supply side, there was a corresponding shift away from industrial policies toward active labour market policies, which became the centrepiece of economic programs in continental Europe. In the US and UK, efforts to expand consumer demand were at the heart of policymaking, and governments encouraged financial innovation. The ready availability of debt was used to help people whose incomes were stagnating cope with economic fluctuations in this post-Keynesian era. Although median wages grew modestly in the US, higher prices for housing and rising equity markets combined with cheap imports of goods from Asia to create an illusion of wealth that fuelled the expansion of consumer demand.

In sum, each historical period has had a distinctive set of policy prescriptions, which can be understood as the governmental response to the economic and political challenges of that era. What lessons can be drawn from this analysis for the current period? Most importantly, this account suggests that we should not neglect the role that politics will play in the development of new economic policies. The European and American electorates are still fragmented along multiple lines, which will limit the extent to which we see a return to class conflict in the electoral arena. In the context of this ambiguous fragmentation, electoral outcomes will depend heavily on electoral rules.

Conventional wisdom in comparative political economy holds that electoral systems based on proportional representation (PR) are more likely than majoritarian electoral systems to promote redistribution. Coalitions between social-democratic and centre parties are more likely to form under proportional representation systems, and they tend to provide more generous social benefits than the governments elected under majoritarian systems that are forced to compete for the allegiance of the median voter. Thus, political progressives on both sides of the Atlantic tend to prefer PR over majoritarian systems. During good times, there is much to admire in the politics of proportional representation.

During bad times, of the sort associated with economic crisis, however, proportional representation is less attractive, as the case of the Weimar Republic famously illustrated. Splinter parties, on both the right and left, also tend to prefer proportional representation because they are more likely to secure seats in the legislature under proportional representation. Even large parties carrying 30% of the popular vote cannot win elections in majoritarian single-member constituencies. In the midst of economic crisis, splinter parties – including both radical right anti-immigration groups as well as radical left socialist groups – are likely to gain support. Because most European states have PR systems, their mainstream parties will be forced to deal with the difficult challenge of incorporating such groups or maintaining support in the face of them, as the recent European elections have demonstrated. By contrast, under majoritarian systems, discontent arising from economic crises tends to lead to alternation in government between mainstream centre-left and centre-right parties. The US has witnessed this, as the economic crisis helped bring the Democratic Party back to power, and in the UK, Gordon Brown will likely soon be defeated by the Conservatives. Developments in the US may have sparked the crisis, but it is Europe that is likely to have to pay the political price.

When speculating about how systems will change as a result of the current crisis, therefore, it is imperative to bear political considerations in mind. Although the current economic juncture may call for specific policies, whether those policies are implemented or not will depend on the character of the political cleav-

ages that mark a particular era, and on the ways in which national institutions organise those cleavages into politics.

EUROPEAN INTEGRATION

In the short term at least, European integration is also a casualty of this crisis.
Given the electoral rules outlined above, radical right-wing groups (which tend
to be nationalist and anti-EU as well as anti-immigrant) are likely to gain influence in Europe. Although these parties will not muster the strength to take office
in most countries, their growing support will put pressure on existing governments to expand nationalist responses to the crisis and limit their commitments
to European integration.

Economic crises tend to exacerbate existing tensions, invariably decreasing
satisfaction with existing governments. During the recession of the 1970s, nearly
every government that was in power going into the crisis was overturned as it
progressed. Over the past two decades, one of the most prominent sources of
tension in Europe has been immigration. Anti-immigrant sentiment has been
growing across Europe for at least 25 years, and most opinion polls indicate that
between 20-25% of the European electorate is, broadly speaking, resentful of immigrants. Therefore, it would not be surprising if citizens turned to radical right
parties to give voice to their current frustrations, and if those parties demanded
that brakes be put on the process of European integration.

Political integration has been a challenge for the EU since its inception. With
enlargement to 27 member states, moving ahead with political integration will
be even more difficult. Moreover, Europe's response to the economic crisis has
left many citizens questioning the value of the EU. Whereas the European Central Bank carried its weight admirably during the post-crisis period, finding innovative ways to loosen monetary policy, political leaders failed to find parallel
innovations in the fiscal domain. National governments were wary of introducing robust fiscal stimulus measures because the closely intertwined continental
economies are prone to spill-over effects. Instead, many promoted mildly protectionist measures, playing into the hands of nationalist parties. The EU's inability to coordinate fiscal measures was a serious failure. This issue provides a
classic example of the kind of coordination problem that can best be solved by a
supranational body, yet the only such body in Europe failed to rise to the challenge. National governments jealously guarded control of their domestic spending, and as a result, many EU countries had sub-optimal and uncoordinated policy responses.

European countries currently find themselves on the horns of a dilemma. On
the one hand, to maintain their generous welfare state expenditures, they require

significant long-term economic growth. To achieve this, they urgently need to re-establish the prosperity of their economies, even if this requires fiscal stimulus measures that may lead to domestic deficits or inflationary pressures. On the other hand, bailouts to the troubled financial sector, which cannot be avoided, are usurping funds that might be used to sustain vocational skills or invest in technology-led growth. As many European voters have observed, the current situation has turned the re-distributional ambitions of European welfare states upside-down, as social expenditures are restrained to free up resources for financial bailouts.

Although market optimism has dwindled, a new era of optimism about what states can do will not necessarily follow.

Nevertheless, the European welfare states are likely to weather the storm. If European countries can restore even 2% per year of GDP growth, they will be able to sustain their welfare systems in the long run. Although the crisis has thrown some sand in the wheels of redistribution, it has highlighted the need for those wheels to keep turning. The crisis has reminded many Europeans of the importance of social programs to support the unemployed, the disabled, and others negatively affected by the crisis. In this respect, the economic crisis may reinforce, rather than undermine, the legitimacy of the welfare state as well as the Lisbon strategy, by strengthening demands for more active labour market policies.

Not all EU states are fully developed welfare states, however, and one of the biggest challenges the EU faces in the coming period will be to rescue the newly acceded member states of Eastern and Central Europe. The economic crisis has had disproportionately damaging effects in these new member states, which have not been widely appreciated even in the rest of Europe. As Wade Jacoby has noted, these countries made the transition from communism at the height of the neo-liberal era, and were sold the most radical version of the market model. Their governments truly believed that markets could work miracles, and now they are suffering more than other countries as a result of this irrational exuberance.

To its credit, the EU has taken significant steps to shore up the Eastern and Central European economies. Both the ECB and the European Bank for Reconstruction and Development have been important players in the immediate aftermath of the crisis in this region. However, many of the accession countries are undergoing a serious adjustment, similar to the 1980s debt crisis in Latin America, and the levels of defaults occurring in this region are already putting a significant strain on the EU. Under these conditions, it is unclear how much more the EU will be willing to contribute to an urgently needed second round of recovery assistance in the region.

Despite the problems it has posed for the EU, however, the economic crisis is likely to increase the international standing of the euro. Because the aspirations of the EU have been so high, there is a tendency to judge its performance harshly, as it forever falls short of extraordinary goals. It could have done more in the realm of fiscal policy coordination and integrated the new member states more effectively. Nevertheless, the establishment of the euro was an incredible feat. In less than two decades, the EU has created a currency that has integrated the economies of continental Europe.

In global terms, the euro is likely to emerge from the crisis stronger – both in prestige and in economic value – as a result of the American dollar's post-crisis tribulations. The American economy has lived for several decades on debt and loose monetary policy. Ordinary Americans maintained their consumption through borrowing, decreasing the savings rate ratio virtually to zero over the past two decades. However, the crisis has brought the inherent imbalances of this system – especially vis-à-vis China – to light, and the model has begun to appear increasingly unsustainable. After losing several trillions of dollars in household wealth over the past year, Americans have dramatically increased their savings and decreased their consumption. As a result, the attractiveness of investment in the US is declining and, over time, that may reduce the global demand for dollars. As the dollar exchange rate falls, the euro is likely to strengthen against it and to join the dollar as a desirable reserve currency.

THE STATE-MARKET STANDOFF

Can we expect the crisis to usher in a more active economic role for governments? As we compare and evaluate policy responses to the crisis, it is important to remember that different types of political economies demand different types of responses. Many continental European governments have faced criticism – especially from the US and the UK – for adopting labour-preserving programs. What critics in liberal market economies fail to appreciate, however, is that in these coordinated continental economies, it is essential to try to preserve industrial and service sector jobs, because the organisation of labour and capital markets in these countries makes it difficult to re-establish these jobs once they have been lost. Conversely, critics of the British and American focus on stimulating consumer demand need to appreciate that this is appropriate for economies in which the primary engine of growth is consumption.

That said, however, one caveat remains pertinent to all countries as we anticipate the long-term policy response to the economic crisis: although market optimism has dwindled, a new era of optimism about what states can do will not necessarily follow. Neo-liberalism's recipe for resource allocation might have turned
out to be catastrophe-prone, and government regulation of financial markets
will certainly increase as a result. However, citizens currently have as little faith in
states as they have in the market. Because they are presiding over recession, whatever governments do during an economic crisis is usually seen as a failure, so
states should expect some popular backlash regardless of what governments do
in the crisis period.

This is true on both sides of the Atlantic. The US was founded on a fear of big
government, and scepticism about government's capacities runs deep in the
American psyche. The popular saying, "In God we trust, all others pay cash," still
resonates with the American people and brings to mind recurrent states' rights
movements. Scepticism about Obama's stimulus plan is already on the rise in the
media and among conservative political circles, and although these voices remain in the minority, an extended economic downturn could tip this balance. In
Europe, the problems are more institutional. Any 'return of the state' would have
to happen at the EU level; national governments already play a larger role than
they do in the US, and the problems of economic coordination stretch well beyond the borders of each member state. Since the EU is currently the scapegoat-
of-choice for anti-immigrant and Eurosceptic complaints, its legitimacy may be
too low to allow it to rise to such a significant challenge.

As we consider the post-crisis rebalancing of state versus market power, however, the role of firms should not be neglected. They are critical actors in the
development of political economies. Economic adjustment is driven by both
governments and firms, each guided by different incentive structures. The post-
crisis strategies of Ford, Siemens, and EADS have already had larger effects on
the lives of their thousands of employees than any single government intervention.

TOWARDS A NEW LEGITIMISING NARRATIVE

As we contemplate what might happen to the balance between state and market
power, we should also recall the importance of developments in the realm of political discourse. If they want to move to heightened levels of intervention, governments will have to find new legitimising narratives for that role. The narratives of the past no longer suffice. Throughout the era of modernisation in the
West, the democratic state was often presented in grand historical terms as the
political vehicle for the establishment of enlightenment ideals. As Samuel Beer

observed, democratic states were seen as the reflection of a voluntarist impulse: their actions reflected the will of the people. As creatures of the enlightenment, they were thought to be able to harness the power of science and technology on behalf of their citizens. In this respect, the democratic nation-state was seen as the legitimate vehicle for technological and ultimately economic progress. One of the most striking features of the contemporary era, however, has been the questioning of enlightenment values inspired by post-modernist thought. At a popular level, that has gone hand in hand with increasing distrust in governments.

Governments will need some successful projects to restore popular confidence in their capacities.

If governments hope to take on a more activist role in the economy, therefore, they will have to re-establish the terms on which such a role can be said to be legitimate. This will not be easy, even in North American and Western Europe, which have long democratic histories. However, the task will be even more challenging in Eastern and Central Europe, where the historical experience with democracy has been shorter and the legitimising narratives of the distant past are mediated by a half-century of communist experience. Despite the declining legitimacy of neo-liberal governments, these countries have few sound alternatives. On one side of the political spectrum are parties committed to market fundamentals; on the other side are nationalist parties that are often protectionist, anti-immigrant, and Eurosceptical.

Moreover, if governments are to take on a substantially larger role in the economy, they will need some successful projects to restore popular confidence in their capacities. In the short run, it may be easier to engineer some changes of this sort in the US than in Europe. The Obama administration was elected, in large measure, as a backlash against eight years of a Republican administration devoted to market competition. Therefore, the new administration has plenty of room in which to generate new policies for which it can claim credit. Obama's campaign platform included innovative measures to tackle energy shortages, climate change, health care, and education. To his credit, he has continued to pursue these policies despite the setbacks presented by the economic crisis. This is not to say that Democrats are going to win the next election, but they are in a position to restore some faith in government in a country where it has been deeply eroded.

In Europe, where governments have long devoted considerable resources to social support, there is less room for novel projects that might inspire new confidence in government. Few of the mainstream parties in any country include innovative planks in their platforms, and many contenders for power are simply waiting for the crisis to bring down existing governments. Successful though this strategy may be, it does not promote new ideas or innovative programs that can revitalise the body politic. In more than a few cases, political leaders have demonised 'globalisation' while using the EU to expand competitive markets. Electorates understand this hypocrisy, and it has left them jaded about the candour of politicians and the credibility of governments. As a result, the challenge these governments now face is not simply a technocratic one of finding more effective economic policies. The contemporary challenge is more political: governments must articulate moral visions capable of restoring their legitimacy in difficult times, and ideally visions that breathe new life into a European Union discredited by the role it took on as the agent of market competition. This will not be easy and is rendered more difficult by the absence of EU officials elected by Europe as a whole. There are grounds for hope, however, in the fact that time and time again the EU has reinvented itself, showing the creativity and dynamism needed to overcome the myriad of challenges it has faced since its inception.

The economic crisis has brought the world to a new policy crossroads. Deciding which direction to take from here entails not only economic, but also political choices. The relevant developments will require international cooperation, but national implementation. As a result, no government will be able to forge ahead without shoring up its domestic legitimacy, and after two decades of neo-liberal excess, that will require some fundamental re-imagining of the role of the state in the economy. Nowhere is this challenge more apparent than in Europe, where the tasks of national economic and political reform are compounded by the necessity of coordination within an ever-changing European Union.

Troubleshooting Economic Narratives

Suzanne Berger

PROFESSOR OF POLITICAL SCIENCE,

MASSACHUSETTS INSTITUTE OF TECHNOLOGY

"Looking back at the run-up to the crisis, it is difficult to pinpoint exactly when things went wrong. Certainly the origins of the disaster pre-date the subprime crisis. Some analysts like Martin Wolf argue that the underlying problem was excess global liquidity, so both Asian savers and American spenders are to blame. If global imbalances were at the heart of the economic collapse, then the run-up to the crisis can be traced to the 1997 Asian financial market crash. Following this disaster, Asian governments felt increasingly insecure and ramped up their reserves, primarily in US dollars, to avoid vulnerability to such a scenario in the future. As they over-saved, the US over-spent, and the savings glut intensified. Greenspan's monetary policies of very low interest rates only intensified these problems. As for banking and investment regulations and the regulation of non-bank lenders and the shadow banking system, Basel II was too little, too late."

QUESTIONING ASSUMPTIONS

The crisis has cast many old assumptions about the economy into doubt. Neoliberalism no longer seems a body of self-evident truths; market fundamentals are being overturned; and the appropriate role for politics in markets is once again open for debate. It's time to go back and rethink some assumptions about the foundations of post-war economic growth and stability. Specifically, in light of the crisis, misunderstandings about the embedded liberalism of the 1950s and 1960s as well as of the globalisation period starting in the 1980s have been exposed. It has become apparent that our models of globalisation were limited to real economy models: financial markets only had an auxiliary function. In the varieties of capitalism approach, for example, finance is considered as a subsystem in the overall industrial economy. The links between the real economy and the financial economy were not conceptualised.

Embedded liberalism

European post-war historical accounts invariably include references to the embedded liberalism era, a label coined by John Ruggie. This period is understood as one in which citizen consensus on open economies was obtained in exchange for welfare-system security guarantees provided by the state.

It has become apparent that our models of globalisation were limited to real economy models.

As consensus erodes, the power of alternative explanations for post-war stability may come to be better appreciated. In their book *Capitalism since 1945,* Armstrong, Glyn, and Harrison, for example, emphasised the role of repression of wages and workers' demands. Alan Milward saw the post-war establishment of the welfare-state as an emergency policy of last resort for governments that had been completely de-legitimised. They had been unable to protect their citizens against either the 1930s depression or World War II. Welfare states in Europe were introduced as a way of re-establishing this legitimacy and rebuilding the capacities of the state. As Milward explains in his book *The Rescue of the European Nation-state*, the connection between the emergence of the welfare state and a societal agreement on economic openness required consolidation at the EU level.

Milward's theory is reinforced by the economic realities of the times. Despite claims to the contrary, the move towards market liberalisation in the post-war period was ambiguous at best. Bretton Woods did not establish open markets – it instituted a regime of capital controls. Both John Maynard Keynes and Harry Dexter White insisted that such controls be maintained on a permanent basis, in order to give societies the ability to manage both employment and growth.

In the standard narrative, embedded liberalism was eventually eroded as the US and the UK pioneered new neo-liberal reforms, which undercut the consensus on the welfare state. Paradoxically, however, while the US and the UK did indeed champion neo-liberalism, they were not the most ardent advocates of the new international regime of capital mobility. Rawi Abdelal found that in fact it was the French – and later the Germans and the rest of Europe – who pioneered the norm of capital mobility, which is now considered one of the most fundamental neo-liberal reforms. Abdelal's research, as can be read in his book *Capital Rules: The Construction of Global Finance,* suggests that the Europeans established the norm in an attempt to increase European economic integration, although in the end they failed to push this norm through to implementation at the level of the IMF.

The boundaries of globalisation

Historically, this points to a second questionable historical assumption. In the current neo-liberal era, starting in the 1980s, people have claimed that globalisation ran rampant and broke down individuals' identities as citizens of their domestic nation-states. While globalisation did resume with new vigour in this period, it did not break down domestic ties to the extent that is often assumed.

The globalisation process that began in the 1980s can be interpreted as the second of two globalisation regimes. The first globalisation regime, lasting from roughly 1870-1914, was driven almost entirely by technological advances. Transportation advances, such as the railroad and steamship, lowered the cost of immigration as well as that of shipping goods. Communication advances – for example the transatlantic cable – brought people into immediate contact. Whereas previously there had been a three-week delay in transatlantic information sharing, now it was possible to instantaneously communicate London stock prices to investors in New York. Nevertheless, as soon as World War I broke out, this era ended as governments raised the barriers to the flow of capital, goods and services, and human beings across borders. Although the technologies of communication and transportation remained intact and continued to be utilised, lowering the borders to the free movements of capital did not begin anew for another 70 years.

The second globalisation regime was driven not only by new digital technologies but also by acts of government, like opening their economies to trade and the deregulation of financial markets. Since it depends so heavily on politically negotiated regimes, globalisation today might even be more vulnerable to shocks than the first globalisation regime was. Starting in the 1980s, economic liberalisation and market de-regulation have been consistently advanced through internationally negotiated agreements, such as the Single European Act of 1986. Unlike technological advances which are nearly impossible to undo once conceived, negotiated contracts are easily broken and nullified. Whereas it took a world war to bring down the first regime, weaker triggers could lead to significant reverses in the current globalisation regime.

Real economy restrictions, such as increased energy prices, have already begun to undermine globalisation.

Real economy restrictions, such as increased energy prices, have already begun to undermine globalisation. It is likely that, in the future, energy will become less plentiful and therefore more expensive. This will promote the creation of regional-level supply chains, as transportation costs rise. Therefore, companies are increasingly looking closer to home for their components. Rather than looking only to China, the US may re-evaluate its outsourcing towards Mexico and Latin America, while the EU turns towards Eastern Europe. Especially in heavy industries such as steel, automobile manufacturing, and aerospace, there is an increasing understanding that distance to markets really does matter.

In terms of identity and legitimacy, even before the economic crisis there was no evidence that citizens were shifting allegiances away from the nation-state. In Europe, which was perhaps one of the most globalised enclaves in the international community, this did not seem to be the case. Quite to the contrary, in the 2005 referenda on ratification of the European constitution, the strength of nationalism was clearly demonstrated. Various public opinion polls of citizens overwhelmingly reaffirmed that they held their national governments accountable for their security and wellbeing, and felt largely betrayed by the globalising ambitions of the EU.

For years, multinational corporations presented themselves as companies that span borders and have no particular dependence, allegiance, or even responsibility to their home societies. The crisis has revealed this to be a myth.

The economic crisis heightened such sentiments, but also brought the centrality of the role of the nation-state back into the limelight from a purely economic perspective. In fact, looking back on it now, it seems that nation-states remained vital throughout the globalisation period. Whereas in good times the hand of the state may be hidden, in hard times it re-emerges in a visible and powerful way.

The bailout and bankruptcy proceedings of banks and investment firms over the past year (2008-2009) of the financial crisis are sharp illustrations of how firms which once proclaimed themselves to be global actors with no national home territory in fact depended on domestic rules and, ultimately, national support. The clean-up after the collapse of Lehman Brothers provides a telling example. When the accountants came in to take charge at Lehman's European branch in London, they found no cash on hand. As in most multinational corporations, all cash was sent back to headquarters at the end of every working day, and in the case of Lehman's, $ 8 billion had returned to New York City on the Friday before the collapse. The London office did not even have a domestic bank account, and had to turn to the Bank of England to help get them through the difficult period that followed. This was made clear by Jennifer Hughes in her *Financial Times* article, 'Winding up Lehman Brothers'. Suddenly, one appreciates why it might be important to keep the headquarters of 'global' corporations located within one's own national territory.

Similarly, in the US automobile industry, government bailouts for companies have varied depending on the ownership of companies. Toyota, for example, whose finance division was even located in the US despite it being a Japanese-owned business, received no assistance or financial guarantees from the US government. The General Motors financial arm (GMAC), in contrast, was treated as a bank by the government; as such, its deposits were legally protected by federal insurance (FDIC).

For years, multinational corporations presented themselves as companies that span borders and have no particular dependence, allegiance, or even responsibility to their home societies. They have argued that the national location of their headquarters is little more than a historical accident. The crisis has revealed this to be a myth. At a time when corporate survival depends on the support of national governments and taxpayer funding, suddenly it is clear who belongs on which side of which national border. Iceland's troubles presented this dilemma on a blown-up and tragic scale. As territoriality has become increasingly visible and important in the crisis period, globalisation has begun to recede on many fronts.

BLINDSIDED BY FINANCE

Just as the globalisation of the financial sector was restricted by the little-understood constraints of national economies, many academic models of the real economy were likewise limited by their failure to address the financial sector. The 'Varieties of Capitalism' approach to analysing the different strengths and weaknesses of the advanced industrial economies was an enormous advance in academic understanding. However, there are many countries that are neither liberal market economies nor coordinated market economies, and as the exceptional cases have multiplied, the utility of the model was bound to be called into question. In addition, the model is static. It predicts that the pressures of globalisation will likely reinforce rather than undermine the distinctive features of both liberal market and coordinated market structures by emphasising their different institutional competitive advantages. However, the patterns of change and response to global market competitive pressures appear to be more complex, and to reveal a greater internal heterogeneity in the 'pure' cases than was originally contemplated.

The greatest deficiency of virtually all of our theorising about national models of capitalism in an era of globalisation was a failure to link our conceptions of the real economy to financial markets. Throughout the neo-liberal era, there was a significant 'financialisation' of the economy. The financial sector grew ever larger and more integral to the real economy, while at the same time becoming ever less regulated. Yet despite the breadth and interdisciplinarity of research on capitalism and production systems, somehow the subject of financial systems came to be the specialised domain of experts in an encapsulated subfield of economics and business school finance. In political economy literature on the varieties of capitalism, financial markets were conceptualised as a source of funding for the real economy, rather than as a sector with a life of its own, earning profits on its own terms, with, however, real consequences for the real economy.

Scholars failed to identify the potential weaknesses and dangers of complex new financial instruments.

In addition, scholars failed to identify the potential weaknesses and dangers of complex new financial instruments and the emergence of new non-bank entities in financial markets. New derivative instruments and securitisation contributed to the distribution of risk and the allocation of high risk to those actors most willing and able to take it on. In so doing, finance not only funds productive activity across the economy but, through its allocations, makes the economy more innovative and efficient. This, at least, is the theory – but in the wake of the financial crisis, many wonder whether the virtues of finance beyond plain-vanilla banking may not have been oversold.

GLOBAL CONSEQUENCES OF THE CRISIS

Once it hit, the crisis spread globally, and different countries are now discovering different strengths and weaknesses that the crisis uncovered. Here, too, the crisis has raised new questions which we are poorly prepared to answer. Take, for example, the *Economist's* claim that the relatively milder fallout of the crisis in France is evidence for a specific and possibly superior French economic model. It's true that Germany has been harder hit. But it is only natural that in the short-term a country that exports heavily – Germany – will suffer more from an international decline in consumer demand than a country that runs deficits of 6-8% of GDP per year and has a relatively weak export performance – i.e. France. But in the long run, it could be the case that Germany will still have its highly qualified manufacturing sector, and France will be left with more debt.

Once the immediate crisis has been surmounted, the United States will need to find a new model of growth that will halt and narrow the widening in income inequalities of the past 20 years. They are both morally and politically unsustainable. The greatest new disparities have been between those at the very top of the income distribution scale and everyone else in society – and these disparities are closely linked to the vertiginous expansion of the rewards for financial actors. It has become clear that the regulation of pay for those employed in the financial sector is not only a matter of equity, but also a matter of preventing incentives for the kind of reckless risk-taking that pushed the system over the edge into disaster. How to create more equality along with a more innovative and productive economy is not only a question of compensation. It is involved in virtually every issue on the political agenda today. Health care reform, for example, could potentially have significant egalitarian redistributive effects. Not only would the 46 million Americans who currently hold no health insurance be given security, but providing for them would open up many new jobs. In addition, it would improve American corporate competitiveness. The costs of health care overall in the United States are greater than in any other advanced economy, and the burden on individual employers, for example at GM and Ford, has been a significant factor in their recent financial difficulties.

To lay out opportunities for improving both economic performance and social outcomes in the midst of a deep crisis may seem to be wildly optimistic. Certainly, there are significant political hurdles, as the bitter and even violent debates over health care reform in the US demonstrate. But this is a time of unsettled beliefs and the emergence of new generations into politics. As such, it presents opportunities that ought to be grasped. For scholars of political economics, there is a pressing obligation to offer a better understanding of the constraints and possibilities for political action, in a world in which national governments are still our main hope for regulating a global economy.

Leadership Imperatives for a Post-Crisis World

Stephen Roach

CHAIRMAN,

MORGAN STANLEY ASIA

"As the former Chief Economist of Morgan Stanley, I had been warning about the problems in the US economy for at least five years before the crisis hit. I never believed for a second that the US could continue to sustain a record consumption binge in a weak income environment. My concerns were amplified by the ultimate perils of the asset-led US economy: the bulk of the excess consumption was supported by unsustainable asset and credit bubbles.

"My timing in predicting the onset of crisis was early – I began to truly get worried already in 2003 and 2004. The macro-economic approach gives you the framework to understand the tensions that exist, but it doesn't allow you to predict the trigger that will spark the crisis. Unfortunately, the longer one predicts a crisis that fails to materialise, the more people begin to discredit you. They stop listening.

"Being only human, in the end, self-doubt started to creep in. I began thinking, "Maybe I'm missing something… Maybe I'm looking at things too pessimistically…" But although I questioned myself, I always came back to the same conclusion that there were fundamental problems with America's bubble-driven, asset-dependent growth model."

Like all crises, this too shall pass. But the severity of the current debacle points to a very different post-crisis healing than that which has taken place in the past. Most importantly, over the foreseeable future, the macro-economic environment is likely to be characterised by the combination of lingering problems in a damaged financial system together with an unusually anaemic recovery in the global economy.

Tensions will undoubtedly persist in such a tough post-crisis climate. In sharp contrast to the V-shaped recoveries of yesteryear, when relief was quick and powerful, the next several years are likely to reflect a persistent fragility, punctuated by periodic setbacks. Politicians and policymakers should continue to lean heavily on their fiscal and monetary arsenals in an effort to overwhelm the headwinds of a weak and tenuous recovery.

Contrary to the buzz of neo-Keynesian thinking, the post-crisis world needs far more than the brute force of anti-cyclical policies aimed at forestalling a relapse. A break from the broken strategies of the past is an urgent imperative. To the extent that actions are aimed at resurrecting the failed unbalanced growth models of the past, yet another wrenching crisis is a distinct possibility. Mindful of such perils, the authorities need to be tenacious in uncovering the problems and mistakes that got the world into this mess in the first place. Only then can a crisis-torn world transform imbalances into balance, and turn angst into opportunity.

This is not a crisis of capitalism but a crisis in the governance of capitalism.

This is not a crisis of capitalism. Ultimately – albeit with long lags in many cases – the invisible hand of creative destruction worked with brutal efficiency. It is, instead, much more a crisis in the *governance* of capitalism. An ideology of self-regulation replaced the discipline and oversight that an increasingly complex system required. It will take bold and visionary leadership to reverse that trend and to regain control of a precarious financial system and an asset-dependent global economy. But there is really no other choice. The global body politic must get governance right in this post-crisis world.

THE POST-CRISIS SCENARIO

What will the post-crisis world look like? Different regions face different diagnoses. After the collapse of its asset-based growth boom, the US will now probably enter into an extended low-growth period. Over the past 12 years, US consumer demand expanded, on average, at a nearly 4% annual rate. In contrast, over the next three to five years, this number will probably be closer to an anaemic 1.5 % annual increase. This will be sufficient to return America's consumption to GDP ratio from its current reading of 71% (as of mid-2009) to pre-bubble levels of 67%. In this regard, American citizens should prove to be smarter than policymakers such as Bernanke or Obama, who are urging consumers to maintain excessive levels of spending. While politicians are pushing to re-inflate consumption levels, American consumers have now begun to increase their rate of saving. Although stimulus policies were well-intentioned, based on the fear that the recession could evolve into a depression, they were nevertheless ill-conceived. They perpetuate existing macro imbalances in the US, and they were based on an exaggerated threat of depression.

Despite the necessity of increased savings, the coming retrenchment of the American consumer is likely to push the US into a prolonged low-growth period, akin to the Japanese lost decade after their own domestic bubbles burst. In the Japanese case, this was a difficult period, but certainly not catastrophic for the world as a whole. The global economy held together, and new sources of international growth were revealed. However, if the same were to happen for the US, it would be far more serious, as the US is much larger and has much higher import penetration. A repeat of the Japanese scenario at this scale would pose serious sustainability issues for the broader global economy.

In Europe, however, the outlook may be even worse. Unlike Asia or the US, the EU went into the crisis with no cushion of strong economic growth to shield it from the global crisis: US pre-crisis growth rates were around 4%, whereas in Europe this figure was 2%. Moreover, the engine of European growth was Germany: an export machine. Now that the global economy is in recession, exports will no longer provide a way out. Additionally, the ECB recognised only too late the dangerous risks in the global economy. Moreover, unlike the US Federal Reserve, it has been unwilling to champion stress testing of European banks. This is a critical process as it eases people's fears and restores confidence in the banking system. Also, the ECB's fixation on price stability has been executed in a disturbingly backward-looking fashion. Had the ECB been more concerned with the forward-looking inflation prognosis, it would be running more pro-growth policies today. The ECB's backward-looking inflation phobia, in combination with the euro's unfortunate strength and Europe's structural rigidities, make hopes for a quick EU recovery look increasingly unfounded.

In Asia, every major economy is either in the midst of a sharp slowdown or has tumbled into outright recession. However, although the Asian economies are currently very imbalanced, with a burdensome overemphasis on exports, with sufficient reform they may actually become an important new driver of growth in the post-crisis period. China is illustrative of this situation. Its economy is one of the most imbalanced globally, having benefitted enormously from investment and export-led growth over the past 30 years. With booming external demand, this was a spectacular growth model, but now the crisis has dried up this source of growth. Recently, the Chinese government has realised that internal consumption could be a new driver of growth, but they have yet to make the necessary investments in health care and welfare to support such a development. This would not only revitalise their own domestic growth, but also serve as an international growth driver to aid in recovery from the crisis. Asia has a population of 3.5 billion people, with China comprising 40% of this number. There is no way that

Asian production alone can satiate its demands. Nevertheless, this would still not be enough to compensate for the lost US consumption: China and India combined are only about one-fifth of the consumer market in the US. It is therefore mathematically impossible for these countries to offset the shortfall of US consumer demand.

Thus, as the US and the EU reel from the impact of the crisis, Asian economies (China in particular) may be given a long overdue chance to expand their consumption and their role in world markets. While this may not completely counter the slowdown in the West, it will be an important force for growth in the challenging period ahead.

FAMILIAR PATTERNS

Like most crises, this one has already given rise to a cottage industry of investigations and commissions aimed at correcting flaws in the system and thereby avoiding a recurrence of such turmoil in the future. This is a very familiar pattern. Experts invariably produce a detailed post mortem of what went wrong, and release numerous reports with great fanfare. These are sometimes followed by action but, more often than not, greeted with blank looks, polite applause, and little follow-through.

The very concept of a crisis dooms this approach to failure. History demonstrates that the next crisis is never like the last one. Yet diagnoses and cures are almost always backward-looking. It's akin to the ever-mutating virus that forever complicates human disease control, spawning internally generated immunities, which continually frustrate new vaccines. That is not to say that obvious flaws in financial systems or policy architectures should not be uncovered and addressed, but rather that there is a limit to any cure that arises from a backward-looking diagnosis.

For example, the Asian financial crisis of 1997-98 was, at the time, billed as the world's worst financial crisis since the 1930s. Post-crisis commissions focused on the architectural reforms that would prevent the replay of this powerful pan-regional contagion. Follow-through, in this instance, was impressive. Among other things, Asian currency pegs were largely abandoned, current account deficits were transformed into surpluses, depleted foreign exchange reserves were rebuilt, and exposure to short-term capital inflows was sharply reduced. Lessons were well-learned – at least in the context of what went wrong in 1997-98.

Eleven years later, Asia is in trouble again. While the post-crisis remedies developed after the financial crisis of the late 1990s worked well to mitigate that period's turmoil, they failed to inoculate Asia against the inevitable next crisis – in this case, a massive shock to external demand that left its increasingly export-led economies ripe for the fall. Developing Asia's backward-looking fixation on financial repair did little to prepare it for a shock that was aimed at the heart of the structural imbalances in its real economies. That does not mean Asia should not have adopted the menu of widely recommended post-1997-98 crisis measures. It just should have done more. Unsurprisingly, the problems of the past did not turn out to be a good guide to the stresses that were to hit Asia a decade later.

Asian economies may become an important new driver of growth in the post-crisis period.

Unlike the crises of the past 25 years, most of which originated in the developing world, this one arose in the rich countries of the developed world. Plus, it was the main engine of the developed world – the once-thriving US economy – that was the principal source of a problem that quickly became global in scope. Once again, the rush to judgement is on. This time, the focus is on the flaws in the modern-day financial institutions and the toxic financial instruments that have presumably given rise to this crisis. Calls for regulatory reform are louder than ever, both at the national and at the global level. The recently unveiled proposals of the Obama administration are leading the charge in this area. Can the American body politic break the mould of the backward-looking reform process and draw more prescient lessons for the future?

A MACRO CRISIS

The political response will be effective only if it avoids the incremental thinking that typically dominates post-crisis debates. While that may be a lot to ask of myopic politicians, it is necessary given that there is a deeper meaning to this crisis: a macro overlay that made the micro flaws especially serious. At work was a lethal interplay between the bursting of asset bubbles and the unwinding of destabilising imbalances. Both of these were major sources of disequilibria that had been all but ignored during the pre-crisis era of excess. Deepening our understanding of these powerful macro forces is essential in order to promote sustained healing in the post-crisis era.

The saga began in America. Starting in the late 1990s, the US economy went through an ominous transformation. Income-short consumers discovered the miracle drug of a new source of purchasing power: the seemingly open-ended wealth creation of ever-growing asset markets. First through equities, and then through residential properties, American households drew on asset appreciation to consume well beyond their means (as delineated by the US economy's internal labour income-generating capacity). Real private-sector compensation – the broadest measure of the economy's endogenous income flows – currently stands only about 13% above its early 2002 levels in inflation-adjusted terms. That represents a staggering $ 1 trillion shortfall from the path that would have been implied from the average trajectory of the previous four long-cycle expansions. Yet personal consumption surged to a record 72% of real GDP in early 2007 – a spending binge without precedent in US history, or for that matter in the history of any leading economy in the modern era.

Wealth creation closed this gap, driven in recent years by the self-reinforcing feedbacks of housing and credit bubbles. Courtesy of new 'breakthroughs' in mortgage finance – breakthroughs, in retrospect, that were more destructive than constructive – American homeowners tapped the open-ended home equity till as never before. Net equity extraction from residential property surged from about 3% of disposable personal income in 2000 to nearly 9% in 2006. This provided newfound support to spending and saving that allowed households to more than compensate for the extraordinary shortfall of labour income generation. The result was not only the consumption binge noted above, but also a profound shortfall of income-based saving. The personal savings rate slid to 1.2% in mid-2005 – the lowest reading since the Great Depression of the 1930s.

The story didn't stop there. Lacking in income-based saving, the US imported surplus saving from abroad in order to keep growing. But it had to run massive external deficits in order to attract the capital, pushing the current-account deficit up to a record 6.5% of US GDP by the third quarter of 2006. The impact of that development was global in scope, as deficits must always be matched by surpluses elsewhere in the world. Courtesy of America's gaping external shortfall, global imbalances (the absolute sum of the world's current account deficits and surpluses) soared to 6% of world GDP in 2006, nearly triple the 2% reading of a decade earlier. Joined at the hip, asset bubbles and global imbalances stretched the macro fabric of the global economy as never before.

As in all eras of excess, tantalising explanations were offered as to why these problems should be ignored. The so-called Bretton Woods II framework was a prominent excuse: a purported symbiosis between the US and a China-centric Asia, which many argued cemented the financial underpinnings of the world's biggest consumer to the world's major exporters. In the end, there was one fatal problem with this line of reasoning – it all hinged on ever-expanding property and credit bubbles. When those bubbles burst, a deadly feedback mechanism came into play, as powerful post-bubble adjustments hit the world's most overextended consumer, setting in motion forces that sapped external demand for the world's export-led surplus savers. The once virtuous cycle quickly became vicious, with wrenching macro adjustments exposing the micro flaws of a precarious financial system and setting the world up for the worst financial crisis and recession since the 1930s.

THE MACRO SOLUTION

The above argument implies that the crisis-torn world needs more than micro-based regulatory reform. That very consideration is now being actively debated in the world's major political capitals. One of the most contentious aspects of this debate involves the thorny problems of systemic risk, including the cross-product and cross-border interdependencies of financial institutions, complex securities, market structures, and economies. A consensus has coalesced around the concept of a systemic risk regulator: a new or existing authority that should be charged with managing these complex interdependencies.

The wheel need not be reinvented. Systemic risk is nothing new. It is only jargon for the complexities that have always been at the core of interdependent macro systems. True, these complexities have morphed into different forms over recent years, compounded by the cross-border linkages of globalisation, new technologies of financial engineering, and a massive increase in the scale of global financial institutions. However, that doesn't mean that market-based systems have lost their ability to contain such risks. Central banks, by setting policy interest rates that, in turn, provide important benchmarks for the price of risky assets, can still exercise ultimate control in fulfilling this function. It is just a question of whether they have the political will – or the independence – to do so. Rather than attempt to create a new systemic risk regulator, it is more important to take a careful look at the central banking function itself; namely, considering the possibility of making explicit changes to policy mandates that would force central banks to make systemic risk control an integral part of their mission.

There is also an important global overlay to considerations of systemic risk. As we have seen all too vividly in this crisis, cross-border spillovers are the rule – not the exception – in increasingly integrated global capital markets. Disparities in country-specific regulations have led to a regulatory arbitrage that has compounded global imbalances. This adds unnecessary volatility to markets, underscoring the need for cross-border harmonisation of regulations, as well as for a regulatory authority charged with monitoring and sounding the alarm on the global ramifications of systemic risk. Again, the existing central banking structure should be used to deal with this aspect of the problem, in this case, by empowering the Bank for International Settlements (BIS) with the authority of the global systemic risk regulator. Given its long-standing concerns over mounting global imbalances, as well as the rigor of the analytics it has developed to assess this problem, the BIS is certainly deserving of this important responsibility.

But the reworking of policy mandates needs to start with the central bank that is most responsible for this mess: America's Federal Reserve. There are compelling reasons to believe that the bubble-driven distortions of the US economy, as well as the global imbalances they spawned, would have been considerably different under an alternative monetary policy regime. Had, for example, the Fed run a tighter monetary policy in the early part of this decade, the excesses of property and credit bubbles most assuredly would have been tempered. While it is true that an asset-dependent US economy would probably have grown more slowly as a result (as would the rest of the US-centric global economy), in retrospect, that foregone growth would have been a small price to pay in order to avoid the crisis-induced shortfall that could now be with us for years to come. Before the Fed is given new powers in the post-crisis era, as proposed by the Obama administration's regulatory reform proposals, a careful reconsideration of its old powers is in order.

A NEW MANDATE FOR THE FEDERAL RESERVE

Mindful of the costs of a decade of misguided monetary policy, the US Congress now needs to alter the Fed's policy mandate to include an explicit reference to financial stability. The Obama administration has proposed that the Federal Reserve be empowered as America's new systemic risk regulator. That expansion of power should not be taken lightly, nor should it be granted without greater accountability. Charging the Fed with promoting financial stability would not only force it to aim at tempering the damage from asset bubbles, but also require it to use its regulatory authority for promoting sounder risk management practices. The explicit incorporation of financial stability into the Fed's policy mandate would align concerns over systemic risks with concerns about destabilising bubbles and imbalances – a welcome development after years of neglect and excess.

The wheel need not be reinvented. Systemic risk is nothing new.

There is good reason to believe that the Fed needs to be bound by a new law to avoid bubble-prone mistakes in the future. As was the case with the 1946 Full Employment Act targets, as well as with the 1978 Humphrey Hawkins Act objectives of price stability, Congress need not specify precise targets with respect to financial stability. That should be left up to the Fed, allowing them the monetary authority to develop the metrics and tools that would enable the execution of the expanded policy mandate.

This will require the Fed to adjust its tactics in two ways. First, monetary policy will need to shift away from the Greenspan/Bernanke reactive post-bubble cleanup approach, and towards pre-emptive bubble avoidance. It may be tricky to judge when an asset class is in danger of forming a bubble, but in retrospect, there can be little doubt of the profusion of bubbles that developed over the past decade. These include equities, residential property, credit, and many other risky assets. The Fed mistakenly ignored these developments, harbouring the illusion that it could clean up any mess after the fact. The extent of today's devastating mess is clear repudiation of that hands-off approach.

There is no room in a new financial stability mandate for the ideological excuses of bubble denialists. Alan Greenspan, for example, argued that equities were surging because of a New Economy, that housing markets form local rather than national bubbles, and that the credit explosion was a by-product of the American genius of financial innovation. In retrospect, while there was a kernel of truth to all of those observations, they should not have been decisive in shaping Fed policy. Under a financial stability mandate, the US central bank will have no such leeway. It will instead need to replace ideological convictions with common sense. When investors and speculators buy assets in anticipation of future price increases – precisely the case in each of the bubbles of the past decade – the Fed will need to err on the side of caution and presume that a bubble is forming that could pose a threat to financial stability. The new mandate would encourage the Federal Reserve to deal with financial excesses by striking the right balance between its policy interest rate and the tools of its regulatory arsenal. In times of asset-market froth, they should favour a 'leaning against the wind' approach with regard to the policy interest rate, pushing the federal funds rate higher than a narrow inflation target might otherwise suggest. Yes, the US would undoubtedly pay a short-term price in terms of foregone output, but that price would be well worth the benefits of a more durable expansion.

Second, the Fed's other tactical adjustment should be for its new mandate to require it to be much tougher in exercising its long neglected regulatory oversight capacity. For good reason, the Fed has been equipped with tools in its policy arsenal that can and should be directed at financial excesses, including margin requirements for equity lending as well as controls on the issuance of exotic mortgage instruments (negative amortisation and zero-interest rate products, for example). In addition, the Fed should not be bashful in using the bully pulpit of moral suasion to warn against the impending dangers of mounting asset and credit bubbles.

Of equal and related importance is the need for the US central bank to develop a clearer understanding of the negative linkage between financial stability and the open-ended explosion of new financial instruments, namely derivatives and structured products. Over the past decade, an ideologically driven Fed failed to make the critical distinction between financial engineering and innovation. Complex and opaque financial products were viewed as testaments to American ingenuity. Unfortunately, the Fed understood neither the products nor the incidence of their distribution. Never mind that the notional value of global derivatives hit some $ 516 trillion in mid-2007 on the eve of the subprime crisis (a 2.3 times increase in value over the preceding three years to a level that was fully ten times the size of world GDP), the operative view in US central banking circles was that an innovations-based explosion of new financial instruments was a huge plus for market efficiency. Drawing a false sense of security from the 'originate and distribute' technology of complex derivatives products, the Fed took great theoretical comfort from a presumed diffusion of counterparty risks. These so-called innovations became the mantra of the Brave New World of finance, and were billed as a new source of liquidity to the system that could serve as a shock absorber in times of distress. Yet as the aftershocks of the subprime crisis painfully illustrate, trust in ideology over fact-based risk assessment turned out to be a fatal mistake. The derivatives implosion was not only concentrated in many of the world's major financial institutions, but it was also a critical source of illiquidity and an amplifier of market shocks.

The lessons of the inflation problems of the 1970s, as well as those from the asset bubbles and the Fed's regulatory laxity over the past decade, should not be lost on the US Congress; America's central bank cannot be entrusted to correct these mistakes on its own. Ideological and even political biases can – and have – repeatedly gotten in the way of the policy discipline required of an independent central bank. New targets must be explicitly hardwired into the Federal Reserve's policy mandate. Only then can it be transformed into the systemic risk regulator Washington is now seeking.

POLITICAL WILL

This crisis didn't have to happen. The all too convenient 'inevitability excuse' – the notion that the world has once again been engulfed by the proverbial hundred-year tsunami – is nothing more than a cop-out by those who were asleep at the switch. Of course, cycles of fear and greed date back to the inception of markets, and those powerful animal spirits were very much at work this time as well. However, much could have been done to avoid the devastating repercussions of the so-called subprime crisis. There is compelling reason to hold the stewards of the financial system accountable, both those in Washington as well as those on Wall Street.

In free-market systems, the global body politic renders the ultimate judgement on matters of governance. The emphasis above has been on monetary policy and, specifically, on a new mandate for central banks. That is not meant to take the place of other regulatory reform proposals that have been offered in recent months. But too much attention has been focused on micro remedies, while ignoring the macro issues that have come to a head in this extraordinary period of crisis and recession.

There is no room in a new financial stability mandate for the ideological excuses of bubble denialists.

Politicians and policymakers face a number of other key macro leadership imperatives. Among these, the choice between the quick fix and the heavy lifting of global rebalancing is especially critical. It is tempting in a climate where the first signs of healing are evident to lapse back into the old strain of economic growth that got the world into serious trouble in the first place. Why not, for example, let Americans go back to excess consumption and the Chinese revert to saving and exporting? Despite claims that both societies are culturally inclined toward those extremes, the main support for such views comes solely from the compelling political expediency of maintaining the status quo.

In addition, politicians should not be let off the hook in facing up to the mounting risks of trade frictions and protectionism. The choice between the collective interest of globalisation and the self-interest of 'localisation' is essential in that regard. Since 2004, the drum beat for trade friction and protectionism has been growing ever louder. However, of the 45 anti-China trade bills introduced in the US Congress between 2004 and 2007, none passed, thanks to high prosperity and low unemployment at the time. In such periods, belligerence on trade policy can be dismissed as political posturing. However, this prosperous period has clearly passed, and in the midst of a severe recession and soaring unemployment, politicians are under serious pressure to protect increasingly beleaguered workers. Unwilling to look in the mirror, Congress has been blaming China for all of the problems currently bearing down on middle-class workers. The risks of protectionist policy blunders are especially worrisome in such a climate. Only through a better understanding of today's strain of globalisation can the body politic avoid such dangerous protectionist temptations.

In the end, we cannot delude ourselves into thinking that the lessons of this crisis rest solely in new rules and regulations. They are a necessary – though insufficient – condition for a more robust post-crisis architecture. Our problems also have a very important human dimension – namely, they are an outgrowth of the poor judgement endemic in this reckless era of self-regulation. By purging governance of these ideological biases, the authorities will be better positioned to avoid the dangerous interplay between asset bubbles and global imbalances in the future. While there should be no illusions that such steps will banish the threat of financial crises in the future, to the extent that the body politic rises to the occasion, the inevitable next crisis will be far better contained than this one.

Establishing a New Macro-economic Policy Regime

Willem Buiter

PROFESSOR OF EUROPEAN POLITICAL ECONOMY,

LONDON SCHOOL OF ECONOMICS

"My first concerns about a potential crisis began in 2005, when the British government issued its first 50-year Index-linked Treasury Gilt, and the interest rates on it were 0.36%. This is extraordinary low – the long-term historical average is just below three percent. This gave me my first sense of foreboding that something was amiss. Not only were these long-term risk-free interest rates astonishingly low, but also the credit risk spread across the board were at rock-bottom levels. The only way to explain this was that the inventors of these new financial instruments had found new and improved ways of trading risks by engaging a huge new population of risk-holders. These people tried to convince us that the risk had not just been traded, but had effectively been traded away. I didn't buy it. I knew too many people in the industry to believe that this story was credible. So there clearly was something wrong with global asset markets: risk-free rates were too low, and risk itself was severely under-priced.

"My second indication that a crisis was looming was when BlackRock went public. At this point I realised that something serious was going to happen, and soon. This was an insane institutional transformation. Blackrock's entire purpose had been to take public companies and make them private, and then it turned around and enlisted the advantages of public companies to its own benefit."

PRELUDE TO THE CRISIS

Every crisis is in many ways the same: there is excessive growth and an asset market boom. A sense of euphoria emerges, and everybody becomes convinced that this time they have truly invented the elusive *perpetuum mobile*. The fact that society suffers from such periodic bouts of insanity must be taken as a given. They have happened before and will surely happen again. The important question is whether the given regulatory arrangements and macro-economic policy arrangements lean against or feed the inevitable credit and asset bubbles that accompany these bouts of insanity. In this case, policy arrangements undoubtedly fed the euphoria.

Prior to the crisis, most macro-economists operated in an academic language that had become completely disconnected from the world they were supposed to be modelling. This made it impossible for them to foresee the crisis before it hit. The discipline was based on a common paradigm, which was, at its core, a mix of neo-classical and neo-Keynesian economics. Unfortunately, while this model functioned well in good times, it was useless in times of crisis. Its logical structure did not recognise even the possibility of defaults, insolvencies, or illiquidity problems, instead relying faithfully on complete market structures. Therefore, the problem was not merely that their models could not answer questions on these subjects – they did not even allow the user to ask the right questions.

There were many imbalances in the pre-crisis economic system that could have triggered the crisis: the unsustainable growth of credit, the risky increases in leverage, unbridled financial innovation, and regulatory arbitrage both within and between countries. Any of these could have created conditions ripe for a 'Minsky moment' – the point in the business cycle when investors realise that they hold too much debt and sell off their assets, leading to declines in markets and a severe demand for cash.

Every crisis is in many ways the same: there is excessive growth and an asset market boom.

In actuality, it was the little-understood subprime mortgage market (primarily in the US, although parallel systems existed globally) that triggered the collapse. Sadly, this was, in large part, a social experiment that went disastrously wrong. American Republicans used government-sponsored programs to solidify their political base by turning tenants into homeowners. Eventually, this created a disastrous bubble that, upon bursting, exposed other underlying economic imbalances.

These imbalances had been simmering just below the surface of the past decade's apparent macro-economic stability: high and smooth GDP growth, low and stable inflation, and low and falling interest rates had blinded people to these underlying flaws. First among them was the often cited US-Chinese trade imbalance, reflecting too much US consumption and too much Chinese saving. However, even more important was a far less frequently referenced imbalance: a portfolio imbalance between the global demand for and supply of low-risk financial assets. Countries exporting oil and other commodities – specifically the Gulf Cooperation Council countries – had become a *nouveau riche* in the global community, yet like China and many other New Industrial Countries that had been hit hard by the 1997/98 crisis, they maintained an unfortunate preference for investing mainly in low-risk assets. When their conservative portfolio preferences were not matched by an expansion in the supply of such assets, the low-risk interest rates dropped to ludicrous levels.

In addition to these imbalances, Alan Greenspan (former head of the Federal Reserve) instituted monetary policies that exacerbated the already dangerous pace at which liquidity was being injected into the US economy. The problem was not that he cut rates drastically in 2003, but that he left them far too low for an extended period of time, inciting excessive investment and liquidity flows into the economy. Similar patterns occurred both in the eurozone as well as in Japan.

As a result of these multiple layers of underlying instability, the fallout from the crisis was severe with only slow rates of recovery. Luckily, policymakers learned the lessons of the 1930s and avoided pro-cyclical behaviour, high interest rates, allowing the money supply to collapse, or trade wars. Unfortunately, they also made new mistakes. Specifically, they failed to reform the current problems of moral hazard and insufficient or inadequate regulation. Both the Obama administration and Gordon Brown's government engaged in insufficient re-regulation programs; rather than truly correcting the existing regulatory deficiencies, they simply tried to turn back the clock to recreate the economies that they thought they had in 2005. They refused to tackle the Too Big To Fail problem, and they were insufficiently aggressive in tackling excessive leverage. The US, specifically, was worryingly unwilling to tackle schisms and balkanisation in the regulatory structures. By neglecting this issue, they set the stage for an infinitely worse financial sector boom and bust in the decades to come. Incentive structures remain corrupted, encouraging excessive risk-taking by institutions that are too big or too politically connected to fail.

The already excessive but still rising public debt burden must be reduced, and solutions such as allowing central banks to set negative interest rates should be explored in order to help economies emerge less damaged from the crisis. Yet the most necessary change in the post-crisis period will be the development of new macro-economic models that allow researchers to ask the right questions and explore issues that are central to modern economies. Backward looking analyses may be a good place to start in such a quest, but if they ignore modern developments, these analyses will necessarily be lacking. Keynes and Minsky were certainly important thinkers, but they only offer preludes to what is currently required. Although they asked many of the right questions, they failed to create fully articulated theories.

On the whole, given the magnitude of the financial collapse, it is actually surprising that the economic fallout has not been greater. Despite their oversights and shortcomings, the monetary and fiscal authorities did a remarkable job of mitigating the damage and preventing the crisis from spinning completely out of control. Aggressive intervention by central banks provided external credit to households and corporations when banks were hoarding capital and liquidity. If this is as bad as it gets, the global community got off lightly.

GLOBAL REBALANCING

All of the above-mentioned problems predominantly impacted the North Atlantic region. As a result, these countries are especially likely to undergo slow and painful recovery from the crisis. However, by now it has become plainly apparent that this crisis has spread beyond the developed world and has had especially severe effects on emerging economies. However, the character of these effects has been mixed, with some emerging economies actually having the potential to emerge from the crisis stronger than they went in. Specifically, those emerging economies that (1) did not suffer much damage to their financial sectors, (2) were not too dependent on exports to the West, and (3) were not too dependent on external finance will do better overall. Based on this analysis, India, which satisfies all three of these conditions, may fare quite well in the post-crisis period. Brazil and China, both of which meet two of the three conditions in this analysis, may similarly avoid significant damage if they are able to redirect domestic policy to make up for vulnerabilities in the remaining component.

Given the magnitude of the financial collapse, it is actually surprising that the economic fallout has not been greater.

In addition to the crisis clearing more space for emerging economies to grow, it may also weaken existing powers. Many are speculating that the international system of reserve currencies is likely to shift. Specifically, it is highly likely that the world will move away from the dollar's current dominance, and towards a new multi-polar reserve system. The country issuing an international reserve currency must meet two criteria: it must be a hegemon politically, economically, and financially; and it must act responsibly in its monetary, fiscal, and financial policies. The US no longer satisfies either of these prerequisites, making the long-term prospects bleak for the dollar's standing as the favoured international reserve currency. However, such changes will occur only slowly; in the short-term, China, the Middle Eastern countries, and other newly wealthy nations will still invest overwhelmingly in dollars. Gradually, this preference is likely to be eroded, leaving space for new reserve currencies to emerge.

In the medium term, the euro is likely to be the primary beneficiary of this shift. This currency is an anomaly, seeing as the European Central Bank has no fiscal back-up. This is a negative factor from the perspective that in other countries the treasury guarantees the solvency of the central bank. However, the negative side of fiscal back-up is that if a treasury ever asks the central bank to monetise their deficits, they would be effectively obliged to do so. In this regard, the fact that the euro is a shared currency between many countries is actually an advantage because it is protected from national fiscal irresponsibility. Additionally, although less admirably, the ECB bankers have been extremely conservative throughout the crisis, and have maintained excessively high interest rates. Although this is unfortunate for real investment in the euro area, it is good news for outside investors in euros, increasing the likelihood that the euro will be adopted as a replacement international reserve currency in the medium-term. However, in the long-term, this niche is likely to be shared with emerging markets' currencies. The Chinese yuan and Indian rupee, for example, are likely to emerge as viable competitors to the dollar and the euro.

AVAILABLE POLITICAL TOOLS

The post-crisis response has been described as the coordinated efforts of a 'Keynesian fire brigade'. In fact, this is far from the truth. Keynes was not an advocate of monetary policy, favouring fiscal policy instead. Yet the greatest policy victories against the current crisis have overwhelmingly been won with monetary instruments.

It was the monetary authorities who cut interest rates almost to the floor, and when this was still insufficient, it was again the monetary authorities who began engaging in unconventional monetary policies such as quantitative easing, credit easing, and extending unlimited credit. One should not underestimate the degree to which such practices have heroically broken the mould of central bank dogma. Creativity in central banks is akin to swearing in church.

Fiscal policy, Keynes's weapon of choice, has been weak and insignificant in comparison. Some countries have managed to achieve a limited discretionary fiscal stimulus – the US and, to a lesser extent, France, Japan, and Germany. However, most of the fiscal stimulus that has occurred since the crisis has been purely the result of automatic stabilising mechanisms. Allowing these to function was certainly a preferable fiscal stance to blocking them and initiating pro-cyclical policies, but it did not constitute a true fiscal reaction. This was largely the result of the fact that most countries – especially in the West – entered into the crisis with dismal underlying fiscal capacities.

However, the weak fiscal policy response may not be as much of a tragedy as it appears to be on the surface, as there is little evidence that discretionary fiscal policy actually works. In 2008, Spilimbergo and others published a report for the IMF, outlining their fiscal policy recommendations for the crisis period. Ironically, the appendices – which were supposed to contain the empirical support for increasing fiscal policy expenditures – were all at best inconclusive, and often showed a negative effect from fiscal stimuli.

This is not to say that fiscal policy should be avoided altogether. Clearly, pro-cyclical policies remain detrimental. However, further increasing government debt could prompt a panic about the all too real threat of sovereign debt default. Automatic stabilising measures alone created 10% of GDP deficit in the UK, with discretionary fiscal policies accounting for another 2%. The US maintains a similarly disheartening annual deficit. At the same time, government revenues have dried up. The British government had been heavily reliant on the housing sector for its revenues. Both the British and the US governments counted on the financial sector for income – in the US, this sector alone accounted for 40% of the country's total corporate profits in 2006. With the crisis severely impacting these two industries, governments currently face a structural deterioration of their revenues. As the tax buoyancy of GDP declines, governments have increasingly less fiscal elbow-room before they are confronted with concerns about fiscal sustainability. Suddenly, the once ludicrous idea of sovereign debt default appears worryingly plausible – even in some of the world's largest economies.

There is little evidence that discretionary fiscal policy actually works.

There are two additional reasons that this particular crisis was unfit for a predominantly fiscal response. First, to be effective, counter-cyclical policies in the downturn require that the markets believe counter-cyclical policy would be implemented in the next upturn as well. If not, they will spook the financial markets. This condition is unlikely to be satisfied, because counter-cyclical policy during the upswing would run exactly counter to the policies of the past eight years, especially in the US and the UK, where pro-cyclical policies during boom times had actually become the norm. Second, fiscal policy becomes emasculated by excessive private and public sector debt. Textbook macro-economics maintains that once monetary policies such as interest rate reduction and quantitative easing begin to create a liquidity trap, the time is ripe for Keynesian fiscal policies to save the day. However, when debt is as high as it is currently, even fiscal policy is unable to salvage these losses.

In such a context, tackling unemployment is difficult, if not impossible. Monetary policy is useless in such an endeavour, and fiscal policy is unhelpful in the current crisis for the reasons mentioned above. Wage moderation is also unconstructive if every country tries to achieve it simultaneously. It is largely a beggar-thy-neighbour policy of last resort, and only works if the country implementing it is facing a domestically isolated downturn while their neighbours are overheating. Finally, policies of work sharing must be avoided, as they only institutionalise inefficient and distortionary employment patterns that tend to linger long after their necessity has passed. In fact, short of creating a condition where negative interest rates can be implemented, there is little that can be done to combat unemployment. Like old age, it has become, quite simply, a fact of life. Despite the difficulty that the Western mind has in accepting such a reality, it is crucial that policymakers do not get ahead of themselves, making irresponsible interventions in the labour market. If anything, now is the time to increase labour market flexibility, not rigidity. If this cannot be achieved – for example because of unions or other vested interests – it may be better to do nothing, as poor institutional reform is infinitely worse than none at all.

Nevertheless, at the core of the problem of unemployment is a far more tangible problem: debt. Unemployment has been amplified because the crisis caused a demand problem, and this demand problem, in turn, was caused by excess debt and lack of credit. The neo-liberal period triumphantly claimed to have reduced the public debt, but in fact this was little more than a smoke screen for shifting contingent public debt on to the private sector. The average debt to GDP ratio in the eurozone is currently 70%. Leverage increased dramatically in the past decade, especially in households and in the financial sector. Naïve neo-liberal market optimism led policymakers to take their eyes off the ball; they assumed that as long as debt was private, it was innocent. Sadly, as the current crisis has made clear, unsustainable private deficits are just as much of a problem as unsustainable public deficits. This is particularly true in cases where there is an implicit option for policy authorities to socialise and take over or guarantee private sector debt, as has been done in Europe in Sweden, Latvia, Ireland, the UK, Germany and many other countries. In a way, all private debt of entities deemed systemically important is, at its core, contingent public debt.

Private debt also makes countries vulnerable to international capital markets and speculative attacks. New EU countries that have not yet joined the euro have suffered tremendously under pressures from international speculators. In order to attack financial institutions of, say, Romania or Lithuania, international speculators were able to buy Romanian lei or Lithuanian litas on liquid markets and sell them for other currencies, most notably, for euros. This has made joining the eurozone an urgent imperative for many of these countries, in order to protect their financial standing. However, it should be noted that acquiring the euro does not entail acquiring the fiscal credibility of the entire EU, let alone of its best members. As an illustration: recently the basis point credit spread between German and Irish or Greek bonds reached 300 points. Clearly, the markets do not believe that there is a de facto pooling of sovereign default risk in the eurozone. This proves, once and for all, that although joining the common currency brings financial benefits, it does not mean that countries become responsible for each other's debts.

> *The neo-liberal period triumphantly claimed to have reduced the public debt, but in fact this was little more than a smoke screen for shifting contingent public debt onto the private sector.*

Unlike the problem of unemployment, if the international community could agree that debt (public and private) was the core issue delaying a recovery from the current crisis, there are a variety of ways in which they could tackle it. Many people argue that debt could best be reduced with inflationary policies. They suggest aggressive monetary policy and extensive quantitative easing that would essentially wipe out the real value of the current debt. However, a less-bad policy would be to agree to an international Jubilee: an agreement to force forgiveness of all debt. While this is certainly not a policy that could be repeated, it may be an appropriate measure for such extraordinary times. It essentially means cheating people out of their loans, but it would at least cheat people upfront and honestly rather than the more legal – but less moral – method of cheating them through unanticipated inflation.

HOW MUCH EUROPE?

In Europe, there is an ongoing battle between those who favour giving more power to the EU, and those who favour ridding them of the powers they already hold. Regardless of one's position on this spectrum, it seems pathetic that Europe has resigned itself to an uncompetitive international position for its banking and financial sectors because it cannot agree on a fiscal burden-sharing rule. All banks must be backed by a central bank, a regulated supervisor, and a treasury. Because these three institutions do not all exist at the EU level, banking must necessarily be done nationally. In order to use its unification to its competitive advantage, Europe must set up cross-border institutions of supervision and fiscal burden sharing, including a minimal European-level fiscal authority that could solidify these commitments.

When Europe established a customs union, it realised that it could not set separate tariff policies for each of its member states. To solve this problem, it made trade a supranationally determined policy component of the EU. Similarly, if Europe wants to truly establish a single market – for financial products and services as well as for the free mobility of capital and people – it will need to put regulation into the supranational domain of the EU. Sadly, there is insufficient leadership at the EU level to implement such drastic reforms.

Therefore, if EU level regulation proves impossible, legal space should be provided for countries to create sub-EU level international regulatory institutions. These sub-groups of countries would be able to broaden the reach of their financial services beyond their own borders, even if they were unable to expand their presence throughout the entire EU. Such agreements would avoid future repetition of shameful catastrophes like the Fortis debacle. For a week, the Benelux governments tried to reach an agreement on how to share the burden of capital to be injected into this international bank while maintaining its cross-border character. Eventually, Fortis was split into three parts – Dutch, Belgian and Luxembourgian – essentially recreating a Dutch territorial 'rump' of ABN and insulating it from foreign competition. Yet insulation of national banks has already caused decreased competitiveness in the Netherlands, where ABN AMRO, ING, and Rabobank essentially control the Dutch financial market as an oligarchy.

The crisis has highlighted the need to create a new role for the ECB in Europe.

In addition, the crisis has highlighted the need to create a new role for the ECB in Europe. In response to the current crisis, the ECB will be formally mandated to perform a variety of new functions, including liquidity and credit-enhancing measures, becoming a lender of last resort, and maintaining general financial stability. Whereas its previous functions (primarily limited to interest rate adjustments) allowed it to remain politically independent, such an expanded role requires political accountability. Realising such a change in the US or the UK is relatively uncomplicated; governments simply have to pass a law. But in the EU, the ECB is based on treaties that are extraordinarily difficult to amend with 27 member countries. While aspects of the ECB's behaviour and governance can be changed without opening the treaties in their entirety, changing its mandate is not as simple.

However, this may have to be done, as the only alternative proposal on the table is downright unacceptable. EU leaders have proposed creating a European Systemic Risk Council that will be authorised to make binding decisions on the regulation of banking and financial institutions. While on the surface this appears to be exactly what is needed, the proposal puts the politically unaccountable ECB at the head of the organisation. It allows the ECB to continue working within the same politically insulated policy-space it had been operating in previously. However, the decisions that it is entitled to make in this new capacity are unquestionably political.

THE BOTTOM LINE

In the upcoming crisis recovery period, five reforms are to be recommended. First, the public debt burden must urgently be reduced. Otherwise, by the time the next major downturn occurs, countries will be completely incapacitated by public debt overhang and unable to respond with aggressive stabilisation policies. Second, policymakers should introduce innovative new institutions. Specifically, they should allow central banks to implement negative interest rates.

Third, Europe must create an EU level regulatory structure to manage cross-border banks and other systemically important financial institutions, such as insurance companies. Once these are established, they should be expanded to include agreements with other countries and regions on new globalised standards. This will prevent European financial institutions from being undercut by global regulatory arbitrage again.

Fourth, as the crisis changes the relative wealth and power of nations, these changes should be reflected in international institutions. The US's veto in the IMF must be abolished, and EU's combined weight should similarly be dramatically reduced.

Fifth, the "Too Big To Fail" problem must be addressed. Banks should not be allowed to grow so large that they no longer can be left susceptible to the vulnerabilities of their own risk-taking. Their size could be constrained, for example, by creating vertical splits in banks (re-inventing Glass-Steagall-type distinctions between commercial banks and investment banks, or other splits between 'narrow banking' and other, riskier banking activities) as well as by establishing capital requirements that are not merely counter-cyclical, but also higher for larger banks. In addition, rating agencies should be banned from engaging in activities that constitute conflicts of interests. No company should be both broker and dealer; no proprietary investor should also be entitled to act on behalf of clients. Aggressive anti-monopoly policies would also significantly check the size of companies. Finally, high-risk financial institutions should be prevented from having limited liability constructions – instead they should be required to operate as partnerships, as investment banks used to be.

Many factors aligned to contribute to the current economic downturn, and many policies and institutions will have to be revised in order for the international economic community to pick itself up again. In the search for new policies and institutions, policymakers must be realistic, recognising inadequate instruments for what they are (fiscal policy comes to mind) and attacking the roots of problems, rather than their symptoms (unemployment is an unavoidable side-effect of its policy-susceptible root cause: namely excessive debt, both public and private). In this endeavour, the EU faces the added policy challenges of insufficient coordination between the national and supranational policymaking levels.

Varieties of Capitalism;
Varieties of Reform

David Soskice

PROFESSOR OF POLITICAL ECONOMY,

OXFORD UNIVERSITY

"In hindsight, the bankruptcy of Northern Rock in 2007 was probably the first sign of the economic crisis, although at the time, few realised the full significance of the event. As the crisis continues, it develops differently in different economies. Different countries have institutionalised different varieties of capitalism, which display different strengths and weaknesses in the face of the crisis' turmoil. In the post-crisis recovery period, it is important that reforms be considered within the framework of the varieties of capitalism already established in different countries."

VARIETIES OF CAPITALISM

The varieties of capitalism approach is a framework for understanding the similarities and differences among developed economies. This firm-centred political economy differentiates between two varieties of capitalism: liberal market economies and coordinated market economies.

Liberal market economies include the US, the UK, and other economies where firms coordinate their activities primarily via hierarchies and competitive market arrangements. In these economies, competition and formal contracting characterise market relationships. Actors adjust supply and demand in response to price signals, often based on the types of marginal calculations emphasised by neo-classical economists. There is general education, a flexible labour market, dispersed shareholder corporate governance, and market-based technology transfer.

In contrast, in coordinated market economies such as Sweden and Germany, firms depend more heavily on non-market relationships to coordinate their activities. They have extensive relational or incomplete contracting, network monitoring based on the exchange of private information inside networks, and reliance on collaborative rather than competitive relationships. Equilibrium outcomes of firm behaviour are the result of strategic interaction between firms and relevant actors rather than the demand and supply conditions of the market. These economies emphasise vocational training, regulated labour markets, bloc shareholder corporate governance, and organised technology transfer.

The varieties of capitalism approach is explicitly not about judging which variety is superior or more productive in world markets. Each variety has different strengths and weaknesses. The economic and institutional aspects of the two varieties influence political systems differently, which, in turn, influence the way the economy is structured. This feedback ingrains the models of capitalism and makes them resistant to change except in cases of dramatic technological developments or significant adjustments in world markets.

Globalisation has led to increased cooperation between coordinated market economies and liberal market economies in areas such as corporate governance and finance. In addition, neo-liberalism has expanded as the dominant intellectual framework beyond the liberal market economies into coordinated market economies. Remarkably, despite these real-world pressures, no hybrid model has emerged between the two theoretical models. However, although the systems are too fundamentally different to be fused, there have been many successful cases of cooperation.

To compete in the global economy, coordinated market economies have had to find ways to obtain the benefits of liberal market economies for their own firms. Yet despite this collaboration, the two models of capitalism have remained distinct, splitting tasks according to their relative strengths rather than adopting each other's institutional structures. In the financial sector, for example, German companies have merged with companies in liberal market economies in order to take advantage of their high-risk activities. Deutsche Bank acquired Morgan Granville in 1990, and Dresdner Bank acquired Kleinwort Benson Bank in 1995. In both cases, the companies were able to build models of collaboration despite their differing organisational structures. The most common solution was to do the high-risk investment banking in London or New York, and the more stable banking in Frankfurt.

In fact, in some cases, the pressures of globalisation have reinforced existing domestic economic models. For example, as Germany became a more open economy and companies became more susceptible to foreign competition, elements of the coordinated market system were strengthened. Increased competition brought the previously conflicting interests of various stakeholders into line with one another. Suddenly the survival of the company became the primary concern of skilled workers and the works councils, who had previously been more interested in advocating the rights of labour at the industry level. Similarly, attempts to improve profitability led companies that had previously concerned themselves with the capacities of the entire industry to focus on the individual company's competitive position. These combined effects have led to increased bloc shareholding and a shift in the role of the works councils from one of co-determination to one of co-management. Counterintuitively, these represent a reinforcement of – rather than a divergence from – the coordinated market economies' emphasis on cooperation and consensus.

It is likely that the economic crisis will be prolonged and cause profound damage.

This cooperation has made the two types of economies heavily dependent on one another, with the result that neither is immune to economic shocks in the other: both systems suffered severely from the economic crisis. Yet given the fact that no hybrid model has emerged, each variety of capitalism will need to determine a unique path to recovery in the wake of the crisis.

LOW GROWTH: CONSTRAINTS AND OPPORTUNITIES

In both types of economies, as the economic crisis progresses, one of the most telling indicators to watch will be average household expenditures. There are two potential future scenarios. In the ideal (but perhaps unlikely) scenario that household spending recovers in the United States, there will be a revitalisation of the economies of Germany, Japan, and China. Although this will entail a recovery of sorts, it will also mean a return to the status quo, an unbalanced world system in which the savings of these countries finance continued consumption in the United States. Nevertheless, this scenario may eventually lead to the increased regulation of risk, potentially giving the global system the opportunity to rebalance.

Unfortunately, a second scenario may be more plausible. The economic crisis actually consists of a number of interlinked crises, including financial, housing, and pension crises. It is therefore more likely that the economic crisis will be prolonged and cause profound damage. Reinhart and Rogoff performed a historical study in 2008 of financial crises, and found that when economic crises occur in conjunction with a run-up in housing prices – as they did in this crisis – the recession following them will tend to be severer.

The stock market crash negatively affected peoples' pensions, which, combined with the housing price crash, means that many households have seen their savings completely wiped away. This will make fiscal policy decisions more complicated. Generally, in a financial crisis, central banks would reduce interest rates and use quantitative easing to encourage people to begin borrowing again and to stimulate investment. However, low interest rates also translate into low accumulation on future savings. Therefore, if people are concerned about their pensions, even economic stimulus packages may be unable to trigger a revival of average household expenditures, as people may use this money only to rebuild lost savings.

What will pull the economy out of this recession? The world economy urgently needs a new demand driver. Historically, different processes have played key roles in sustaining growth. These have included electrification in the mid-19th century, preparation for the World Wars in the early 20th, and a dramatic increase in consumer durable purchases as working class families' consumption capacities grew in the post-war period. Since the 1980s, information technology and electronics have been significant demand drivers, as has the dramatic increase in secondary and tertiary education. Unfortunately, it is still unclear where future demand drivers might come from.

Unfortunately, neither the financial nor the business sector is well-positioned to act as a demand driver or to aid in the recovery process. Financial institutions are not yet ready to begin lending to people with risks. Instead, the emphasis in the near future will be on increasing risk rules and improving supervision. Proverbially, such measures would be "closing the stable door after the horse has bolted." Although these measures may be necessary to avoid future crises, in the post-crisis period they should be avoided, as credit is urgently needed to rebuild the economy.

Liberal market economies would do well to improve their social services.

Businesses, similarly, will probably not provide new demand drivers. Whereas consumption rises and falls apace with growth, investment tends to lag far behind economic recovery. This is a result of the investment accelerator principle, which says that small changes in consumer spending can cause large percentage changes in investment. When businesses see their markets declining even slightly, investment expenditures may drop significantly. Some have predicted that investment may fall as much as 30% as a result of the crisis. This is a significant component of GDP, and will perhaps have as large a negative effect on aggregate demand as the stimulus packages had a positive effect.

The verdict is still out on the impact of the crisis on businesses' research and development investments. On one hand, businesses may see that they must become competitive in order to survive in declining markets; on the other hand, they may retreat from new product development, prompting implicit cartelisation. What is clear, however, is that the focus of businesses in the near future will be on increasing cash reserves and cutting back investments. Any investments or technological developments that occur are likely to be cost-cutting and labour-saving, further compounding the damage wreaked by the crisis.

SPECIFIC REFORMS FOR DIFFERENT ECONOMIC SYSTEMS

Both liberal market economies as well as coordinated market economies will need to implement significant reforms in the post-crisis period. The reforms that will be needed differ according to the problems that the respective economic systems have developed, although using fiscal policy to promote growth may be possible in both types of economies. Each of these situations will be considered here in turn.

Liberal market economies

Liberal market economies' primary concern should be reforming the financial sector. Deregulation of this sector was a significant cause of the financial crisis and, even before the crisis, did not provide aggregate benefits to society. The high-risk-taking activities that liberal market economies developed led to astounding growth and high tax revenues, yet the financial sector sucked the best and the brightest labour away from the public sector. Previously, many of the best-educated workers would opt for careers in the government or in education, whereas now, in the US, the smartest students find work on Wall Street, and in the UK, they solicit employment in the City.

Yet the most pressing reason for financial sector reform is that in many financial activities, the value added for society is dubious, unclear, or even negative. Imagine a spectrum of regulation, running from 0% to 100%. Towards 0%, anything would be allowed, including criminal activities such as lying, cheating, or fraud. Unfortunately, some hedge fund activities approach this end of the spectrum, making money by skimming funds off pensions or private investors who cannot play the stock market as cleverly. This money moves out of households and into rich firms, making finance a redistributive rather than a productive activity. Worse, the redistribution flows exactly contrary to egalitarian principles: stealing from the poor to give to the rich. This urgently needs to be revisited. Unfortunately, governments gain the bulk of their tax revenues through the financial sector, making the prospects for reform bleak.

In addition, liberal market economies would do well to improve their social services. Yet reforming sectors such as health care, housing, or education has proven difficult. These sectors lack autonomy as well as qualified personnel.

Change has been limited to top-down readjustment of targets and increased micro-management, as disconnected bureaucrats set ever-changing standards. In addition, many liberal market economies have majoritarian political systems where the middle-class vote is paramount. In such a setting, the public sector can become highly politicised as both sides adopt 'name and shame' tactics aimed at destroying the credibility of their opponents' public sector management. Sadly, destroying the credibility of management also destroys the credibility of the services provided, as frequent politically motivated yet inconsequential reforms never gather enough political clout to address fundamental problems.

Coordinated market economies

Inequality has risen dramatically in coordinated market economies. In Germany, for example, the ratio of inequality between the middle 50th percentile and the bottom 10th percentile of income earners has widened significantly since the 1990s. This has created rising problems with poverty. In addition, criminality and punishment have increasingly become the domain of immigrants and the poor. As the economic crisis further increases unemployment and forces more people into the informal economy, these challenges will be amplified.

These problems affect coordinated market economies disproportionately. Immigrants (both internal immigrants from within the EU, as well as external immigrants) face very different prospects for employment in coordinated versus liberal market economies. In liberal market economies, literate hardworking immigrants can get decent jobs regardless of where they received their education, and slowly work their way up in the system. In coordinated market economies, on the other hand, it is virtually impossible to get decent work without having graduated from the domestic school system. As a result, immigrants are stuck in the informal sector, working sporadically and often in illegal trades such as drug trafficking.

Inequality has risen dramatically in coordinated market economies.

Facing such contrasting employment prospects, well-educated immigrants will generally choose to move to a liberal market economy. Only less-educated workers face the same prospects in both systems and move to coordinated market economies. Thus, for example, Germany receives a disproportionate amount of less-educated immigrants, further perpetuating the criminality at the bottom of society and increasing the anti-immigrant sentiments of native Germans.

Compounding this problem in Germany is the fact that the *Hauptschule* (the lowest level of high schools) have displayed declining educational quality. They are increasingly attended by immigrant children and children of less-educated parents. In addition, the recent reshuffling of the country's political affiliations has led to decreased political will to maintain the quality and opportunities provided by these schools. Previously, *Hauptschule* students received help obtaining apprenticeships that could lead to stable jobs, but in most schools, this has ended. Although the recent movement to incorporate *Hauptschule* and *Realschule* (the middle-level high schools) would be a positive change, it will not solve all of these problems.

The financial crisis is unlikely to lead to fundamental regime change.

Worsening inequality, increased immigration, and the declining quality of the school system have led to increased fragmentation in the lower half of German society. As a result, many children are losing their connections in labour markets. Previously, even the poorest children generally had a family connection or a friend who was employed and could help to connect them with employers, but this has become increasingly rare. For Muslim families, these problems are especially acute. It has been noted that while Indian children tend to do quite well in German schools, Pakistani and Bangladeshi children do very poorly, a difference that may be partially accounted for by the role that women play in their families. In the broader population, women are often employed part-time in the service industry. They are sometimes the only family members still employed, and become the only link to labour markets for many children. The children of conservative Muslim families, where women rarely work outside the home, thus face an even greater disadvantage. For all of these reasons, reform in Germany must involve innovative changes. Attempts to adopt the flexible labour markets of the liberal market economies will only increase the difficulties of the most vulnerable members of society.

In addition, reforms will be needed to help integrate significant flows of new immigrants. The crisis will increase unemployment across the EU, and especially in Eastern Europe, prompting increased internal immigration from the East to regions with relatively lower unemployment rates. However, as this exacerbates the unemployment problems of the host countries, there is likely to be a significant increase in anti-immigrant sentiment.

Europe has recently witnessed the development of a new brand of right-wing parties. In contrast to traditional right-wing politics, these parties have become pro-welfare state, but vehemently anti-immigrant. This could have damaging consequences both for immigrant populations across Europe as well as for existing left-wing parties who may lose their constituencies to the right. This has already occurred in Denmark and the Netherlands, for example with Geert Wilders' 'People's Party for Freedom and Democracy' (PVV).

Both liberal and coordinated market economies

Major demand drivers have seldom originated at the government level. Yet in the context of the current crisis, it may be possible to use fiscal policy to restore growth in both liberal as well as coordinated market economies. However, there is a large divide between the different economies' willingness to use this tool, with coordinated market economies generally being less willing to do so.

This difference can largely be explained by the differing role of unions. Coordinated market economies tend to have strong unions that are powerful actors in industrial relations. They have the power to set wages, which can drive up the interest rate and, thus, also the exchange rate. Facing these conditions, central banks are less likely to use discretionary fiscal policy. They are forced to take a tough stance on interest rates from the outset in order to gain bargaining power, because opening fiscal policy up to negotiation would quickly politicise it. In Germany, for example, the government has so far not been willing to finance investment in labour training programs, fearing that this would push fiscal policy into the political arena. This could usurp the power of the government, and may even give unions the impression that fiscal policy is available for purposes such as bailing out failing companies. The opposite is also true; in liberal market economies where there are multiple, poorly coordinated unions, central banks can be more flexible in their use of discretionary fiscal policy.

Despite these differing challenges, discretionary fiscal policy has the potential to act as an important demand driver in both types of economies. There are two areas where its use could be especially helpful: first, in providing public sector employment for women; and second, in investing in education and training programs.

Scandinavian countries used fiscal policy to create nearly unlimited employment possibilities for women in the public sector. They provided flexible work that allowed women to take time for having children and caring for families. This was very effective in Scandinavia, perhaps because even the bottom tiers of their society are very well-educated. The Swedes recovered from the financial crisis relatively quickly, and some speculate that this may have been because female public sector employment served as a good insurance policy against concerns about pensions and unemployment. Swedish families knew that even if a man lost his job, his wife was virtually guaranteed a well-paying position in the public sector.

However, the politics are more complicated in places like Germany, where there is a profound split between the educational levels of the poorest and the richest in society. Middle-class voters are not comfortable paying higher taxes to provide high-wage jobs to poor or less-educated women. In addition, in Germany, many voters (especially Christian Democrats) prefer the tax breaks associated with women staying at home to incorporating women into the workforce.

If political conditions make expanding women's role in the public sector workforce unrealistic, then getting unions and businesses to back the idea of training existing employees may be the next best option for using fiscal policy as a demand driver. To date, training expenditures have gone primarily to two groups: (1) the young, and (2) the unemployed. The unemployed have proven very difficult to train, and are not generally a good investment in the long-term. Training the young, however, has been very successful and has actually been a major driver of growth: whereas in the 1970s, 60% of children left school at age sixteen, today these numbers are down to about 25%. Pushing more people to pursue tertiary education may be a good way to further exploit this driver. In addition, training expenditures could begin targeting a third group: existing employees. Creating training programs within companies to up-skill their workers may be a productive demand driver, and would ensure the cooperation of businesses in the recovery period.

The financial crisis is unlikely to lead to fundamental regime changes, and will probably reinforce rather than unify the two varieties of capitalism. However, in light of the crisis, each of these economic models has its own unique problems that must be attended to in order to promote recovery and restore future growth.

PART 3

COPING WITH PARADISE LOST

In order to determine the social-cultural impact of the economic crisis, the interviewees in this part primarily analyse the culture of discontent that seems to have emerged in the wake of the hegemony of neo-liberal doctrines over the past quarter-century. Their views are, however, not entirely despondent. The crisis offers a window of opportunity to revisit social and cultural issues of national identity and international solidarity, long believed to be unmodifiable concepts.

As Mark Elchardus explains, we currently stand at a crossroad. The crisis will either fuel resentment and discontent against the ruling political elites, or, by contrast, it will usher in a reappreciation and modernisation of the welfare state. The tilting of the scales will largely depend on how political actors capitalise on the crisis.

Both Richard Sennett and Amitai Etzioni claim that the crisis undermines the moral legitimacy of free-market fundamentalism. They radically differ, however, in their cultural understanding of the crisis. According to Amitai Etzioni, neo-liberal ideologies tore down the normative constraints of deferred gratification and made way for immoral consumerism. Richard Sennett draws more attention to the overlooked fact that, for the foot soldiers of the new capitalism, credit debt compensated for appalling public housing conditions and exclusion from affordable health care. Both end their analysis on a positive note. Amitai Etzioni hopes the crisis will instigate a renewed normative dialogue in capitalist societies, while Richard Sennett sees the crisis as an opportunity to establish more equitable distribution of welfare.

As Dominique Moïsi asserts, for any new moral departures to take root on this side of the Atlantic, Europe needs not only to become more unified and cohesive, but it also must assertively communicate its comparative social advantage at the global level. Collectively, these arguments reveal a constructive element of the crisis: it has demonstrated the merits of the European economy. Despite its flaws, the European social ideals of a more civilised form of capitalism have thus far helped European citizens weather the crisis.

Social Discontent in European Welfare States

Mark Elchardus

PROFESSOR OF SOCIOLOGY,

UNIVERSITÉ LIBRE DE BRUXELLES

"In 2007 I was in the United States for a conference. I hailed a cab and struck up a conversation with the driver. Proudly, he told me that he was about to buy his third house. It struck me as odd that a cab driver could own three houses, though I hesitated to inquire further. Luckily, he was eager to explain his plan to me, and that, in fact, it would not cost him anything.

"He was able to buy the third house with no down payment. Five years earlier, he had purchased his second home, and since then, it had almost doubled in value. In order to pay the instalments on his third house, he could take out a loan on the market value of his second, and the only portion that he would have to pay out of pocket would be the interest on the loan. The plan was to sell one of the houses in five years' time, with the net result being that he would own his second house without having paid anything for it.

"Still confused, I asked a Belgian friend in the insurance industry how this was possible. He explained to me that in the United States, they gave high-risk, low-interest loans to people without demanding down payments. To make this possible, they counted on steady increases in value of 10-15% per year. The danger was that if these increases ever declined, companies would have to demand higher interest rates on loans, leaving many debtors unable to repay. Two months later, the subprime mortgage market collapsed."

THE NORTHWESTERN EUROPEAN WELFARE STATE

Northwestern Europe is unique in the non-Asian OECD region (i.e. Europe and North America). It has its own political structure, economic system, cultural traits, and historical narrative. Politically, it is unique in its development of a strong welfare state. Claims that the welfare state is declining in this region are largely over-exaggerated. However, this is not the case for the rest of the non-Asian OECD region: these states never developed welfare systems to the same extent that Northwestern European nations did, and those elements that they did create suffered under neo-liberal policies during the last quarter of the 20th century.

In economic terms, differing approaches to the welfare state created distinct forms of capitalism. Northwestern European capitalism developed a close symbiosis with the functions of the welfare states, whereas the rest of the non-Asian OECD region developed more liberal forms of capitalism. Liberal capitalism is most apparent in the Anglo-Saxon world (i.e. the United Kingdom and English-speaking North America), where financial institutions took over many of the functions that are fulfilled by the welfare state in Northwestern Europe.

In addition to the differing forms of capitalism, a cultural divide has formed reflecting differing degrees of secularisation. Northwestern European societies have tended towards secularism, leaving little space for the traditional morality of religious doctrine. This diverges from other areas of the non-Asian OECD region, most notably southern Europe and the United States, where religion and traditional morality still play a prominent role, even in politics. The role that traditional morality plays in society influences the way people relate to their bodies, and the way they relate their bodies to society. This, in turn, characterises the way that citizens relate to the state, and their conception of what issues can legitimately be legislated. Secular states tend to perceive government regulation of abortion, marriage, euthanasia, or other religiously influenced decisions as less legitimate than more religious societies do. Among rich nations, those with underdeveloped welfare states tend to be more traditional in terms of religion and ethics. That creates a cultural divide among rich societies.

Finally, Northwestern Europe has its own historical narrative and its own way of situating itself in history. After World War II, the countries in this region instigated profound reforms of their domestic governance structures, moving away from the policies of the 1930s, when poverty and insecurity had been widespread. They built strong welfare states and designed far-reaching social security systems. Progress became the norm. Citizens expected to be wealthier in retirement than when they had been working; they expected their children to have greater opportunities in life that they had.

Citizens of Northwestern European states have developed a nostalgic and utopian narrative of a lost Golden Age to describe the period between World War II and the financial shocks of the 1970s. That quarter-century has become the defining period in their history. In the nostalgic narrative it is described as a time when society was well connected, people cared about and respected each other. They felt safe, there was a low crime rate, no dangerous traffic, and children could play in the streets. People slept with their doors unlocked, there were no foreigners and no threatening conflicts between ethnic groups. People could work in peace without stress or insecurity, and they often stayed at the same jobs their entire lives. People were financially secure and did not worry about retirement. Such a Golden Age only exists in the imagination, but it heavily influences how people perceive the world around them.

Citizens tend to agree that the golden age of the welfare state is over. They claim that since the 1970s, unity, connectedness, values, and respect have all been lost. The multicultural society has derailed and in its place, there is conflict, threat, and crime. In their eyes, economic globalisation has undermined their economy and their security by destabilising the welfare state and promoting migration.

> *The majority of citizens in Northwestern European welfare states are profoundly convinced by the narrative of 'the decline of the virtuous and peaceful welfare state'.*

This is the narrative of 'the decline of the virtuous and peaceful welfare state', and the majority of citizens in Northwestern European welfare states are profoundly convinced by it. It influences the way that they understand and relate to politics, and politicians who link their rhetoric to this narrative find a sympathetic ear among a large segment of the population. This narrative leads people to feel insecure and fearful. It relates to a feeling of discontent that has been growing in Northwestern European states, not only among the vulnerable in society, but even in the middle class. Discontent can be described by four elements that usually arise in conjunction with each other: (1) feeling unsafe, (2) feeling unsatisfied with interpersonal relations and disrespected, (3) feeling that the community is becoming intolerant and aggressive, (4) feeling that work is becoming too demanding.

Although partially affected by people's personal realities, feelings of discontent are primarily influenced by the media. People turn to popular media to help them clarify and conceptualise their more indistinct and intangible feelings of fear. However, by codifying people's fears, the media actually reify them. Images of villains, malevolent immigrants, and calculating terrorists fill the collective imagination, providing tangible evidence of why people feel unsafe. In this way, the media drive out rational political logic. They concoct risks to rationalise fear; fear, in turn, generates increased perception of risks, hereby creating a feedback cycle that fuels further feelings of discontent. Thus, in addition to their unique economic and cultural systems, Northwestern European welfare states are increasingly unified in their culture of discontentedness and malaise.

The media not only affect the way citizens feel about society, but also the way they interact with their governments. People can vote on the basis of two questions: first, "How am *I* doing?" and second, "How is *society* doing?" There has been a discernable shift over time in the relative weight people ascribe to these questions. Whereas they used to premise their votes on the first question, they are increasingly relying on the second.

When citizens ask, "How am *I* doing?" they look at their personal experience, their financial situation, employment stability, general wellbeing, and happiness. In contrast, when they ask, "How is *society* doing?" they generally turn to the media for an answer. People feel that the state of society, as a whole, should determine their vote choice. Well-intentioned though this may be, it breaks down the relationship between the elected and the electorate, uncoupling the politicians' policies from their electoral rewards.

In welfare states, politicians aim to improve the living conditions of their citizens and to reduce unjust inequalities. They aspire to create policies that allow citizens to improve their lives and give everybody a fair chance at happiness. In short, they try to please their electorate. However, when voters stop voting based on their personal wellbeing, this system breaks down. When people vote on the basis of the question, "How is society doing", they are primarily led by their malaise, discontentedness, nostalgia and the media, which tends to be responsive to those feelings. A discontented electorate which votes based on media-driven fear may not vote for parties that will improve their welfare. Voting for radical or extremist parties is often based less on personal experience than it is on media-influenced feelings of societal discontent. Extremist parties are aware of this and may cater to the discontented, consolidating not only a constituency, but also a heightened climate of fear.

In fact, despite the commonly voiced claim that the economic crisis will strengthen socialist parties, 20th-century history supports the opposite view. Socialism thrived in the 1960s, a period of great prosperity. In difficult economic times, populism and right-wing politics have gained influence, most notably in the late 1930s through early 1940s and in the mid 1970s. Based on these precedents, one would expect the current economic crisis to increase feelings of discontent, thus strengthening right-wing and populist parties as well.

The origin of this shift in voting behaviour is unclear, although two explanations are possible. The first, and most plausible explanation, is that people have always had a noble conception of politics: they want to vote on the basis of how society is doing, not on the basis of their 'petty' personal concerns. Ideologies linked their personal concerns to the fate and future of society. Working-class parties told working-class people that their personal concerns were noble and of societal importance. Confessional parties did the same for religious people. Ironically, the end of these ideologies has brought about the end of voting on the basis of personal interest. Alternatively, it could be argued that the relative welfare and security from the quarter-century Golden Age in Northwestern Europe changed peoples' relationship to society and politics, making personal interest less pressing. This explanation is less convincing however.

NEO-LIBERALISM VERSUS THE WELFARE STATE

Recently, Northwestern European welfare states have faced interlinked challenges from both sides of the political spectrum. From one side, neo-liberalism has created an anti-state mentality that negatively affects the legitimacy of welfare state systems. From the other, government over-commitment has reached dangerously high levels since the economic crisis, threatening the future viability of these states.

Internationally, the dominant model of the state for the past 20 years has been neo-liberal. The emphasis has been on creating a passive state that is continuously retreating from the economy. The neo-liberal critique of the state has invariably led to anti-state policy prescriptions: whenever state actions were found to produce undesirable results, critics demanded that the state halt these actions rather than reform or improve them, which has weakened our capacity for governance.

The economic crisis has brought to light two linked legacies of neo-liberal over-dominance. First, neo-liberalism led to excessive deregulation and non-regulation of many economic and financial activities, allowing high-risk financial instruments to thrive. Second, it has left an intellectual vacuum. The orthodoxy of non-intervention left little intellectual space for modelling growth-promotion, equality-promotion, or other desirable forms of intervention. It was as though non-intervention was a virtue in itself.

Since the economic crisis, governments have been called upon to play a more active role in the economy. Barack Obama and various European leaders led the way, advocating a temporarily expanded role for the state. Governments were in the unique position of being able to make the long-term commitments necessary to mitigate the effects of the crisis. Especially in Northwestern Europe, where citizens expect government interventions in the interest of social security, allowing banks and private savings to collapse was unthinkable.

As the crisis hit, the non-intervention orthodoxy was cast aside, but there was nothing available to replace it. While government intervention was undoubtedly necessary, there has been no institutional or intellectual framework to guide it.

As a result, states have woefully over-committed themselves. The scale to which states intervened in the economy was blatantly irresponsible. Governments went beyond what they could institutionally manage or foresee, and while markets can cope with unforeseeable risks, states cannot. For example, the Belgian bank, KBC, was recently given € 2 billion by the Flemish government, and guaranteed € 14 billion by the Belgian government if its American reinsurers should fail. However, nobody knows what would happen if the Belgian government was suddenly forced to make good on this promise and raise € 14 billion from the financial markets. How many billions can a state raise for the purpose of long-term guarantees in financial markets they cannot control?

The economic crisis has brought to light two linked legacies of neo-liberal over-dominance: excessive deregulation and an intellectual vacuum.

The same people who, only a few years ago, advocated state retreat and non-intervention now advocate using the state as an almost limitless instrument. One of the biggest political challenges in the coming years will be to renegotiate a proper role for the state, and to return to reasonable government commitments.

SOCIAL IMPACT OF THE CRISIS

A drawn-out economic crisis could have damaging repercussions for the Northwestern European welfare states. Specifically, it may undermine middle-class security, as well as further aggravating inter-ethnic tensions and scapegoating.

Financing a welfare state is expensive. As the crisis shrinks the availability of public funds, and governments run up state debt, it may be compelling to make cutbacks in social programs. This should be avoided at all costs: in welfare states, citizens derive a sense of ontological security from the welfare system. This security runs deeper than the immediate security of a pension fund or unemployment benefits. Even in the middle class, the relationship of citizens to society runs through the welfare state. Undermining the ontological security of the middle class, while simultaneously jeopardising the immediate security of the most vulnerable in society, could be politically dangerous, triggering a decline in societal cohesion and increasing discontentedness.

Another potential repercussion of a long-lasting recession is increased inter-ethnic tension. As the middle class becomes discontented and welfare recipients become vulnerable to state cutbacks, tensions between natives and non-natives are likely to increase. While this is likely to happen everywhere, Northwestern

European welfare states are especially vulnerable to such a development. Historically, integration of immigrants in this region has been very difficult. Ironically, in countries with weak welfare systems, this is less of a problem: integration is easier because there are many low-paying jobs, and there is less scapegoating since citizens have only limited rights to make claims on the government. In contrast, in welfare states, citizens are able to make more claims on the government. This places a larger burden on public resources and tax revenue, which can lead to scapegoating of immigrants.

Parallel to this, there has been a disconcerting shift in the way non-natives are perceived in Northwestern Europe. For example, in Flanders, surveys show that indicators of ethnic prejudice and ethnocentrism have remained relatively stable or even declined over time. However, in the intellectual community, even among self-styled progressive or left-wing thinkers, a new process has emerged, which can be described as the 'Islamisation of the stranger'. Non-natives are no longer seen as migrants or outsiders, but as Muslims, who, as a group, are perceived as incompatible with the local culture influenced by the Enlightenment. This incompatibility is not based on culture, background, or even on race, but on religious identity and belief. This religion-based framework of stereotyping is a throwback to movements in Europe between the two World Wars, and even to Europe in the 17th century.

IMPROVING WELFARE

In the more optimistic scenario that the crisis will be brief and cause only limited damage, it may provide Northwestern Europe with a window of opportunity, serving as a catalyst for reform. There is a growing consensus in these countries that reforms are needed to steer systems away from neo-liberalism, meritocracy, and the over-emphasis on personal responsibility. Specifically, the role the educational system plays in the perpetuation of inequalities should become an important focus.

In all of the Northwestern European welfare states, there is a growing cleavage between the well-educated and the poorly educated. The welfare system provides families with child support, childcare and good schools in order to promote high levels of education across the population. Many families are able to take advantage of this; however, there is a clear link between the educational level of parents and of their children. This is a direct result of the competitive, meritocratic nature of the school systems. From a very young age, children undergo competitive selection procedures, streaming them into different tracked educational programs that determine their future life chances. However, at such a young age, these children's academic capacities still depend heavily on their parents' level of education and the cultural resources available in their homes. Less educated parents are less able to help their children with their schoolwork and to push them to excel in the education system, with the result that their children are placed in less promising educational tracks. Thus, many children are lost to the education system before they even begin. In Flanders, statistics show that indicators of health, housing, mobility, and life expectancy are strongly related to the level of education, and that in all of these areas the divide is growing between the well-educated and poorly educated.

Immigrants and their children are particularly affected by these kinds of inequalities, because of language barriers and societal isolation in addition to, on average, having parents with lower educational levels. This leads to increasingly isolated and depressed immigrant communities.

In upcoming years, these challenges are likely to become compounded, as ever more immigrants will be needed in Northwestern Europe. The baby boom generation will soon retire, and with the low birth rates Europe has experienced in recent decades, there will be even fewer people in the workforce to replace them and to care for them as they grow old. Even the economic crisis has not severely influenced the labour market. There is still a shortage of qualified labour. While allowing increased immigration will solve this problem, it will also further aggravate inter-ethnic tensions, especially if the educational cleavage stifles immigrant communities' development.

What types of policies could avert future inter-ethnic tensions? One option is implementing a more selective model of immigration, based on the Canadian model, which would ensure that a high percentage of immigrants are professionals and skilled workers, as opposed to unskilled workers entering in the interest of family reunification or as refugee immigrants. This would be positive for Northwestern European societies, but very negative for the Third World countries that lose people with important skills. It is also likely to be insufficient to fill all of the gaps in the labour markets. Instead, more should be invested in current citizens, helping more people to acquire skills that will help them in society, investing in the children of immigrants, and generally, following the Scandinavian model. The children of immigrants are a great reservoir of talent that is being wasted, sometimes even turned into a reservoir of crime. There is still a lot to be done: domestic opposition, fuelled by insecurity and rising right-wing politics, might make such reforms difficult to implement.

TOWARDS A NEW THEORY OF THE STATE

People today complain about the political system in the same way that people before the French Revolution complained about the king: they see government as inaccessible, inefficient, and illegitimate, yet fundamentally unchangeable. There is therefore a pressing need for an international dialogue to renegotiate the nature and the role of the state. Is the current system of representation still sensible? What is the role of parliaments? What is the role of the state? Who is empowered to act in the state? Hopefully, the economic crisis will provide people with the courage and the occasion to address these fundamental questions.

The basic goal of democracy is to give people influence over the circumstances that affect their lives. Current models of representational governance were designed using the intellectual tools of the 18th century. A debate today would certainly create more just and efficient systems than those we are currently using. In modern politics, the political decision-making process has, in many cases, become divorced from democratic representation. The politics of representation in national campaigns deal with malaise; the European Commission deals with policy, and the European Parliament is elected under conditions of general disinterest. Such a condition was never intended by the generations who have fought for democracy.

Cutbacks in social programs should be avoided at all costs: Citizens derive a sense of ontological security from the welfare system.

More broadly, in the globalised world, economic, political, and cultural systems all operate on different scales. Trying to integrate them is problematic, and the nation-state may no longer be the appropriate level at which to do so. However, if state-level governance is no longer appropriate, how can these systems be linked to democratic decision-making? For example, how can the impact of banks, insurance companies, media, and research institutes, all of which have enormous impact on society and people's lives, be brought under democratic governance?

In Europe, the dialogue should begin with a discussion of the European Union, which includes an assortment of different systems. The European Commission is post-representational, the Council is a representation of nations, and the Parliament is a (quite ineffective) mix of other older models. The European Union should be the focus of reform, as even specialists are unsure exactly where or how it is possible to influence this complex political machine.

Northwestern European welfare states have a special need for institutional reform in the wake of the current crisis. Their welfare systems have been undermined twice by neo-liberalism: first, by the neo-liberal agenda that pushed an anti-state mentality; and second, by the neo-liberal intellectual dominance that allowed for no alternative visions of the state and has left an intellectual void in its wake. In addition, a growing climate of discontent has left societies in these states ontologically vulnerable to the cutbacks in state funding that the crisis will produce.

The economic crisis has soured the appeal of neo-liberalism for future generations. If Northwestern European welfare states avoid the pitfalls that serious cutbacks could produce, they will be able to use this change in the intellectual climate as an important instigator of institutional reform; not only re-establishing welfare institutions where neo-liberalism uprooted them, but also – and more importantly – adjusting welfare state policies that have proven ineffective in the past.

A Crisis of Consumerism

Amitai Etzioni

DIRECTOR OF THE INSTITUTE FOR COMMUNITARIAN POLICY STUDIES,
GEORGE WASHINGTON UNIVERSITY

"Like many people, I was worried by the huge global imbalance caused by the US consuming more than it earned, and basically living off the savings from countries like China, Japan and Germany. Anyone could see that the American housing market was unsustainable. The financial repackaging would certainly, in one way or another, endanger the financial institutions. I believe that deregulation was a major intermediary variable that enhanced the vulnerability of the financial system, but I did not foresee the timing of the crisis or its impact."

With the economic crisis currently at its peak, the time is ripe for a moral conversation on what defines a good society. Is a society governed by consumerism desirable? Can material objects be used to express affection and to seek self-esteem? How can self-actualisation best be realised? Is society ready to face the consequences of utilising a different – more transcendental and communitarian – definition of a good society? Do we dare to ask ourselves not only whether we think our children will be better off than we are, but also what exactly it means to be better off?

Cultural transformations have occurred throughout history – some have elevated and others have degraded the human condition. In this context, it is important to remember that society's current obsession with work and commerce is not a timeless phenomenon; the primacy of these pursuits is only as old as the widespread acceptance of capitalism. Yet crises like the current one can help to initiate and accelerate such shifts into predominant cultural norms. In the words of Rahm Emanuel: "Never allow a crisis to go to waste."

CONTAINING CAPITALISM

Recent economic theory has been guilty of misleading society by failing to explain societal phenomena in psychological or cultural terms. Instead, economists have unforgivably tried to incorporate these phenomena into their rational behaviour paradigm. Unfortunately, these economists were granted too much latitude, allowing them to work in a vacuum where they were shielded from those offering alternative explanations. This prevented the emergence of a broader consensus or theory. Although economists were continually consulted on predicting the economic situation, they were almost always misguided, if not entirely wrong in their predictions, because they failed to incorporate the bigger picture.

Benefiting from capitalism is akin to exploiting nuclear energy: as long as it is well-contained by the walls of a normative culture that favours self-restraint and government regulations, capitalism can generate an abundance of good without undermining the society that surrounds it. Societies are based on normative cultures. This is not a philosophical abstraction, but rather a concept that is deeply embedded in human relationships. Over time, the normative culture that could contain capitalism became less and less discernable, particularly in the US. It was never all-pervasive, but following the Progressive Movement and the various reforms introduced during the New Deal and the Great Society, a measure of self-restraint was integrated into the normative culture, and underlined by various government regulations. Many advanced economies experienced a shift towards a culture based more on libertarian and hedonistic values in the course of the 1960s and 1970s. These changes are inextricably linked to various emancipatory currents, as for example embodied by the women's rights movement. Although different countries experienced different paces and styles of transition during this time, all experienced a move away from the self-restraint so dominant in the immediate post-war decades.

Self-restraint was further eroded under the influence of Reaganism and Thatcherism, which celebrated unfettered self-interest and weakened both government regulation as well as the importance of a self-regulating culture. In economic terms, the lack of self-restraint is reflected in the modern willingness to max out credit cards, whereas in the 1950s, debt was considered a sin. The lack of self-restraint is compounded by the fact that, over the past fifty years, the American public has held a strong yet schizophrenic ideology: on the one hand, Americans demanded low taxes and small government, yet on the other hand they appealed for a full range of public services in the fields of education, housing, and health policy. National security is another area of ideological discrepancies. While most people agree that the potential threat of terrorist attacks using nuclear weapons is real, they have difficulties accepting the restrictions government has to put into place to contain those security risks, such as security checks at the airport.

The metaphor of family groups is useful when we consider the normative structures of cultures at a societal level. A family – just like a society – cannot perpetually spend more than it earns. Moreover, a civil society requires some form of self-government; citizens must have the capacity to restrain themselves. Citizens must undergo a learning process similar to that which is imposed on children, when they are corrected so as not to grow up without restraints or the ability to oversee their own actions. Many societies are concerned with an apparent lack of moderation and civility, which is manifested in the tendencies to consume without paying, or working for a brief period only to collect unemployment and pension benefits afterwards.

Over time, the normative culture that could contain capitalism became less and less discernable.

All of this boils down to the inability to defer gratification and the inability to control impulse. When people feel the urge to do something inappropriate, two things are required to restrain it. First, the person must be able to delay the impulse long enough to examine it, requiring finely tuned psychological facilities. Second, they need to reflect on what is right and wrong and form a judgement based on their internalised values. The problem is that these internal controls have been eroded, while the external controls – for example priests, governments or other authorities – have simultaneously lost moral standing.

This brings us back to an age-old debate: what is the inherent nature of man? When societies lose their moral constraints, suddenly the Catholic view – that all people have inherent beasts that must be restrained and controlled – appears more feasible. This stands in clear contrast to the recent prevailing liberal view, which says that all people are good essentially, but are sometimes corrupted by society. Impulse control is something we must acquire, or else we can face situations where there is willingness to kill or steal based on incomplete and perilous ideologies.

A REVITALISED NORMATIVE CULTURE

The current consensus about the need for new, stronger, and more vigorously enforced regulations is somewhat misguided; it lacks a broader understanding of the way regulation works. There can never be enough regulators, inspectors, or police to ensure that all transactions are carried out legally and ethically. Instead, laws are designed to correspond to moral codes, and regulators try to focus their efforts only on the outlier cases that try to circumvent them. Despite claims that people only act positively when they fear punishment, numerous studies show that in orderly societies, most people engage in pro-social behaviour because they heed their internalised sense of right and wrong and their sense of duty and responsibility. Of central importance is what a culture values, including its attitudes towards the economic behaviour that regulation aims to contain. Regulation is needed as a secondary enforcer when culture fails, but it cannot be the mainstay of good conduct. Sometimes legislation – or the attempt to implement legislation – can trigger a moral conversation on that topic, but on its own, legislation is insufficient to change behaviour. In the wake of the excesses that brought on the economic crisis, many have called for re-regulation. However, they fail to realise that re-regulation can only be successful if the underlying normative culture is also changed.

Impulse control is something we must acquire, or else we can face situations where there is willingness to kill or steal based on incomplete and perilous ideologies.

The idea of normative culture is not a philosophical abstraction, but a concept that is deeply embedded in the web of human relationships. Its scale can vary from that of a small community to an entire nation. Unfortunately, the international normative culture that used to constrain capitalism has been largely eroded in many parts of the world, especially in the US. Although public leaders such as President Obama call for less consumption and more saving, his stimulus package was more aggressive than any in Europe, suggesting that a return to the status quo ante – of gross overconsumption – is quite feasible. Yet the American president finds himself in a difficult position. Most Americans believe they do not have enough money to provide for basic necessities, whereas in fact they do. Trying to educate the public to give up things they do not need is much too dangerous for a politician. Public intellectuals have a vital role to play in such a situation. Unlike the paralyzed politicians, they can initiate a new societal dialogue, thereby preparing the ground for politicians to take the lead in the future.

However, governments generally cannot be the primary agents in major cultural and social changes. These shifts tend to arise instead from social movements, such as civil rights movements, nationalist dynamics, or religious organisations. Nevertheless, governments still have to govern according to transcendent moral codes. Prime Minister Balkenende of the Netherlands is a good example in that respect. Although he was mocked for his actions, he did succeed in setting up an agenda on norms and values, engaging in a moral conversation while avoiding the pitfalls of a moral debate by acknowledging that the government could not provide all the answers. Balkenende even managed to continue this conversation at the European level, during the Dutch EU Presidency in 2004

.

There is no feasible alternative to the market system. Large redistribution of income from high earners to low earners conflicts with democratic values and goes against human nature. We should not expect too much from more moderate redistribution efforts either. Top executives cannot be monitored, and it is impossible to lift the lower classes out of poverty through income redistribution alone. On the other hand, large income disparities and asset inequalities stand in the way of strong social cohesion. Even though Europe has a more even income distribution in historical terms, that too is changing. Europe is becoming more Americanised, with bigger discrepancies between the largely immigrant underclass on the one hand and the middle and upper classes on the other. Japan is moving in the same direction. In the US, besides the black minority, which to some extent has moved up to the middle class, the Latino minority is growing rapidly. They came for economic reasons, work hard, have a strong family tradition and are more religious and communal. The Latino minority will have a profound effect on American society and may make it more communitarian.

Capitalism – in its rawest form – is centred on the quest for perpetually maximising one's utility (largely measured by the volume and quality of goods and services one consumes and by the income one garners to pay for them) by granting work priority over all other pursuits. In considering the question of at what point consumption turns into consumerism – that is, into obsession – and work becomes invasive, Abraham Maslow's hierarchy of human needs is a useful tool. At the bottom of this hierarchy are basic creature comforts; as these are sated, more satisfaction is drawn from affection and self-esteem, and finally, from self-actualisation. It follows that as long as one's consumption is focused on satisfying the need for creature comforts, it meets not only essential but the most basic human needs. Obsession with goods and services takes place once these are used to try to satisfy the higher needs. Consumption turns into an 'ism' when material objects are used to express affection and to seek self-esteem, and when they dominate the quest for self-actualisation. It is especially psychologically damaging when the labour required to pay for consumerism cuts into human relations that are sources of affection, by neglecting family and friends, and undermines non-material sources of self-esteem. It is this 'ism' that turns consumption into a social disease.

The desire to consume ever more leads to working weeks that leave too little time and energy to spend on those aspects that contribute to a good life: family, friends, community services and contemplation. Fulfilment should not be something deemed to be derived from work alone. Religious duties, family events and volunteerism are a few options to curtail the working week. Here we see how culture influences the work ethic, and this explains why work is distributed unevenly across the globe. In the emerging countries and the Western world, people work very hard, sometimes too hard, whereas in some developing countries people approach work differently or suffer the consequences of too much idle time.

THE MEGALOGUES IMPERATIVE

There is a distinct possibility that the economic crisis is deep enough to have a serious impact on our cultural norms as well as to trigger the development of new shared understandings, or in other words, the revitalisation of a normative culture that extols positive meanings and purposes such as communitarian and transcendental sources of human flourishing. Communitarianism refers to investing one's time and energy in relations with the other, including members of one's family, friends, and members of the community. The term also encompasses service to the common good, generated by voluntarism, national service, and public life, politics included. Transcendental pursuits refer to spiritual endeavours including religious, contemplative, and artistic activities.

There is no feasible alternative to the market system.

There are numerous sociological hints that members of high-consumption societies are embracing some behaviours conducive to building a society that is less obsessed with consumption. These include: a decline in the purchase of luxury goods; a suspension or scaling back of lavish celebrations during holidays and rituals; voluntary caps on executive compensation; workers accepting fewer hours, lower pay, lower benefits and unpaid furloughs; a shift from cars to public transportation; more time spent with family and friends and less at work; decline in geographic mobility; a growing number of people opting to purchase smaller houses (McMansion sales have fallen even more than those of other houses).

What is needed next is to help people realise that contained consumption – one limited to creature comforts – is not a reflection of failure. It is rather the liberation of society that grants people new freedoms from an obsession; namely, to engage in projects that are more truly fulfilling. Thus, those who always wanted a modest wedding limited to close friends and family members, and recently using as the perfect excuse that they cannot afford a lavish wedding, now need to be held up as a model for sensible conduct. Dressing down was once the mark of the respected old money – only the nouveau riche displayed their wealth by dressing up. Dressing down must again become a source of communal approbations. We are moving in the direction of a flourishing society, to the extent that such scaled-down levels of consumption are not viewed as deprivations but as positive expressions of a new lifestyle approved by a new normative culture.

Changing the normative culture would shift public perceptions to view these changes as an opportunity to abandon consumerism.

Critics argue that a modern economy cannot survive unless people consume ever more, and hence produce and work ever more. But there is no reason an economy cannot function well if both parts of the equation are scaled back: if people consume less and produce/work less. This is, in effect, what the French do, with their 35-hour workweeks and personal income per capita that is somewhat lower than that of the United States. To varying extents other 'old' European societies do the same. Mainstream American economists have long scoffed at these societies and urged them to Americanise. To some extent they actually did, especially the Brits. However, this assumed that these societies seek to scale back non-materialistic values and promote consumerism ever further. The opposite now recommends itself; the United States ought to move closer to the 'old' European model. This is happening during the current fiscal crisis, but so far much of this scaling-back has been involuntary and felt as a deprivation. Changing the normative culture would shift public perceptions to view these changes as an opportunity to abandon consumerism (by definition for those whose basic creature comforts are well and securely sated) and focus more on communitarian and transcendental pursuits.

The main way societies will determine whether the current crisis will serve as an event that leads to cultural transformation or merely constitute an interlude in the consumerism project is through a process that could be described as 'moral megalogues'. Societies are constantly engaged in dialogues on right versus wrong. Typically, only one or two topics dominate these megalogues in any given time period. Key recent issues included the legitimacy of the United States' 2003 invasion of Iraq, and whether gay couples should be allowed to marry. In earlier decades, women's rights, minority rights, the rights to asylum and to euthanasia were topics of such discussions. Megalogues involve millions of members of a society exchanging views with one another at workplaces, during family gatherings, in the media and at public events. They are often contentious and passionate, and while they have no clear beginning or endpoint, they tend to lead to changes in a society's normative culture and in its members' behaviour.

The megalogue about the relationship between consumerism and human flourishing and what might replace consumerism is now once again flickering, but has not yet become a leading topic like regulation. Public intellectuals, responsible media, and public leaders are those best positioned to focus the megalogue on the proper topic and, above all, on the proper scope. The main question is not how to pass some laws to keep the marketplace in check, shoring up the walls of the container that restrains capitalism from breaking out, but rather, "What makes a good life?" What purposes should replace the worship of consumer goods by those whose basic creature comfort needs have been sated?

Similar precepts have been explored often enough before, for instance by early socialists and by religious orders that favoured an ascetic lifestyle. Societies are constantly engaged in debates on right and wrong, for instance recently on environmental issues and climate change. However, it will not suffice to tell people what they cannot do; they need a positive agenda as well, by which to ensure the global character of moral dialogues.

The Moral Bankruptcy of New Capitalism

Richard Sennett

PROFESSOR OF SOCIOLOGY,
LONDON SCHOOL OF ECONOMICS

"This crisis was already underway in the 1990s when the economy was still booming. My understanding of it actually began with an understanding of the social crisis that predated it. During the 1990s I began interviewing mid-level workers – the foot-soldiers of the new capitalism. I realised that the conditions that were creating wealth in the economy as a whole were actually producing a sociological crisis for them - making their lives embittered and miserable.

"These people had high-stress jobs, their work days were forever being stretched, and their relationships to corporations were becoming ever more problematic. They were constantly stuck in short-term labour, which was disempowering for them as individuals and did not allow them to build up their skill-sets. Their workplaces were focused on transactions over relationships, and this produced a type of procedural and structural injustice: there were no long-term relationships where their needs, grievances, and contributions to their companies were recognised.

"The foot-soldiers of this new capitalism were having a terrible time even as the economic boom was peaking, leading me to believe that something was not right about this new and glorified economic model."

THE SUBTLETIES OF INEQUALITY

The dominant narrative of the economic boom and its recent bust has been told from the perspective of intellectual and societal elites. These people have largely ignored or even misinterpreted the role played by the mid-level workers in society. As such, the dominant narrative has grossly distorted some of the underlying causes of the crisis, specifically the story of American profligate lending and spending. Rather than truly exposing underlying economic distortions and imbalances, many elites have contented themselves with blaming the consumerism of the middle and lower-middle classes for the downturn.

Intellectuals study inequality; they look at Gini coefficients and presume to understand the nature of the underlying social patterns. However, people in the middle of society measure social patterns completely differently: by focusing on wealth stagnation. Wealth stagnation became the norm for these people even during the economic boom, and this reality depressed them much more than the relative gap between the richest and the poorest in their societies. In the Anglo-American systems, people facing wealth stagnation turned to credit as the only remaining tool to build up their wealth.

The dominant share of consumer credit card purchases was spent on health care.

Since the crisis, the same elites who once pushed cheap credit and easy money on consumers are now condescendingly scolding 'irrational consumers' for having taken on credit they could not afford, through subprime mortgages and credit card debt. But what else were the people in the middle to do? They were not using credit to buy mink coats. They used it to counteract wealth stagnation. Specifically, the dominant share of consumer credit card purchases was spent on health care. The 49 million Americans with no health insurance were forced to buy health on credit.

Subprime mortgages, similarly, were not used to buy country villas. Many of the people who tapped into the subprime mortgage market had previously been living in absolute squalor. The United States has appallingly poor housing arrangements to provide for working class and lower-middle class citizens. Therefore, when subprime mortgages were introduced, the push factor to buy housing was enormous, even for families that could not technically afford it.

Another often over-looked subtlety of inequality has been the persistent moralisation of elite status. In the cultural domain, this has become a sickeningly common phenomenon. Big businessmen, who have never in their lives had to worry about putting food on the table, lecture as authorities on the proper conduct of working life. They preach about the necessity of hard work and putting in long hours as though these were the solution to the economy's woes.

Unfortunately the much bigger problems are the lack of work, and the stigmatisation of existing work. As technology becomes increasingly advanced, many routine tasks that were previously done by human beings are now being done by machines. In addition, this technology allows countries to move many existing jobs overseas. The result is a decreased market for mid-level employment, and an expanding need for lower-level employment. Yet many jobs – especially in the service sector – remain stigmatised, even as the labour force becomes increasingly over-educated. A prime example of this is nursing home caregivers, most of whom are immigrants. Despite their low levels of education and the elitist dismissal of their labour as low-skilled, these caregivers have some of the most astute social skills of any workers in the economy. Every night they deal single-handedly with huge crises: patients have heart attacks or strokes, and the only person available to attend to them is the caregiver on the midnight cleaning shift. Despite these trying responsibilities, they are considered – and paid as – nothing more than an unskilled pair of hands. Restoring the dignity and prestige of such welfare-promoting work would do far more for society than moving more and more people into the corporate sector the elite hold so dear.

On the other side of this elite moralisation is the issue of bonuses paid to those at the top of the system. The word 'bonuses' has recently actually become what sociologists refer to as a 'cover emblem'. Cover emblems naturalise issues that actually have more controversial underlying characteristics. The recent American frustration with corporate bonuses actually had little to do with the quantity of money paid – the sums themselves were naturalised. What really got to people in the middle was the notion that the elite had access to these rewards regardless of their performance. Did they deserve them? Were they competent? They were no more deserving or competent than anybody else. The issue that the 'bonuses' cover emblem obscured was one of injustice: they defied a theoretically meritocratic system. People in the middle tier of society looked at the work that they were forced to do, and then looked at the glorified elite with their big bonuses, and wondered: how could someone so stupid get that much money? It is a good question.

In the same way, the entire concept of 'inequality' has become a mystifying cover emblem, obscuring more disturbing issues, such as wealth stagnation and the glorification of elite status.

THE CRISIS AS A HISTORICAL JUNCTURE

The economic crisis has not only shaken the economic system, but also the social and the cultural systems. As such, it entails an important historical juncture, which will have profound effects on the lives of people everywhere. While some of these effects will be positive, some will also be profoundly negative.

There is reason to be optimistic: since the economic crisis, capitalism has lost its moral authority. The crisis has been an enormous wake-up call to those in the middle that they ought to be a bit more wary of those at the top. With taxpayers being asked to bail out the big-shots, the moral authority of the elite position suddenly seems quite fragile.

Realising that the top-down system has failed them, the middle class may alter its passive behaviour. Perhaps it is true that societies need structure and legitimate authority; perhaps people do need to have faith in their leaders. But that argument has limits. At some point, a disabused people must take their fate into their own hands. Even if the availability of credit were restored to its pre-crisis levels, many people in the middle of society would hesitate to return to borrowing. In fact, they are already focusing on finding ways to avoid this, for example by pushing Obama to provide a new health care system.

The entire concept of 'inequality' has become a mystifying cover emblem, obscuring more disturbing issues, such as wealth stagnation and the glorification of elite status.

On the other hand, the crisis has wreaked damage that people will be living with long into the future. In the Anglo-Saxon countries, the crisis has wrecked the retirement years of a large number of people. Many workers with only small government pensions turned to investment to pad their retirement resources. In the crisis, many of these people lost 40-45% of their resources – a devastating blow to their retirement prospects.

In addition, the crisis looks ever more likely to result in a jobless recovery, akin to Japan's lost decade in the 1990s. Unemployment is devastating not only in economic terms, but also in social terms. When you ask employed people how important their work is to them, they often downplay its significance. But the moment they lose their job and depend on unemployment support, they become devastated. For this reason, institutional creativity is urgently needed. For example, the Dutch have pioneered job-sharing programs, investing in employment projects that at least keep people in work half or one-third of the time. These programs work wonders for people's psychological well-being, by allowing them to do something productive every day.

Although such programs do require government support, they actually work out to be not only socially but also financially beneficial. If you include the marital problems, alcohol abuse, and other social by-products of long-term unemployment into the societal cost of unemployment, suddenly job-sharing programs appear quite inexpensive. In an ideal future, if such programs could be organised at the supranational level, tax on multi-national corporations that are contributing to over-production problems would be more than sufficient to subsidise workers who were willing to limit their hours, without in any way restricting globalisation.

In the coming years, however, the people most likely to suffer from increased unemployment are those in their early to mid-twenties, who are just entering the job market. Their employment contacts are thin, and they have only a short employment track-record. Yet the idea that staying in school and off the job market will somehow help them improve their employment chances is entirely illusory. If they are competing with hundreds of other equally over-qualified applicants for a position, whether or not they have a PhD – or even two of them – becomes irrelevant.

One wrinkle in this gloomy forecast is the continued demand for employment in trades despite the downturn. Yet whether or not the Anglo-American systems will chose to exploit this remains to be seen; to date they have virtually neglected developing practical skills in their workforce. Developing the skill-sets of electricians, computer repair personnel, and other unglamorous trades is not included in their educational programs. Instead, students focus on developing the skill-sets of stock brokers or CEOs – careers that have become increasingly rare, especially since the crisis.

CITIZENS AND THE STATE

In the post-war years, many governments provided truly welfare-enhancing social programs for their citizens. These increased societies' security and well-being, not only through economic incentives, but also through social and cultural initiatives. Sadly, starting in the 1980s, many of these programs were abolished, and the only remnants of such systems – especially in the Anglo-Saxon countries – are purely economic in nature. These initiatives, such as the welfare-to-work program, have become heavily stigmatised.

Although economically the 1990s was a boom, socially it was a bust.

Thatcher and Reagan both came to power on the heels of the 1970s labour unrest, and promoted brutal forms of capitalism designed to diminish such disturbances and promote greater economic growth in the future. The seeds of the new capitalism were planted as though the prior system had been an abject failure. Yet ironically, despite the labour unrest, the 1970s had actually been a period of prosperity in both the US and the UK. Nevertheless, Thatcher and Reagan seized the day, and shaped an entirely new economic system, based on new relationships between the state, the market, and citizens.

Cajoled by these iron-willed reformers, domestic populations began to increasingly place their faith in the private sector. They came to trust markets more than governments and, therefore, became immobilised as a political body. Even Tony Blair's Labour party activists would advocate market-based reforms, as they had come to believe that the state had no role to play in industrial policy. Over time, citizens became increasingly uncomfortable with the idea of the state as a positive social driver.

In the wake of the crisis, this passive attitude must change. Despite the economic fallout, the crisis has actually given populations new empowering tools. Suddenly, as a result of government bailouts, societies own their own banks. Rather than impatiently waiting for these banks to pay back their loans, why not treat this as an opportunity? Why not use this bizarre turn of events to the advantage of society, by forcing banks to finance small businesses, green businesses, and other welfare-promoting endeavours? The state has acted boldly since the onset of the crisis, and instead of hiding its role, it is high time it began claiming credit for its accomplishments. This is an ideal historical moment to bury – once and for all – the Thatcher/Reagan attitude that the state is the problem rather than the solution.

Economic indicators should always be considered in conjunction with the social conditions that accompany them. Although economically the 1990s was a boom, socially it was a bust. The current crisis, in the short-term, has been a devastating bust for both the economy and society. But in the long-term, while the economy may remain stagnant and depressed, the seeds of social growth and progress may have already been planted. However, such a dramatic shift will require political mobilisation, policy innovation, and a fundamental reconsideration of what welfare really entails.

Transcending the
European Nation State

Dominique Moïsi

PROFESSOR OF POLITICAL SCIENCE,
INSTITUT D'ETUDES POLITIQUES

"Just after the crisis, I became particularly concerned about Europe's loss of confidence. At first, there were calls for a coordinated European strategy, including Europe-wide economic governance to combat the crisis. But over time, illogical elements, such as emotions, eventually thwarted such rationally coordinated responses to the crisis. Although Europe was initially considered a lifeline for the national economies, other factors besides logic or economic imperatives ended up determining the haphazard crisis-related policies. Europe appeared to lose its appeal as a platform to negotiate solutions and instead came to be seen as a threat to national agendas. Emotionally, economic objectivity alternated with feelings similar to that of a disenchanted lover.

"As this happened, my generation's dream of a vital and forceful Europe moved out of reach. With the results of the Irish referendum in 2008, the last nail was hammered into the coffin of the dreams of the older integrationist generations. The crisis may impose an indefinite delay on Europe regaining a confident attitude towards ensuring social and economic growth.

"Emotions matter, and the culture of hope is slowly shifting from West to East. Asia, in a spirit of optimism, has fared better during the crisis, managing to retain some growth. In contrast, Europe – with its emotional discontent – has not been living up to its full potential."

COMPARATIVE ADVANTAGES

The world is currently changing, and with the economic crisis, many of Europe's presumed strengths have actually been proven void. In this new context, Europe must develop a new narrative of comparative advantage. It must develop its strengths and cover for its weaknesses in order to stay competitive and relevant in a shifting world. Strong winds of change are blowing, and in order for Europe to resist this wind, it must readjust the position of its body.

Unlike the collective hope currently experienced in the US, the EU suffers from a collective moroseness. Ideally, to overcome this, Europe should focus on creating growth in order to restore its emotional confidence in the European project. Sadly, in the wake of the economic crisis, such growth simply may not be in the cards. Europe's financial and economic foundations, once presumed to be exceptionally strong, have recently been exposed as flawed. In this field, Europe has neither a comparative advantage in knowledge for export, nor legitimacy upon which to build a more optimistic European emotional climate.

Similarly, the combination of demographic challenges and exceptionally strong social systems make Europe a poor example for integration in a globalising world. All Western countries face declining populations, and this challenge has forced them to incorporate new immigrants into their economies. Unfortunately, xenophobia tends to triumph over integration in the European context. This stands in stark contrast to the nearly innate American ability to incorporate immigrants. So integration of immigrants is also not Europe's comparative advantage. Unfortunately, the combination of the demographic and economic challenges points to a third European weakness: the military. Without sufficient resources or populations, it is very difficult for Europe to invest in defence.

Strong winds of change are blowing and in order for Europe to resist this wind it must readjust the position of its body.

Implicitly, the EU is often compared with the US. This is unfair. America has been able to build a kind of secular civic religion around the constitution, which gives it a powerful and unified legitimacy. In addition, its common language and common historical narrative of one united country make it much easier to forge unified leadership. Europe has none of this.

Yet on the other hand, comparisons with the US may be fitting. They reveal what Europe is missing – what it has yet to achieve to truly become a unified entity. In many ways – given its much shorter history of unification, linguistic and cultural diversities, and lack of a unifying narrative – Europe has a lot to be proud of. In fact, although its unification project may not rival that of the US, Europe is a powerful example of the potential for reconciliation. The European project has unified and integrated European nations in a way that Latin American or Middle Eastern countries can still only dream of. Since the world wars, they have overcome tremendous differences and forged a stronger unit out of many previously divided entities.

Thus, Europe's comparative advantage lies in exporting its ideals and ideas. First, European countries have managed to create a more civilised version of capitalism; they have created a marvellous system of social protection. Despite Europe's feeling of discontent and moroseness, this does give it an edge over the US, which tends to experience collective hope but also incredible individual fear. American society is violent – lost employment means lost income, health care, and benefits. There is little in the way of unemployment benefits, and people who lose their jobs when they are ill may also thereby lose their life because they are denied access to health care. This is not acceptable for an enlightened country. Therefore, the European model is a powerful example for other countries.

Europe's comparative advantage lies in exporting its ideals and ideas.

In addition, the European democratic model is crucial both internally and externally. Internally, it provides a platform from which ideas can be shared, discussed, and developed. Externally, Europe's experience with democracy makes it admired as a place of ideas and ideals.

Finally, despite its difficulties in reconciling differences with immigrants, Europe has done a remarkable job of reconciling its *internal* differences. Europe has overcome many of its previous conflicts, most significantly those of the world wars. Germany, specifically, has become a prominent power in Europe, and somehow its past has even helped it. Because it underwent such a dramatic transition in the post-war period, it has almost been vaccinated against wrongdoing. France and Germany have always been at the forefront of any European undertaking, and Germany's position should not be underestimated. Currently, Angela Merkel is the most popular European leader.

TOWARDS A NEW EUROPEAN VISION

Yet despite these striking advantages in the European system, Europe faces a variety of challenges that will make it difficult to utilise and export these ideas. Most notably, despite the relative successes of forging a unified EU, nationalism remains strong in Europe, and often makes collective EU action difficult.

However, it is precisely this feeling of national identity which can be a positive force in this globalising age. Despite movements towards internationalisation, the nation-state remains of vital importance. This means European states should not renounce their national identity in favour of a European identity, but should trust in their core national identity to help them feel at ease with multiple identities, including a European identity. If a person loses confidence in their core identity, they tend to reject external elements, and this can jeopardise the chances of social and political progress in a society. One's country should not be one's prison. Ideally, after a French coffee in the morning, eating like a Spaniard during the day and dining as a Italian, one would notice how multiple identities complement each other. Similarly, in the political and economic realms, utilising the benefits of different identities effectively could serve to improve the societies at both the member state and the EU levels.

The greatest barrier to Europe benefiting from its comparative advantages is the growing mediocrity of its politicians.

However, sociological by-products of globalisation also serve as challenges to Europe's capacity to benefit from its comparative advantages. Europe is currently dominated by feelings of diffidence and fear of losing control in a complex world. Globalisation precipitated worries, as it created new winners and losers and had challenging effects on society. The twin fears of losing control and of societal changes are the two main faces of the perceived globalisation threat. Faced with these, many Europeans have begun to yearn for more simplicity. Often, this has taken the form of fear of immigration or of Asia's rising strength. It also rears its ugly head in the form of xenophobia. Yet while such challenges seem to affect Europe disproportionately more than the US, it should be recalled that this is largely the result of Europe's laudable emphasis on social security. A society like the US, which promises fewer welfare provisions to its citizens, will necessarily be less concerned about an influx of immigrants with relatively higher welfare needs.

However, the greatest barrier to Europe benefiting from its comparative advantages is the growing mediocrity of its politicians. If anything, this is what is, in fact, destroying Europe. Europe lacks someone with the ideological skills similar to those of President Obama; his election was miraculous in that he brought back the spirit of the American founding fathers, as well as showing deep pragmatism and intellectual strength. Europe lacks such a figure. While Nicholas Sarkozy does have a unique energy, Silvio Berlusconi in Italy has been little more than a mockery of democracy. In fact, the best and the brightest people seem to have avoided political positions. In the recent past, these people tended to opt for careers in the financial sector, which was an unfortunate loss for society. The leaders that do emerge are often pragmatic, but lack intellect, ideology, and pedagogy. This lack of leadership and unifying ideals has caused a lack of faith in Europe and has led to political polarisation.

Specifically, it is hard to find a strong European leader who is able to rise above the stricture of the nation-state. While the President of the European Commission should ideally have the potential to do so, this person is usually chosen based on the fact that they pose no real threat to national European leaders. As such, this person tends to be politically weak. As long as this criterion continues to be imposed by national leaders, it will be very difficult for anyone to forge a unified leadership that transcends and defies national interests. It is much easier for national leaders to rely on the anti-Europe segment of the electorate than to break the mould and attempt to develop a unifying platform.

A NEW EUROPEAN GENERATION?

The current generation of decisionmakers is spoiled. They are intent on defending the comfortable status quo, and thereby project an indifference and negativity towards the European Union as a whole. This is detrimental to the hopes and political aspirations of future generations. While current leaders can afford to be either moderately pro-Europe or passionately anti-Europe, their children will not be able to enjoy such luxury. Europe is already coming under threat of disappearing from the global scene and is already becoming less visible around the world. US journalists have showed no special interest in France's new president or its return to NATO. Even within Europe, Spain, for example, prefers to discuss its economic issues only in an exclusively Spanish context.

> *The next generation of Europeans will be called upon to create something of their own.*

The next generation of Europeans will therefore be called upon to create something of their own. They will have to come together as Europeans and imagine Europe as part of the solution. In this endeavour, the new Europeans, such as the Poles, may provide guidance. They tend to have a more ambitious appetite for success at the EU level, and this has the potential to generate enthusiasm across Europe in the new generation. However, Europe will have to be imagined not only internally, but also externally. It must band together to prevent losing its international presence. If it does not, in 20 years it will be little more than an association of politically insignificant nation-states with a negligible GDP and declining populations. In international organisations, the EU must unify its power or risk becoming de-legitimised. Specifically, it should propose occupying one seat for the entire EU at the UN Security Council and other international bodies. Either Europe will learn to speak with one voice, or with none at all.

PART 4

EMBEDDING A NEW GLOBAL CONTRACT

The economic crisis presents enormous challenges to policy repertoires and the architecture of international organisations. In addition, as pressing global problems such as climate change, energy scarcity and water management gain in urgency, this has consequences for strategies of concerted supranational action.

André Sapir considers the crisis as the end of the second wave of globalisation. Just as the world wars of the 20th century ended the first wave of globalisation and ushered in a moment of global institution-building, so too does the current crisis present a window of opportunity for institutional recalibration. According to Sapir, addressing the crisis requires, at the very least, that the BRIC countries be welcomed to the table. In this respect, the move from a G8 to a G20 is promising. Consequently, he adds, Europe will become a smaller part of a bigger world.

Dani Rodrik reminds us that the institutional and intellectual legacy of a world of national political economies cannot easily be dismissed. He therefore proposes a new departure for global capitalism: a modus of balancing international economic integration while respecting diversity in domestic institutional arrangements.

Nancy Birdsall shifts the focus towards possible consequences for economic development. She argues that institutions such as the World Bank and the IMF have to adopt more heterodox policies, tailored more to the specific needs of the developing economies that are affected differently by the crisis than the developed world.

Anthony Giddens discusses the issue of climate change. The crisis, in his view, is a moment of unsettled beliefs that creates room for a different type of politics based on inspirational optimism to address the long-forestalled problems related to climate change.

Similarly, Tony Atkinson perceives the crisis as a moment to forge a new global deal, realigning the attack on global poverty, improving child welfare and ensuring climate sustainability. Atkinson underlines the importance of a recurring theme in this volume. A new global deal, he asserts, requires establishing new indicators of measuring social and economic progress, far beyond the narrow scope of GDP growth. Concluding this section, Amy Chua looks at how the crisis will challenge the power balance between the United States and China as world superpowers.

The Crisis of
Global Governance

André Sapir

PROFESSOR OF ECONOMICS,
UNIVERSITÉ LIBRE DE BRUXELLES

"The economic crisis has hit during a period of intense globalisation. Financial problems in the US and the UK triggered a world-wide recession that can only be reversed with globally coordinated solutions. Unfortunately, this will be difficult, as existing institutions that are responsible for global governance have ceased to reflect the current international distribution of wealth and power; emerging economies such India and China are key global economic players, but their economic fortitude is not reflected by their share of power in international institutions. Urgent reform is therefore needed to prevent these institutions from completely losing their efficacy and legitimacy. The previous wave of globalisation ended in the early 20th century with World War I and the Great Depression. Equitable and sustainable reforms of international institutions are urgently needed to prevent the current economic crisis from escalating into a similar collapse.

"On its own terms, the European Union as an institution has been deeply affected by the current economic crisis, and one of its primary challenges in the years to come will be to reinvent its role in a changing world order. Europe can no longer claim the institutional influence that it was accorded in the course of the post-war decades. Nevertheless, the important institutional knowledge that it developed through the process of establishing the EU may give it the potential to act as a key architect in re-designing future models of global governance. These two challenges, for the global and for the European community, are the most pressing issues that emerge out of the crisis."

TWO WAVES OF GLOBALISATION

Understanding the challenges that Europe and the world face today is aided by turning our vision to the processes of globalisation that have characterised the last 150 years. Essentially, the world has witnessed two successive waves of globalisation: the first from the mid-19th century until World War I, and the second one starting at the end of World War II, taking full flight after the crisis of the 1970s and perhaps ending with the advent of the current crisis.

The first wave of globalisation was the product of the second industrial revolution in the mid-19th century. During this period, industrial societies transformed profoundly in terms of their political, economic and social structures, prompting unprecedented rates of growth. This period was characterised by liberal economic policy and little regulation, facilitating the rapid expansion of global industry. These transformative advances had an unsettling effect on international relations, reshuffling and redistributing the cards of power, creating clear winners and losers from the globalisation process.

The BRICs have become increasingly significant players in the international economy, but their influence in global institutions has not increased apace with their growth.

At the outset of this period, the European colonial powers such as the United Kingdom, France, Belgium, and the Netherlands had held the bulk of the cards, and wielded substantial power over developing regions. They faltered, however, by being too slow to recognise the increasing strength and capacities of the newly emerging economies, most importantly of Germany and Japan. These emerging countries began their industrialisation processes much later than the colonial powers, but in so doing incurred an advantage. To catch up to the developed economies, they mimicked the cutting edge of their technologies, saving substantial costs on research and development, and creating a more comprehensively modern industrial infrastructure.

The first wave of globalisation eventually came to a jarring halt with the advent of World War I and the dramatic collapse of the global order. It marked the beginning of the gap between the two waves of globalisation that encompassed the devastating economic depression of the 1930s and culminated in World War II. The world wars and the interbellum period can, roughly speaking, be considered as the fall-out from the first wave of globalisation.

After World War II, the movement towards globalisation began anew. This time, however, the international community was resolved to contain the political and economic instabilities that came out of the first wave, and committed itself to a frenzied institution-building project. The United Nations, the World Bank, and the International Monetary Fund (IMF) were all launched with an eye to avoiding the crises of the early 20th century. Domestically, the post-war years marked the incipience of a set of national welfare policies and other state institutions to protect the more vulnerable members of society. With similar motives of facilitating international dialogue, the G6 (later the G7/8) was created in the wake of the 1970s oil crisis to avoid future vulnerability to such shocks.

Yet despite this project of erecting institutions, there appeared a worrying parallel between the second wave of globalisation and the first: once again, little room was prepared to accommodate emerging economies once they had made their entrée on the global stage. In the first wave, countries like Germany and Japan fell beyond the pale of global political and economic coordination; during the past few decades this fate befell the emerging BRICs. Of course, history never repeats itself, but the parallel is striking. Again, we come from a period of intense economic globalisation, aided by liberalisation and deregulation. Again, this process clearly separates winner from losers. Therefore, it does not affront the boundaries of imagination to consider the current crisis – which has so thoroughly shaken the global economic order – as closing the chapter of the second wave of globalisation, hopefully ending its deeply engrained instabilities and exclusionist structures. It at least marks the end of the unconditional trust that the global order as we knew it could be sustained. In retrospect, the 20th century was an accident of history, in which a small part of the world was able to sway power over a much larger majority. The crisis may be a pressing incentive to move to a more equitable global order.

THE ECONOMIC CRISIS AND THE CHANGING GEOPOLITICAL BALANCE

Prior to the economic crisis, there was a general feeling of optimism. Although globalisation presented challenges and hurdles, the international community felt that it was institutionally equipped, both globally and domestically, to overcome these challenges and to sidestep the pitfalls that had led to the crises of the early 20th century.

Unfortunately, these organisations had an inherent weakness. They institutionalised the global distribution of economic power from the post-war period into static, inflexible governance structures. However, in many ways the balance of power in the mid-20th century was an accident of history, with China and India, for example, accounting for the lowest combined share of world markets on record. Nevertheless, in international institutions, the global community inflated the power of the US and the European states and left little flexibility for expanding the powers of emerging economies. For example, of the 185 IMF member states, the United States currently controls nearly 17% of the vote, and the combined EU states control 32%. In contrast, China and India together have only 5.5% of the voting power.

Over the past fifty years, the emerging economies, most notably the BRICs (Brazil, Russia, India, and China), have grown rapidly. They have become increasingly significant players in the international economy, but their influence in global institutions has not increased apace with their growth. This has made them profoundly wary of global institutions. Although they respect the goals these institutions promote, they are opposed to the distributional hierarchy they represent. Emerging economies insist that they become truly multilateral, emphasising that it is no longer acceptable for an elite core to set the rules that the rest must follow. Policymaking must become multilateral from the outset.

The creation of the G20 will, hopefully, be remembered by future generations as a profound institutional regime change.

Of all of the global governance structures, the IMF has been the most frequent target of developing and emerging countries' frustration, with different writers labelling it a tool of the industrial countries, the West, the G7, or the United States. In the aftermath of the Asian financial crisis of 1997, Asian countries were especially vocal in their criticisms of the IMF. They blamed it for the initial onset of the crisis, as well as its broad contagion and the region's painfully slow recovery. These countries reacted to the crisis by dramatically increasing their reserves, which led to global imbalances. As a result of all this, many Asian nations even called for the creation of an Asian Monetary Fund to provide an alternative to the Western-dominated IMF. This proposal, to completely scrap and rebuild an international institution locally, underscores the declining legitimacy that these organisations face, as well as the urgent necessity of reform.

In the automobile industry, the economic crisis brought to light aspects of the business model that had become uncompetitive and outdated. If the same process occurs at the international level, the economic crisis will have profound effects on geopolitical relationships, as emerging countries' economies are likely to suffer relatively less than those of developed countries.

Developed and emerging economies differ in their proximity to what Philippe Aghion describes as the 'world technology frontier'. Those economies that sit close to this frontier (the developed economies) depend on research and innovation for their growth, whereas countries farther from it (the emerging economies) grow through traditional accumulation processes, oriented around the goal of 'catching up' with the developed economies. The BRIC countries have benefited enormously from a period of rapid traditional growth, in the same way that Europe did during *les trente glorieuses* – Europe's 'Golden Age' of capitalism, lasting from roughly 1945-1970, when countries saw high levels of economic growth combined with full employment.

In the current economic crisis, those farther from the technology frontier may gain an advantage, as their growth is only marginally dependent on the financial sector. In contrast, developed economies depend heavily on financial markets for their growth. While the financial sector has the potential to yield enormous benefits, including rapid growth, it also carries substantial risk, as the economic crisis made plainly apparent. In response to the damage wrought by the crisis, governments are likely to increase regulation of financial markets in order to decrease these risks. Regardless of the necessity of such measures, this will almost certainly lead to a decline in potential growth rates. Regulation will most heavily affect those economies that are most reliant on financial markets for their growth, translating into relatively larger reductions in growth rates for developed economies than for emerging economies. Emerging economies will continue to expand more rapidly relative to developed economies, further aggravating the need for institutional reform to accommodate these changing geopolitical trends.

THE G20: A BEACON FOR INSTITUTIONAL CHANGE

Fortunately, signs of change for the better can already be identified. The establishment of the G20, which has recently come to overshadow the G7, is one promising new development. Like the IMF, the G7 had become outmoded, meeting only with the old industrial powers and giving little or no space to the capacities and needs of the emerging economies. It was a hangover from an earlier time, when the Quad (Europe, the US, Japan, and Canada) had been the primary agenda-setters in trade negotiations. This had been unacceptable even in 1995 when these four nations accounted for 50% of world exports. However, by the time the economic crisis hit in 2008, this figure had declined to 35%, and their legitimacy was fading.

In contrast, the creation of the G20 will, hopefully, be remembered by future generations as a profound institutional regime change. Its significance lies in the fact that it brought the emerging economies out of the peripheries and onto the centre of the world stage. As such, it is an institutional reflection of a changing geopolitical order.

The organisation is obviously still young, but already it can account for some significant achievements. Its decision to provide increased support to the IMF will increase the resources available to developing countries and ease peoples' fears that future IMF policies will replicate those during the Asian financial crisis. In the future, it will be important that the G20 become an increasingly integral part of global dialogue, giving emerging countries a voice in addressing such issues as climate change, the economic crisis, and trade regulations.

CONSOLIDATING A EUROPEAN VOICE

Turning from the global to the European level, two significant challenges for Europe immediately present themselves, both of which will, without a doubt, be exacerbated by the economic crisis. The first is the internal challenge of the ageing population, and the second is the set of external problems associated with Europe's shifting position of the global playing field, as outlined above.

The ageing population in Europe is, at its core, a challenge for public finances. The baby boom generation is nearing the age of retirement, and soon an unprecedented number of citizens will claim their pensions. This will entail a heavy drain on public finance, both through the pension system as well as through health care funding. With declining population levels across Europe, there will be a shrinking workforce and therefore significantly reduced tax revenues. This will make it increasingly difficult for the government to finance the pensioners' growing demands. In a nutshell, this is one of the largest challenges faced by virtually all Western nations.

The economic crisis will intensify this predicament. The crisis will impact growth rates, employment, and tax revenues, further straining the already overstretched public finances. It will also undermine the attempts that governments have made to shore up resources and improve their capacities to tackle the problems associated with the ageing population. Without proper management, the joint impacts of the economic crisis and greying population may have undesirable consequences for the social welfare systems that European states have worked so hard to build.

The second challenge that Europe faces is the set of interlinked changes associated with globalisation, including technological developments, climate change, the altered geopolitical balance, and others. Attempts to grapple with climate change provide an insightful example, as this issue is intertwined with both the altered geopolitical balance as well as the need for multilateralism.

There is no longer much doubt as to the mechanisms needed to curb climate change; the future challenge will be to negotiate burden sharing. A particularly contentious aspect of this will be the distribution of the burden of reform between the developed and the developing/emerging countries. Whereas the developed countries are primarily responsible for the *stock* of the damage, emerging countries currently contribute significantly to the *flow* of continued damage. While emerging countries advocate technology transfers and favour highly cooperative solutions for combating climate change, developed countries tend to favour linking climate change to trade negotiations, using the latter as an enforcement mechanism for the former. However, this would be counterproductive, as it would move climate change into the post-World War II institutions that favour Western developed nations, whereas it is a problem that can only be tackled with emerging and developing nations incorporated as full partners in policy negotiations. The other challenges of globalisation, for Europe, will similarly be centred on the problems of institutional reform in the changing geopolitical order.

The economic crisis has made the institutional shortcomings of global governance institutions painfully apparent.

In 1957, the Treaty of Rome brought the European Economic Community into existence, and since then, Europe has developed and expanded. It has successfully incorporated 21 new member states, witnessed the fall of the Iron Curtain, and developed a currency that has become the second largest reserve currency globally. Just as economic integration was the prevailing narrative for the past 50 years, Europe must develop a new narrative based on multilateralism and globalisation for the upcoming 50 years.

In developing the EU, Europe became a guinea pig of multilateral governance. Through its experiences, it has developed an institutional knowledge base for successful international governance unrivalled globally. To maintain its international legitimacy, it must use this knowledge and become a true advocate of multilateral reform in global governance.

The difficulty is that long-term legitimacy may only be possible at the expense of short-term benefits, both at the level of individual EU member states and for the EU as a whole. Individual member states must be willing to aggregate their sovereign policies to allow for unified EU representation internationally. In order to benefit from the unity that the EU has nurtured, it will be necessary for Europe to learn to 'speak with one voice' internationally. For the EU as a whole, its role as a credible advocate of multilateral reform can only come at the expense of renouncing some of its antiquated institutional privileges in global governance institutions. It must be flexible towards fundamental reforms of institutions, even when this means decreased voting power or reduced direct influence. Europe's role in future global governance institutions will benefit more from its commitment to multilateralism and willingness to share its institution-building experience than it will on the safeguarding of outdated voting privileges.

The economic crisis has made the institutional shortcomings of global governance institutions painfully apparent. These institutions enshrined an overly dominant role for Western developed nations, and as a result are currently facing a crisis of legitimacy. In order for the global community to recover from the current economic crisis, these institutions must reform, fully integrating the emerging countries and promoting equitable and sustainable models of globalisation. Failure to do so, in the best-case scenario, will lead to the continued decline of their legitimacy and efficacy. In the worst-case scenario, their ineffectiveness in promoting a sustainable recovery from the economic crisis could trigger a throwback to the end of the first wave of globalisation, with all of its accompanying economic and political turmoil.

As Europe becomes a smaller part of a bigger world, it faces a critical choice: it must either renounce some institutional benefits in order to gain international legitimacy, or cling to ill-gained voting rights and go down with a sinking ship.

Capitalism 3.0

Dani Rodrik

PROFESSOR OF INTERNATIONAL POLITICAL ECONOMY,

HARVARD UNIVERSITY

"The collapse of Lehman Brothers was the most obvious trigger of the crisis, sparking an unravelling of international credit markets. But this isolated incident was not its cause: the crisis was the result of a wide amalgamation of factors, which proved lethal in combination.

"The economic crisis may have come as less of a surprise to me than to many of my American colleagues, because I had been uneasy about some of these factors previously. Specifically, I did not believe that financial markets were creating any significant added value for the economy. However, even for me, it took a crisis to reveal the extent of the damage: the financial sector had become rotten to the core. It was managing risk appallingly."

MODELS OF CAPITALISM

Over time, the basic tenets of capitalism have changed and evolved, interacting with shifting global trends. Since the 1900s, there have been three broad models of global capitalism, the latter two of which are extensions of one another. They will be referred to here as Capitalism 1.0, 2.0, and 2.1. The current economic crisis provides a valuable opportunity to reinvent these past models and develop something superior: a Capitalism 3.0.

The key element distinguishing these models from one another is the way that the international community has managed the most fundamental tension of an international market system: the balance between the national and international spheres. There is an inherent conflict between achieving deep international economic integration and maintaining the necessary diversity in domestic institutional arrangements. Although there are great benefits to be gained by completely integrating international markets, this should not come at the expense of nations' capacities to provide for their own citizens.

Facing this challenge, Capitalism 1.0 favoured the international agenda, pushing for unrestrained globalisation. During the 19th century, the international community deified the free market as the most profoundly creative and dynamic economic engine known to human kind. The tendency was towards a completely liberalising agenda. This was an era of true globalisation, and the unregulated international market reigned supreme. Under this paradigm, the state played a minimal role, serving as only a 'nightwatcher' for economic interests. Aside from national defence, protection of property rights, and administration of justice, the state was seen as an impediment to growth.

Although this model still survives today in libertarian circles, it was largely re-thought and re-designed after the ordeals of the 1930s and the World Wars. The post-war model – Capitalism 2.0 – imagined a much larger and more fundamental role for the state: it could be described as Keynes plus the welfare state. People realised that markets were not the self-regulating, self-stabilising, and self-legitimising machines that they had imagined them to be. Instead, they had to be embedded in a wide range of regulatory, redistributive, monetary, fiscal, and conflict-management institutions, which, for practical reasons, operated at the national rather than the global level. The Bretton Woods agreement played a key role in institutionalising these new goals by throwing sand in the wheels of international commerce and finance in order to make more space for national solutions. Specifically, it created capital controls and a highly permissive GATT system.

In some ways, the Bretton Woods regime became a victim of its own success. With hindsight, it is apparent that this period prospered because of the vital role assigned to national institutions. The balanced expansion of state responsibilities alongside market expansions created more sustainable and well-distributed growth. However, at the time, the success and rapid growth of the economy led people to overlook the institutional underpinnings of the markets. Economists were still trained in the mentality of Capitalism 1.0, and nothing in their backgrounds prepared them to understand how much the success of the Bretton Woods era rested on the existence of this balance. Instead, they believed that growth had been based exclusively on the liberalisation of the economy, market advances, and increased trade. Worryingly, this same explanation is often still accepted today.

Starting in the 1970s, people used this flawed narrative to justify curbing the functions of the state and pushing for a return to the complete globalisation of markets. This denoted the end of the Bretton Woods era. Capitalism 2.1 returned to the same international emphasis as Capitalism 1.0: the policy mandates of this period were financial globalisation and deep integration under the WTO. Unfortunately, it had two fatal blind spots. First, it pushed for rapid and deep integration of world trade and finance, trusting that the institutional framework could catch up later. Second, it wrongly assumed that deep economic integration had either no effect, or a benign effect, on existing national institutional arrangements. These were both outgrowths of the fundamental imbalance between the global reach of the markets, and the national reach of market limitations. The unintended result of this period was the erosion of the legitimacy of the trade system, as weak financial regulation and the poorly managed interface between national styles of capitalism caused countless problems.

> *The current economic crisis provides a valuable opportunity to reinvent these past models and develop something superior: a Capitalism 3.0.*

The economic crisis was the result of the flaws of Capitalism 2.1. However, it has hopefully had some positive impact by exposing these problems and serving as a warning against repeating them. The crisis will undoubtedly lead to a rebalancing of the world system, and has provided enough of a shock to allow for a complete shift in the global economic system. As the international community moves forward, the biggest question is what Capitalism 3.0 should look like.

SHIFTING POWER STRUCTURES

Although in the short-term the crisis is going to have severe negative impacts, in the medium-term there may be room for optimism. The economic crisis will affect different nations differently, creating new winners and losers in the international arena, and significantly redistributing relative power in the global economy. All countries will have to adjust their national economic strategies, as outdated and inefficient systems will only deepen the negative impacts of the crisis.

Although the US will probably recover from the economic crisis, it is unlikely to regain its former dynamism. It currently has no new driver of growth: on average, households have lost 25% of their wealth, constricting consumer spending; the public sector is increasingly indebted, causing a fiscal drag; the financial sector is in shambles. As a result, Washington's institutional rules – which had previously held great international authority – will become less restrictive. In the past, institutions such as the World Trade Organisation (WTO), the International Monetary Fund (IMF), and the World Bank held significant sway over developing and emerging countries, and were based on these rules formulated in the US. However, as the vibrancy of the US's economic growth model wears thin, so too will its intellectual legitimacy, which had allowed it to control these institutions. As a result, those countries had previously been stuck on the receiving end of development advice may soon find room to establish their own growth models.

While in most cases this will be done willingly, some developing countries may also be forced to reform. As international financial organisations lose their strength, countries that had become addicted to borrowing may find foreign finance becoming more expensive and harder to obtain. Although this will be difficult in the short-term, in the long-term it will have the positive effect of forcing these countries to develop alternative models of growth that are less dependent on current account deficits and loans.

In general, democratic emerging economies will gain the most from the post-crisis rebalancing. Democracy is important, because democratic countries are always stronger in periods of economic turbulence. Incompetent rulers can be voted out and replaced by those better able to meet society's needs and expectations. Emerging economies stand to gain the most because of the loosening of the external constraints posed by the US and its international institutions. Specifically, Brazil and India may achieve a great deal of economic growth in the post-crisis period. Countries like Turkey, with large current account deficits, face greater challenges in this regard, but given proper management may also make significant strides forward.

One of the greatest concerns in the post-crisis period transcends the level of national gains and losses: there will likely be a vacuum of international leadership.

China, on the other hand, is more vulnerable. Its highly authoritarian and centralised political structure, combined with an urgent need for rapid growth, left it both politically and economically susceptible to market shocks. Its initial stimulus package was surprisingly successful in mitigating short-term damages, and was implemented quickly and aggressively despite weak institutional infrastructure. However, in the long-term, China will need to fundamentally change its growth model to one that is less dependent on enormous trade surpluses, and it is unclear whether the current leadership will be able to do this successfully, while maintaining macro-economic stability.

One of the greatest concerns in the post-crisis period transcends the level of national gains and losses: there will likely be a vacuum of international leadership. As outlined above, the power of the US is likely to wane, and it is unclear who will step up to fill this void. Emerging economies are not yet capable of doing so, and despite the talk of the ascendance of China, their GDP is still only one-eighth that of the US.

This may open the door for an enlarged international role for the EU, yet this is far from certain. The reduced constraints of the international system will certainly benefit the EU, with larger EU member states possibly becoming significant international players. However, Europe is still dealing with many internal problems and is conflicted between expanding the depth versus the breadth of the union. It lacks the necessary unity to create coherent supranational economic policies and may therefore be unable to become a global leader independently.

In combination, however, these countries may be able to form unified leadership. Imperfect as the UN and the Bretton Woods institutions may be, no source of leadership should be pushed aside in the post-crisis period. In addition to these, the G20 has become a viable body for future global leadership. Although originally little more than an outreach mechanism for American and European economic interests, it has recently gained legitimacy as a summit meeting for heads-of-state.

THE NEW CAPITALISM

Asking who will lead is essential, but equally important is asking towards what new system they will lead. Capitalism 3.0 must find new and innovative solutions to the fundamental problem of balancing international economic integration with diversity in domestic institutional arrangements. Luckily, the global community has thus far avoided the pitfalls of the 1930s, the internationalisation of embedded liberalism, or a return to the pre-crisis status quo. None of these would be desirable outcomes.

Having learned from the mistakes of the 1930s, monetary and fiscal policies in response to the recent crisis were only minimally protectionist. Despite claims to the contrary, only 78 new protectionist measures have been implemented globally in the past year, and most were extremely minor. Developed countries have clearly come to believe in open economies, and need not worry about the so-called 'slippery slope of protectionism'. Although mildly protectionist measures may occasionally be necessary, they will not spiral into isolationism.

The international community must also resist the temptation to create a global version of embedded liberalism. This would be both impractical as well as undesirable. Impractical, because it places too much faith in the supply of global leadership and the willingness of countries to give up their sovereignty; undesirable because different nations have different preferences and needs and should develop their national priorities accordingly.

There is no way that the international community could simply return to the status quo, an uninhibited trajectory of liberalisation and globalisation. The landscape of finance will be significantly altered by the crisis. Starting in the 1980s, the Washington Consensus became the dominant economic development paradigm, imposed around the world to promote growth in developing

economies. This model was based on elements such as fiscal discipline, trade liberalisation, openness to foreign direct investment, privatisation, deregulation,
and secure property rights. In the 1990s, this model was expanded to include sec-
ond-generation reforms that in addition targeted good governance.

Unfortunately, people's belief in the virtue of this model did not hold up in
light of developing countries' actual experiences with it. East Asia and China
witnessed a boom in this period, yet only partially implemented the Washington
Consensus reforms. Latin America, on the other hand, trustingly implemented
the reforms but reaped little growth from them. This shows that although the
Washington Consensus reforms are based on sound economic reasoning, they
are not a fool-proof recipe for success. Instead, countries must examine their
own individual needs and preferences, and design models that work best for
them. In cases where these goals conflict with the aims of globalised trade, the international community must respect the domestic policy space.

THE IMPORTANCE OF DOMESTIC INSTITUTIONS

Increasing domestic policy space is both politically and practically necessary. Politically, trade adjustments and domestic interventions may be necessary to ensure the support and the security of the population through the difficult process
of globalisation. Practically, increased domestic policy space is not merely a con-
cession to the discontented masses, but also the most efficient way forward. The
world is highly second-rate, but the nature of these second-best problems varies
from country to country. In a world of such heterogeneous initial conditions,
China and the US will certainly require different institutional arrangements –
from a purely economic standpoint. The question is how to interface between
different countries that optimally have different institutions. True free trade is
impossible in such a context, because different institutional set-ups imply trans-
action costs that prevent trade maximisation.

For all of these reasons, Capitalism 3.0 should be developed based on the idea
that markets must become embedded at the level of the nation-state. Democratic governance and political communities are likely to remain embedded within
states, and markets should be embedded similarly. Although economic transactions between these states should be structured with the aim of maximising the
thickness of transactions in trade and investment flows, space must be maintained for heterogeneous national arrangements. Where national models align,
countries can deeply integrate their economies according to liberal trade rules.
However, where national models conflict, 'traffic rules' must be designed to
manage the interface between domestic arrangements.

Democratic governance and political communities are likely to remain embedded within states, and markets should be embedded similarly.

Walking the fine line between protectionism and protecting necessary national arrangements may be difficult in some cases. Many normative questions arise when these interests conflict, and they have no clear-cut solutions. Answering these questions will require new negotiation and dialogue between developed and developing countries. Developed countries call for heightened labour standards to protect their workers from displacement stemming from child labour, regulatory measures to protect them from financial assets traded from poorly regulated countries, and assurances that free trade areas will not provide greater protection from policy change for foreign firms than for domestic ones. They complain that WTO rules permit countervailing for export duties but not for undervalued currencies, and that free trade and increased mobility threaten their social compact with citizens by diminishing access to taxation resources. In addition, they worry about the future of R&D, which had previously been highly regulated by national governments – for example in areas such as stem-cell research.

In contrast, developing countries worry that trade regime agreements on subsidies, trade-related investment measures (TRIMs), trade-related aspects of intellectual property rights (TRIPs), and other negotiations on services that narrow their domestic policy space for industrial policies. They complain that international capital markets impose financial codes and standards, but provide no role for development banking and credit market interventions. In addition, monetary rules such as central bank independence leave no space for using the exchange rate as a developmental policy instrument. All of these difficulties are only heightened by free trade areas and bilateral investment treaties as they are currently imagined.

To create a Capitalism 3.0 with increased domestic policy space, both developed and developing countries must change their tone in trade negotiations. In the past, the global North and South have often been deadlocked, with neither side recognising the others' domestic constraints as anything more than protectionism. As the crisis rebalances economic power globally, a new discussion will become increasingly imperative. Developing countries must come to view themselves as more fundamentally important players with responsibilities, and a stake, in the international system. The quid pro quo must be that just as developing countries need their own policy space so that they can conduct domestic policies of structural transformation and growth, they need to recognise that developed countries may need their own policy space as well to ensure that their own social arrangements are not eroded.

The biggest challenge in this regard will be managing the interface between countries with different domestic policies. This will require a system of 'traffic rules'. These rules must be developed by the nations involved and will necessarily be very complex, but two illustrative scenarios will be outlined here. First, these rules could be designed based on generalised WTO safeguards. This approach would allow countries to re-impose tariffs under certain circumstances and would make the principle behind safeguards negotiated opt-outs with procedural constraints, rather than disorganised opt-outs. This is currently restricted to very limited circumstances: if 'injury' is linked to domestic industry, it must be applied on a most favoured nation (MFN) basis, be temporary, and require compensation. However, the same principle could be applied to a wider set of circumstances where the legitimacy of trade is at stake, those cases should also become subject to transparency, accountability and other institutional and procedural prerequisites, which, in particular, provide standing to beneficiaries of trade. This model creates a 'development box' for developing countries, recognising that structural transformation requires subsidies and other currently prohibited practices. This approach favours an exchange of policy space rather than simple market access.

The second approach to creating 'traffic rules' would be based on rules from the financial sector, creating a nationally based but globally consistent regime of regulation. Under this model, the governance of financial markets could be done at the national rather than the international level, and different countries/ regions could make different regulatory choices. There would be strong pressures towards regulatory arbitrage when regulatory arrangements varied, but governments would be given the right to interfere in cross-border financial flows to prevent their domestic regulations from being undermined.

Although the past quarter-century shows that the price of financial de-globalisation is significant, this is a necessary price to pay for financial stability. Using the 'traffic rules' to limit the damages, in the long-term such an approach would actually be beneficial, as it would allow each country to implement rules best suited to their own development.

THE LIMITS OF FEDERALISM

Although a shift to complete global federalism would be ideal, it is also idealistic and not feasible in the short term. The European Union is currently moving towards becoming a federation, yet struggles with the difficulty of balancing domestic welfare versus EU-wide efficiency. Because EU member states were able to agree on rules for a common market, but not for a common welfare policy, EU institutions – for example, the European Court of Justice – tend to favour economic integration over the national welfare needs of member states.

Nevertheless, a strong benefit for Europe is that it always understood the need for a domestic complement to a single market. This understanding has not been as present in the United States, where it took an economic crisis to trigger the realisation that there may need to be financial sector regulation. Even with the crisis, this realisation has not been extended to include an increased acceptance of welfare state programs.

It is not surprising that the EU integration process has been difficult: creating a federal system in the US required one of the bloodiest civil wars in history. Given these difficulties in creating federal systems, even in limited regions, trying to implement global welfare rules internationally seems absurd.

Instead, the international community should use the window of opportunity provided by the economic crisis to renegotiate a new international capitalism, based on a healthy new balance between domestic policy space and international trade efficiency.

The Global Development Agenda

Nancy Birdsall

FOUNDING PRESIDENT,

CENTRE FOR GLOBAL DEVELOPMENT, WASHINGTON

"I was concerned before the Lehman Brothers collapse that the financial sector in the United States had become much larger than it had ever been historically, certainly since World War II. Like many people, I didn't understand the systemic risk until the Lehman Brothers catastrophe. But even before that, it was clear that the increase in 'financial' globalisation had been very distributionally inegalitarian, including in developing countries, and I had long been concerned about that.

"In fact, throughout much of 2008, it seemed that the subprime market issue couldn't blow up because in numbers it just wasn't big enough. In retrospect, I was naive about at least two things: the tremendous leverage associated with the derivatives markets and the off balance-sheet finagling going on in the big banks. And then there was the regulatory arbitrage, especially in the context of AIG, where their triple-A rating was allowing them to make huge profits selling insurances that did not reflect the actual risks."

CAUSES AND CONSEQUENCES OF THE CRISIS

The economic meltdown was caused by the interaction of two factors. There was the imbalance in the global economy between China's savings surplus and the US's consumption profligacy. The large inflow of capital coupled with expansionary monetary policy made credit too cheap; banks and other creditors took increasing risks in order to stay ahead of the competition with high returns. Plus there were the regulatory failures. (Ironically, in the aftermath there is some risk that the wrong approach to tightening regulation, e.g. on securitisation, could increase the costs of capital in emerging markets.)

Unfortunately, the international community failed to foresee the impending disaster. Obvious signals from Fannie Mae and Freddie Mac, the bust in the Hong Kong housing market a few years ago, and the inherent weaknesses of subprime mortgages were not taken seriously. The main reason for this was a shared conviction, reinforced during the good times, that markets are always efficient

194

and that all actors are rational and well-informed. Neither liberals nor conservatives contradicted what became the conventional wisdom. Also, people tended to think that although they might not completely understand the mathematisation of finance, somebody else surely did. Then there was the unspoken confidence that the US government would guarantee the system – particularly Fannie Mae and Freddie Mac mortgage securities. Finally, the lobby groups and the political influence of the financial sector played a role. The extent to which a crisis might have been prevented by tougher rules affecting the sector, we'll never know. There was resistance to any steps that would seem to threaten US competitiveness – and no doubt there were similar pressures in the UK.

The impact of the crisis has varied across countries. The major emerging markets are doing far better than expected. They were and are less 'globalised' in the financial sector. Most had self-insured with high reserves, a move that provided some protection during the current crisis, but also reinforced the global imbalance which helped trigger the crisis – most obviously in the case of China. Most had for the preceding decade maintained reasonably sound macro-economic policies, and had some fiscal and monetary policy space to adjust to the downturn.

The major emerging markets are doing far better than expected.

Still, what started as a financial crisis is becoming an economic and jobs crisis in many developing countries – Mexico, Cambodia, Ghana, and so on. Those that rely heavily on trade (the majority of countries in the developing world) will experience heightened economic trauma from the crisis if trade fails to recover quickly. Countries and households that rely on remittance income, for example in Central America, are currently suffering dramatically.

GLOBAL IMBALANCES

The crisis could precipitate some policy changes in some developing countries. Large economies may focus more on domestic consumption to minimise their exposure to the reduction in global demand from the once huge US consumer market. For each country, it will make sense to continue to self-insure with reserves, although regrettably the result may be another round of global imbalance. The wisdom of some capital market restrictions will be vindicated. China could become an exception in this regard because of its ambition to make the renminbi a global reserve currency. Even countries with open capital markets, for example in Latin America, may modestly retrace their steps, for example introducing a Chilean-style tax on short-term inflows. Meanwhile, countries will be tempted to keep their currencies undervalued in order to maintain exports.

INCOME INEQUALITY

The crisis will also affect income distribution and inequality in many countries. There are two issues at stake here. First, the incipient middle class in Thailand, China, much of Africa, and many parts of Latin America will be hit relatively hard by the recession. These people are typically semi-skilled workers. They are entering the wage and salary system, becoming the middle-class bulwark of their democracies, in much the same way that European workers took on this role with the rise of so-called embedded liberalism. However, this potential middle class is especially vulnerable in countries that have no automatic stabilising mechanisms and are either unable or unwilling to implement counter-cyclical policies for fear of being downgraded by international rating agencies if they introduce stimulus packages. In countries that depend heavily on external investors and loans, and where voters fear inflation, such concerns may be decisive.

The second issue affecting income distribution is the limited fiscal policy space that many countries face. The recession will have medium-term costs, which may include the permanent loss of human and institutional capital. This may, in turn, ratchet down the potential rate of growth in many countries in the long term. In many countries in sub-Saharan Africa or Central America, revenues are down in absolute, not only relative, terms. Declining trade taxes and revenues have led to flat GDP growth rates, which translate into negative per capita growth in countries with high birth rates – and real costs in human welfare. Because of their limited fiscal policy space, these countries cannot easily implement counter-cyclical measures. Without external help, they will be required to either not pay or lay off teachers, nurses, and other state workers. The long-term cost, as at the time of the 1980s debt crisis in Latin America, is that health education and other delivery systems begin to fall apart – and are hard to reconstitute even when recovery takes hold.

FUTURE GROWTH

Looking towards the future, the global community will be in need of new growth drivers to propel it out of the current downturn. There are two possible growth drivers. First, significant investment in new technologies that could increase productivity in the mature economies would be useful. This would trigger a new round of growth and help boost consumer demand. The US had a period of very high productivity growth of about 2% per year between roughly 1990 and 2003. With high productivity and easy credit, everybody became accustomed to high economic growth and rising consumption. Future productivity growth will have to come from new sources, like green energy and the low-carbon path investments. However, the challenge will be to find funding, from either the market or the government, to finance massive research and development in this new sector.

Of course to make this growth driver operational, policy incentives would help – for example, creating clear signals that the implicit price of CO_2 will rise, and when, and by how much. It is unfortunate that the draft legislation in the US is not strong on this score with, as happened in Europe, many emission permits being given away instead of auctioned off in the early years. Industry pressures have too often prevailed; for example, the section of the bill detailing transparency and information gathering requirements on the consequences of ethanol for various environmental factors – such as forest cover, farmland, or fuel and food prices – was taken out of the bill. However, regardless of the US's domestic policy shortcomings, the international community must take serious action on climate change, agreeing on policies that could influence preferences and steer global investment and legislation in a greener direction.

The recession will have medium-term costs, which may include the permanent loss of human and institutional capital.

The second potential growth driver originates in the developing world, where overcoming existing bottlenecks to production and productivity limitations would significantly increase their growth potential. Private-public partnerships in which risks are shared (with public resources covering typical as opposed to commercial risks) may be an important locus for initiating such change. Tackling bottlenecks and achieving higher productivity levels require intelligent public coordination, which is regrettably perhaps the single scarcest resource in the current global system.

Within the developing world, different countries face different prospects for growth. China alone cannot become a new global growth driver. Even if it does overcome bottlenecks, increase productivity, and focus more on domestic consumption, China is still economically too small to take over from the US as the global demand driver. US GDP (in purchasing power parity) was about $ 14 trillion in 2008, compared to perhaps $ 3 trillion in China. On the other hand, as a group, China, India, Brazil, and other smaller emerging markets could constitute an important source of renewed global demand.

Transatlantic responses to the crisis have differed. The US may start to look towards some of Europe's social policies with envy. The jobs crisis has not hit as hard in Europe, and the automatic stabilisers have been more robust and more effective than in the US.

Hopefully the crisis will lead to greater emphasis on social insurance and safety net programs. The debate over health care reform has usefully raised interest in European systems, with their apparently better results at lower costs. The same will happen with the discussion of pension reform which is bound to come, since the crisis levelled a terrible blow at Americans' private retirement savings. In short, modest moves in the direction of a more European social model seem inevitable, in spite of the American emphasis on low taxes and low government expenditure. Perhaps it will not only be the financial sector that will retreat from the 'cowboy capitalism' approach.

TOWARDS A NEW GLOBAL SOCIAL CONTRACT

The international development community has three objectives; though they are interrelated, it is useful to distinguish amongst them. They are transformation, solidarity, and investing in global public goods that matter for development. Transformation is about growth and good governance. It refers to the conviction that development aid can help transform societies in developing countries so that they ultimately will no longer be dependent on aid. The effectiveness of transformation aid to raise growth – from budget support to big infrastructure – is very hard to show and has been the most difficult to defend to donor taxpayers.

> *Looking towards the future, the global community will be in need of new growth drivers to propel it out of the current downturn.*

Solidarity is about improving people's lives directly, through support for schooling and health and microfinance, for example. The domestic social contract within countries is the national equivalent of such international programs. At the international level, the solidarity objective implies securing some of the basic elements of the domestic policies of embedded liberalism for the entire global community. Although limited global resources make the chance of an international future modelled after the European design of embedded liberalism slim, solidarity-type aid is popular with American taxpayers, and it is relatively easy to demonstrate that it works. Will some new form of embedded liberalism at the international level emerge? In the extreme, this would require a fundamental reconsideration of what sovereignty means, and who is entitled to what security in the international system. An important reform in creating a global system of embedded liberalism would be the liberalisation of the last illiberal market: migration. This would solve problems in ageing societies as well as reducing poverty worldwide. Migration happens anyway, so it is in the interest of the affluent receiving countries to adjust to it in a way that minimises the cost and maximises the benefits for all.

Finally, the third element of the global social contract – global cooperation in provision of public goods – is about international cooperation in addressing challenges such as climate change, pandemic disease, cross-border drug trafficking and corruption, and tax havens, as they affect developing countries. Unfortunately, the scarcest resource currently is cooperation and government effectiveness in worldwide and inter-governmental bodies. In order to be effective at an international level, the world needs forward-looking domestic governments that can get things done. At the same time, however, all countries tend to be plagued by a deep distrust in anything that implies international 'government'. (The current crisis has at least had the benefit of inspiring greater coordination of fiscal, monetary, and financial issues and triggered the creation of the more inclusive G20 at the head-of-government level.)

Transformation is about growth and good governance.

To meet these current coordination challenges, all existing institutions should be utilised. The G8, G20, UN, ILO, World Bank, IMF and the Financial Stability Forum all have a role in ensuring a more prosperous and equitable world. The G20 is a hugely important institution in this regard, because it functions as an implicit steering committee for international financial institutions. However, from a social justice perspective, the biggest challenge the G20 faces is the lack of representation of the poorest countries. The biggest problem in the IMF and the World Bank, similarly, is the over-representation of the 20th century trans-Atlantic powers, and in the case of the IMF, the difficulty of disciplining the biggest economies, for example China and the US, on the global imbalances.

Nevertheless, international institutions like the World Bank and the IMF always undergo processes of cumulative incremental change. For example, in the IMF, Dominique Strauss-Kahn is leading a reform process that will make it easier for the G20 to increase the resources of the Fund to assist emerging markets and the developing countries in coping with the fallout from the crisis. The Atlantic powers have realised that change is needed in order to keep China and other emerging economies engaged.

The economic crisis highlighted a variety of international inequalities and at the same time created new instabilities that urgently need to be addressed. The crisis has both necessitated and facilitated institutional reforms to make the global system more just and sustainable.

The Economic Crisis and Climate Change

Anthony Giddens

PROFESSOR EMERITUS,

LONDON SCHOOL OF ECONOMICS

"*When the economic crisis began, I was busy with my book on the climate change crisis, so my political and economic radar was somewhat deactivated. I probably noticed the economic crisis at the same time as the general public. However, as the discussions around the economic crisis developed, I discovered that the themes in these debates actually paralleled the themes in the climate change crisis debate. When you talk about dealing with the climate change and energy crises, you necessarily have to ask big questions. What should the role of government be? To what extent should markets be allowed free rein? How do you negotiate long-term political arrangements? Perhaps the two crises are two sides of the same coin, in the sense that many of the same fundamental problems lie at their core. The crises may appear completely separate, but the institutional hurdles to fixing them are largely the same.*"

THE RESURGENCE OF LONG-TERM POLICY

The world is at the brink of a new era. Many challenges have come to a head recently and have culminated in three potentially devastating crises that will together change the face of the future: the economic crisis will impact future financial capacities, the climate change crisis will impact future business possibilities, and the energy crisis is already fundamentally shifting the world's resource priorities.

The crisis necessitates a new responsible brand of capitalism.

First and foremost, in the upcoming period the state and the markets will need to negotiate a new relationship. Recovery from the economic recession necessitates more than the current stimulus packages, which are largely based on a neo-

Keynesian model. Keynes' solutions were designed for the 1930s – a completely different era, when solutions were perhaps simpler: the distinction between state and market was clearer, and states' capacities were far broader. While the crisis has demonstrated the need to revitalise state-level planning, the state planning conducted in the 1950s and 1960s cannot be directly transferred to the present. The planning of the past was manifestly flawed in too many ways, specifically in that it did not incorporate markets sufficiently. Therefore, in the current market-driven age, such backward-looking solutions are out of place. Instead, the state must be forward-looking, imagining new solutions and guidelines, and looking not just as far as tomorrow, but also ahead into the next two or three decades.

Therefore, the crisis necessitates a new responsible brand of capitalism, which will build new relationships between the state and markets, and will establish new long-term objectives. In negotiating this new arrangement, policymakers must carefully consider the capacities of markets versus governments for long-term planning. There is a common quip that markets are too short-term to provide secure solutions for the future, and indeed, there is some truth to this. However, compared to the challenges that democratic governments face in long-term planning, markets may often have relatively better prospects for institutionalising future planning.

Pension plans are an obvious example of long-term planning that operates more effectively when coordinated by markets rather than governments. In the climate change realm, insurance is one such market mechanism that could be encouraged to evolve even further to meet future climatic challenges. Specifically, the number of hurricane incidents has increased dramatically over the past years, and this trend looks as though it will continue in the future. While spreading untold risk and misfortune, these incidents also open up a market niche: catastrophe insurance.

Hurricane Katrina proved, once and for all, that hurricane victims cannot expect anything over and above the most limited coverage from governments. Instead, people will need to turn to private insurance companies. Alliance Insurance Company is already innovating in this area, providing catastrophe bonds that can cover this type of extreme-weather damage. Eventually, such insurance innovations will have to be integrated with more sophisticated financial instruments and more accurate future climate predictions that can incorporate major weather events. In such an endeavour, the government can play a role by providing technology and structural incentives for such coverage. Ultimately, though, it must let insurance companies work out a strategy according to market principles. So too, in the wake of the economic crisis governments should be empowered to help provide information and positive incentives for companies to recover, without basing the model on long-term state interference.

However, there are some sectors in which states must also institutionalise their own long-term strategies, and in democratic systems, the long-term holds special challenges. However, overcoming each of the crises currently facing the world requires sustained government action. A fundamental problem with democratic governance is the difficulty in sustaining policies on politically polarised issues – and all of these crises are indeed polarised. On the climate change issue, for example, Democrats and Republicans are completely divided, both in their perceptions of the problem as well as in the solutions they propose. It is therefore necessary to enact bills that will carry long-term policy obligations for successive governments. A solution that works under the Democrats but is stopped again under the Republicans is no solution at all in a politically fluctuating environment. Once policies are in place, they must become shielded from the political pandering of successive governments.

When people are presented with business opportunities and positive investment ideas, they find it easier to act in ways that align their goals with those of the global community.

In many ways, this parallels the difficulties with implementing fiscal and monetary policy in the long term. In Europe, the European Central Bank was initially given a politically determined mandate, but was then insulated from the political tides in a policy space all its own. Similarly, most other global central banks are – to varying degrees – shielded from politics. As post-crisis policymakers discover that past central bank policies require revisions, they will have to find ways not only to temporarily re-politicise and renegotiate these functions, but also to institutionalise and re-insulate whatever new policies are decided.

Governments have a key role to play in mitigating all of these crises, but it cannot be done with ad hoc policies. Instead, policies must, once decided, be insulated from these instabilities. Neither a stable climate nor a stable economy can be achieved with part-time or quick-fix solutions.

INSPIRING CHANGE

The current period is unique in the degree to which these crises have been internationalised. Neither environmental nor economic problems have ever achieved the degree of global recognition that they enjoy today. However, this also means that today's global institutions still do not have the capacities to deal with these crises. Many new arrangements will have to be made in the near future to bring these institutions up to the task of handling such complex challenges.

In the climate change realm, regardless of the Copenhagen 2009 agreements, the biggest challenge will be enforcement of the accords. This happened already after the Kyoto protocol, where many signatories simply ignored their obligations once the conference was over. The EU provides a perfect small-scale illustration of this problem. Although it has proven beneficial for EU members to reach a general agreement on targets and planning to mitigate climate change, it has often occurred that countries simply ignore these agreements later if they cease to align with their national interests.

Similarly, in the economic realm, while it is fantastic that both the left and the right in the EU came together to create a stable currency and sober fiscal policy, it is impossible to push this further without enforcement mechanisms. Nowhere is this structural challenge more apparent than in the implementation of the Lisbon agenda, where the biggest challenge has always been inter-member state enforcement. Outside of the EU, this problem takes on epic proportions. While the EU has at least some disputed level of authority over its member states, the international community has absolutely no common enforcement mechanism.

Because of these difficulties with enforcement, it may be more viable to structure new global policies around incentives rather than threats. In this endeavour, economic policymakers should learn a valuable lesson from the political tribulations of climate-change and energy policymakers to date: stay positive. There is little to be gained by scaring people, and opportunities sell better than warnings. Just as Martin Luther King would have gotten nowhere had he announced, "I have a nightmare....," so too will policymakers fail if they use scare tactics rather than outlining a feasible new vision.

In the climate change arena, policymakers have found that citizens tend to react more proactively to the idea of 'energy security' and 'clean energy' than to the vague yet horrible threat of global warming. When people are presented with business opportunities and positive investment ideas, they find it easier to act in ways that align their goals with those of the global community. Specifically, many emerging economies have been surprisingly quick to shift to growth models based on a future of sustainable energy. China, for example, no longer wallows under the illusion that it can simply copy Western growth models. They and other emerging economies have discovered that they hold an advantage over Western countries: having more recently pulled themselves into the industrial era, they are still more receptive to change.

The response to the current economic crisis should similarly be structured around 'dos' rather than 'don'ts'. As economic institutions are re-imagined, priority should be given to opening up new and socially positive business opportunities that will be profitable in the long term. In coordinating policy action, governments must come to understand that if they do not make short-term investments to allow them to participate in these new and more sustainable opportunities now, they will only be left behind in the future. Businesses, similarly, must be persuaded that participation in sustainable regimes will increase their future competitiveness. Already, emerging economies have proven quicker to adopt more cutting-edge financial policies after the crisis, with the result that they will be whisked ahead, while the West will wither in the quagmire of outdated institutions. This is evidenced by the fact that China has been able to ride out the recession much more successfully than many Western countries.

THINKING OUTSIDE OF THE BOX

Existing societies have been proven unsustainable. In order to survive, they must reform. Therefore, this is a critical moment for the intellectual community. Each of the crises necessitates the development of fundamentally new ideas and concepts; they require new ways of relating citizens to markets, markets to states, and states to their citizens. In terms of environment, intellectuals must rethink what a low-carbon economy really means: claims that we can simply replace one technology with another, for example replacing gas cars with electric cars, are ludicrous. Society will have to undergo a major shift, with people restructuring their daily lives, habits and preferences. It is up to intellectuals to contemplate the knock-on economic impacts that this could have.

Climate change is urgent, and the clock is ticking. Unfortunately, with the addition of the economic crisis to the policy turmoil, these long-term ambitions will have to be developed in conjunction with short-term economic recovery necessities. The idea of a 'climate change New Deal' that would tackle the economic crisis at the same time as the climate change and energy crises is a fantastic example of an innovative idea for this new era. However, this proposal still has glitches. Certainly, government stimulus investments should be used to push for investments in renewable technologies and infrastructure, while trying to bring money back into circulation. But there are wider economic consequences from such investments that should not be overlooked. Most notably, new technologies and infrastructures not only create jobs, but also destroy them. As new sectors emerge, old ones disappear, and this translates into temporary hardship as labour and resources are shifted. Unfortunately, there is still no conclusive analysis of exactly what the employment balance would be from a 'climate change New Deal'. For this reason, while government investments will be critical to building the infrastructure of the new era, they cannot go it alone – creative business people will also be needed to signal lucrative new green industries and entrepreneurial opportunities.

In addition to these large-scare societal reforms, there may be space for more small-scale radical innovation as well. In the social and economic realms, a great deal of both intellectual and practical experimentation is likely to occur in the near future. Just as the post-war period saw a rise in utopian and alternative living arrangements, this crisis period calls for similarly utopian experimentation with financial arrangements. This is not a call for Marxist or revolutionary replacements of capitalism, but rather for small-scale explorations of different community and economic structures.

However, one of the most revolutionary changes is actually surprisingly simple: introducing an alternative measure of growth and prosperity. Focusing on GDP growth exclusively perpetuates environmentally unsustainable and increasingly financially suboptimal policies. Of course, in the post-crisis period everybody is more than ever focused on GDP growth, making such a switch in mentality difficult. However, this may be the best time imaginable for implementing such a reform. Larger indexes reflecting welfare and true development would be better targets for post-crisis recovery than furthering the economic growth that already led to the three crises we are currently entangled in.

Economists for a long time have argued that after a certain level of economic development, growth actually becomes destructive. This concept of over-development can be clearly illustrated by the over-consumption in the US of cars. Personal cars were supposed to be the token icon of freedom and mobility, but instead they are currently producing exactly the opposite, as commuters sit for three hours a day in traffic jams. If we adjusted our economic indicator to welfare indices, our ambitions would change as well, perhaps killing two birds with one stone; not only would models be created whereby the post-crisis low economic growth could be reconciled with increased well-being, but the over-consumption that is pushing greenhouse gas emissions literally through the roof may also be quelled.

The degree to which policy prescriptions correspond for the economic crisis as well as for the climate change and energy crises is truly striking. Yet despite the overlap, reform in these sectors will be no easy task. It will require innovation and experimentation, new methods of coordination, and perhaps even a fundamental reconsideration of societies' goals. However, if international policymakers find the will and cohesion to rise to these challenges, the current era of three-fold crisis may give way to the development of a more sustainable and equitable future.

A Stress Test
for the Welfare State

Tony Atkinson

PROFESSOR OF ECONOMICS,

OXFORD

"Although I certainly cannot claim to have foreseen the current economic crisis, I have long been suspicious of the success stories surrounding the economic performance of the United Kingdom. I have been lecturing for a long time already, especially to mainland European economies, that the economic vigour of the UK was in many ways a mirage. Our external position was, in fact, rather poor due to structural savings deficits, much like in the United States. In addition, I never really bought the idea that the contributions made by the financial sector could be measured as growth. The recorded contributions always seemed exaggerated.

"What particularly worries me now is the effect of the crisis on employment: we seem to be entering a very unemployment-intensive recession. It is paradoxical that, after a decade of relatively jobless growth in Europe, the recession is marked by the shedding of jobs. The employment-generating effect of growth may have been small, but the unemployment-generating effect of recession threatens to be large."

ILLUSORY GROWTH

The crisis has revealed that much of the growth of the last 20 years, both in the UK and elsewhere, was in fact illusory. This is the consequence of the fact that growth was mostly driven by one sector: the financial industry. There were simply few other growth drivers outside of financial innovation and credit creation. Sadly, much of the growth that was created in this sector was simply reinvested in the financial sector, and little of it found its way into the real economy. The national accounts showed households as having increased their use of financial services by 65 percent (to put this in perspective, it is double their increase in health care consumption), but this is purely an imputation. Of course the profits generated by the financial industry did show up as increased incomes, and these went primarily to those at the top of the distribution ladder. People are right to suggest that the pie was not shared evenly, but the larger problem was that there was simply not much pie being baked.

It should not be forgotten that the rapid expansion of the financial sector has deep political roots.

It should not be forgotten that the rapid expansion of the financial sector has deep political roots. In many Western economies, state-owned pension schemes were pared down over the past two decades, with the UK being the most extreme example. This put great pressure on people to make their own financial choices, which partially explains the growth of the new financial instruments that the industry developed. It had to cater to a much larger audience. A similar pattern can be discerned behind the rising housing prices of the last years, as people used real estate as investments for old age. It is striking how rarely people have made the conceptual link between such trends. The financial industry, pensions, and macro-economic trends are all deeply connected and should therefore be treated as such, both in politics and academia.

Fragmentary thinking was also a characteristic of European social policy. The Lisbon Agenda failed to address structural inequalities. This can be explained by its narrow understanding of such issues, suggesting that employment was the cure for all economic ailments. Overall employment rates in Europe have risen by an impressive 8%, but the actual trickle-down effects have been limited. There has been no significant reduction in the proportion of people living at risk of poverty. So while the Lisbon Agenda was successful in improving employment rates, this one indicator alone cannot fully measure success. When judged on the basis of a broader set of criteria, the shortcomings of Europe's dominant paradigm as set out by the Lisbon Agenda are revealed.

Europe's conservative response to the crisis could make these problems even worse. Long-term issues tend to be neglected by many European leaders. There has been an excessive focus on the immediate response, even as the crisis creates potential momentum for structural change. Now would be a good time, for example, to educate voters that tax increases are unavoidable if future problems are to be addressed. In the foreseeable future, living standards in OECD countries are not likely to rise as rapidly as in the past, since additional resources will be largely absorbed by an ageing population and measures aimed at cleaning up the environment. When those costs are deducted, little remains left for consumption.

The crisis, having stunted growth and driven up unemployment, is in many ways a stress test for the welfare states. The crisis is likely to have significant redistributional effects, which in turn are likely to affect social policy. Studying previous episodes of economic downturn reveals that recessions triggered by a financial crisis often result in sharp redistribution from lower and middle incomes to higher incomes. Take the case of Singapore. The percentage share of the top one percent of incomes remained constant for over 30 years, until the Asian financial crisis of 1997, after which it rose significantly. Europe experienced a similar reverse redistribution in the 1980s. This crisis could have similar results. The reason for this is that the very wealthy are the most resilient to economic setbacks; they have both cash and property. In addition, they do not suffer so much from declining stock markets. The principal losers from financial crises are pension funds and other institutional investors, which means the middle and lower classes lose out. There is the risk the welfare state may end up with less egalitarian income distribution as a consequence of the crisis.

> ## There is the risk the welfare state may end up with less egalitarian income as a consequence of the crisis.

Although the crisis may strain many social institutions, it can also have positive consequences. In many of the advanced economies, direct welfare programs and social policies are being reconsidered. The United States under Obama, for example, is pressing for reform of the health care system, and unemployment insurance is being extended. Also, for Europe, the crisis was the final push needed to realise that many member states have serious flaws in their social systems. In this light, politicians could reconsider the old-fashioned idea of an income policy that includes wages, fiscal issues, and social issues in one package. Such a policy would need to be conceived of at the European level. Monetary and fiscal policy are no longer under national control, leaving wage policy as the only tool remaining for national governments, with competitive wage deflation as a result. A European income policy would be an answer to this problem

The debates on income policy should be interwoven with considerations of another crucial social policy: a minimum income for children. As a consequence of the crisis, such a social issue can regain currency in the European political debate. This debate is especially timely now the realisation has come that future generations will not inherit a better and more prosperous world. This creates sympathy for a shift from focusing exclusively on economic growth to creating a model of socio-economic stewardship; that is, trying to ensure future generations are – at least – not worse off. A minimum income for children could be an integral part of this. Although such shifts in political debates are an insufficient basis to herald a *grande rentrée* of the welfare state, they are nevertheless promising signs that long-neglected issues can be once again on the agenda.

Going beyond thoughts of realigning the welfare state, what is most required is a different set of social performance indicators. In fact, the crisis is partially the result of focusing exclusively on economic growth, as measured by the increase in average income and GDP output. According to this yardstick, many Western economies were indeed growing considerably over the last decade. European GDP, for instance, has risen 20 to 25 percent since 1995. However, in a number of countries, median household incomes have risen less rapidly during that same period. This reveals the very uneven distribution of growth. One of the lessons of the crisis is therefore to be very cautious in selecting and weighing indicators for the well-being of the economy. National income may have been a useful indicator for steering economic policy, but by turning it into a monolithic objective, other telling indicators tend to be overlooked. The OECD has already made considerable attempts to design these new indicators by including more socially oriented indicators, such as the output of health care services. Such attempts to formulate a new portfolio of indicators are the beginning of a move towards a more equitable post-crisis world.

FROM THE EUROPEAN TO THE GLOBAL

Whereas the Western countries may be able to solve many of their problems by rethinking welfare state systems, such a solution is insufficient on a global scale. Many of the problems facing the global community – such as climate change and global poverty – are simply too vast in scale and go too far beyond what social policy can achieve. Nevertheless, an analogy can be drawn. As in Europe, many global challenges must be solved collectively. Just as Europe will benefit from co-ordinating its attempts to redesign welfare state systems, many global issues should also be addressed in an integrated manner. The global community needs a package deal just as Europe does.

> ## What is most required is a different set of social performance indicators.

Some signs of regime change can already be identified at the global level. The most significant of these is the move from the highly contested G8 model to the more inclusive G20. This has had promising results. Already, China and the US have taken steps towards coordination that would have been hard to imagine before the crisis. One interesting example is their agreement on increasing Special Drawing Rights. The Americans had refused this for years, and the Chinese seemed to be unlikely candidates to dare to raise such a proposition. However, in the face of the crisis, this issue could suddenly be forced to the foreground. That said, the G20 still excludes many countries that will suffer from the crisis most severely. Many have argued that the direct effect of the crisis on developing economies was going to be minimal, since their economic structures were supposed to be less susceptible to collapse. But as the crisis unfolds, it has become clear that many developing countries will see their incomes through remittances dry up, while at the same being forced to bear the brunt of the consequences of climate change. On top of this, they are likely to suffer from new restrictions pertaining to migration. The question now is how to begin addressing these long-term issues.

The G2 and the Crisis

Amy Chua

PROFESSOR OF LAW,

YALE LAW SCHOOL

"I started questioning the foundation of the economic boom during my time on Wall Street in the 1990s. Most Wall Street investment bankers and lawyers worked hard and were extremely knowledgeable. Remarkably, however, there were also some on Wall Street who seemed less skilled but were still able to become multi-millionaires. People were able to make 40 million dollars in less than two years. There were also suspiciously successful financial instruments. It is now known that many people buying and selling derivatives during this period did not understand them or appreciate their risk. There was too much 'easy money', as they say.

"Various mechanisms were at work leading up to the economic crisis. Some were certainly less benign than others. One dangerous phenomenon was the soulless consumerism in the United States, illustrated by the ubiquity of identical brain-numbing shopping malls, filled with people buying things they could not afford. This, combined with perilous borrowing schemes and the United States' increasing debt to China, led to huge financial problems. One might hope that the crisis would bring about bring a shift in the American mentality and that society would move away from the idea of easy money. Arguably, the idea of credit is a testament to the US's optimism and faith in a more prosperous future. In America, credit is leverage that earns money, as well as justifies borrowing money. While this may be good promoting for risk-taking and allowing hard work to reap great rewards, there are unfortunately many sectors of American society which rely on credit too heavily."

THE UNLIKELIHOOD OF REDISTRIBUTION AND REGULATION

The economic crisis that began in the United States has spread globally. However, as the world's previously unrivalled economic superpower, the US is still in many ways seen as being at the centre of the current crisis. Many still look to the United States for indications of change or reform. However, the US has a distinctive historical tradition with a specific value system that makes many dramatic types of reform quite unlikely.

For example, although the crisis has brought to light the gross inequalities in American income distribution, this has sparked only limited public outrage. Recent Gini-coefficient readings have been closer to those in the early 20th century than to those in the 1950s and 1960s, when citizens were benefiting from New Deal prosperity. This indicates the return to a dramatically skewed wealth distribution system. Yet contrary to the diagnoses made abroad, many Americans do not see people such as Bill Gates or Warren Buffet as symptoms of a flawed system. Instead, they look to them with respect and aspire to obtain the same position one day. Of course, some class antagonism is inevitable: the financial crisis has certainly triggered resentment against 'greedy' Wall Street Bankers and 'overpaid' CEOs. However, this antagonism is still nowhere near as strong as the general American feeling of respect for the well-to-do.

> *Although the crisis has brought to light the gross inequalities in American income distribution, this has sparked only limited public outrage.*

In addition, because of the way political cleavages are arranged, the poor in the US are insufficiently unified to pressure their governments for redistributive reforms. To the contrary, a large proportion of lower-income whites in the US votes Republican and strongly opposes income redistribution. Why is this the case? There are two reasons. First, the ideological power of the American Dream, which says that hard work, not handouts, is the key to success still holds great power. But second, racial cleavages are stronger sources of political identity than are class cleavages. Poor white Americans are more likely to identify with figures like Bill Gates and Warren Buffett than they are with the poor in the ethnic minority communities. This precludes the formation of political groups – such as labour unions – that would have sufficient strength to overcome the institutional hurdles to reform. Black and white labourers have been at odds for so long that even the current crisis, and the dramatic rise in unemployment that resulted from it, will be insufficient to instigate a realignment of their political aims.

Finally, it should be remembered that despite the global nature of the crisis, the US government is focusing on fixing American problems first. Obama has recruited some of the brightest thinkers to lead the way out of the crisis. Yet despite their various internal divisions, they remain largely domestically oriented. There is a danger that not just the US governments but European and other governments will adopt inward-looking, protectionist policies in response to a crisis that is global in nature and that requires global coordination.

Surprisingly, there has been a notable lack of popular backlash or gloom in the US since the crisis. Americans seem to have great faith in Obama's capacities and still hold true to the fundamental belief that sometimes things must get worse before they can get better. In this optimism, they continue to hold true to their very American ideals.

AMBIVALENCE TOWARDS EUROPE

Many US economists and policymakers have argued that the structure of the European Union has actually made it harder for them to respond to the crisis. The United States has traditionally been quite open to absorbing external influences, and this strategic tolerance has served it well. Yet although the country is currently examining the workings of many European social programs, it is highly unlikely that the US would ever embrace such models.

Most notably, there have been many calls for more regulation and more government spending since the economic crisis. Small government has traditionally been one element that set America apart from Europe. However, the extent to which this reveals a true change in institutional direction remains to be seen. Reagan's legacy of deregulation – which was a clear departure from the New Deal – is currently evaporating as increased regulation gains more support, and this marks a clear change. However, the pendulum ought not to swing from one extreme to the other, as over-regulation is not the answer and may only incite over-*de*-regulation in the future.

> ### Even during this crisis, millions of dollars are still being donated to the New York City Ballet, the Metropolitan Museum or universities.

It is true, for example, that Obama's health care plans are similar to European systems. However, a very different ideology underlies the American plans. Most significant is the reluctance in America about creating handouts. Americans do not aspire to become a welfare state, but rather to live in a society in which talent and hard work will ensure that one can provide for one's family without having to rely on the government. Although they may want to ensure that all citizens receive some basic form of coverage, American citizens would be uncomfortable with health care that is as redistributive as the European systems are.

A second trend is that even Republicans are becoming increasingly in favour of regulation. However, there are several strands of Republicans. The big-business Republicans are generally in favour of immigration and are socially progressive. This contrasts with those who are typically in favour of more religion in schools, shutting down immigration, etc. These 'family values' Republicans are often among those who have expressed outrage at the behaviour of the rich Wall Street lawyers and bankers, calling for more regulation. However, this contrasts with the distinctively American (and specifically Republican) distrust of big government.

In addition, despite the steadily expanding role of government since the crisis, President Obama has been unsurprisingly cautious about bringing up the issue of tax increases. If he had said he intended to raise taxes, regardless of the purpose, there is no way he could have won the election. Instead, he promised more social services, and it was the Europeans who expected a corresponding tax hike. In the US it is still maddeningly unclear how people expect these new social programs to be financed.

Finally, despite the controversies that have emerged over the past months about executive compensation and bonuses, President Obama has still continued to voice support for a system of awards based on merit. This reflects the very American ideal of meritocracy, which is rooted deeply in American cultural identity. Americans believe in upward mobility and do not reject an economically stratified society as long as they think the wealth is fairly earned.

Such a mindset essentially bars the prospect of any major departure from the status quo in the US. Interestingly, many of the new reforms are described as public-*private* partnerships, with Obama carefully including the word 'private' so as to avoid triggering fears of big government or the replacement of the treasured meritocratic system with European egalitarian systems. Of course, Americans will want to halt corruption they believe is endemic to Wall Street, but they will prefer seeing dividends of wealth being returned to the community or country voluntarily, through philanthropic channels rather than through government channels. To their credit, this has continued to happen. Even during this crisis, millions of dollars are still being donated to the New York City Ballet, the Metropolitan Museum or universities.

WHAT ABOUT CHINA?

Progressive and liberal thinkers hope for a European and American Union, but there is also the possibility of a G2 emerging in the form of an America-Chinese alliance. Fifty years from now, people may look back and say that the hegemony of the US caused its own decline, and that with the economic crisis the power shifted to China. However, this is an unlikely scenario. Despite its successes and its rise in the global arena, China's ascendance should not be overestimated. China is in many ways still a developing country. In addition, even a Chinese citizen would be forced to admit that the 'empowerment of the masses' probably only applies to roughly 10% of the population. It is also questionable to what extent the population really favours democracy; most Chinese prefer slow and gradual transition.

Internal divisions around class lines within China may impinge on their future global success. China is very concerned that unemployment resulting from the financial crisis will spur widespread social unrest. In the face of this current source of instability, the Chinese government has harnessed Chinese nationalism in an extremely effective way. Using nationalist rhetoric, the government has managed to paint democracy and human rights as impositions from the West.

Internal divisions around class lines within China may impinge on their future global success.

Finally, whereas the US benefits enormously from its reputation of being a land of immigrants and opportunities, China is a quintessentially ethnically defined nation, and therefore is not in a position to attract the world's most talented and enterprising. This puts China at a disadvantage when it comes to technological innovation. There are far more Chinese people trying to obtain US citizenship than Americans trying to enter China. This gives the US a structural advantage over China that it is unlikely to lose, even with the crisis.

China also has to deal carefully with its southeast Asian neighbours. In Indonesia, for example, the Chinese minority – constituting 3% of the population – controls as much as 70% of the economy. Whenever a poor majority believes that an ethnic minority controls all the wealth, there is typically majority-based ethnic resentment and risks of confiscation, anti-market backlash, and even violence directed against the wealthy minority. With the recent financial crisis, unemployment has risen dramatically in Indonesia. If the economy does not improve, there is a risk of backlash and violence against the Indonesian Chinese, similar to what occurred in 1998. All this puts the Chinese government in a perilous diplomatic situation.

AN AMERICAN FUTURE

The crisis struck at the heart of modern capitalism: the United States. As a result, it placed the US in a unique position. The US was both held responsible for the crisis as well as called upon to end it. In searching for a solution, the international community must remember that any solution originating in America will carry distinctly American qualities. In the US, the ideologies of upward mobility and self-reliance have deep roots. Because of the robustness of the American Dream, even poorer Americans will not support the idea of entrepreneurial success being taxed too heavily as they risk being taxed themselves should they become rich. More importantly, Americans will strongly resist any unwarranted government seizure of private wealth. The rest of the world should bear these cultural eccentricities in mind before relying too heavily on any American-born solution.

PART 5

REALIGNING EUROPE

As an integrated political economy, it is to be expected that the global economic crisis also affects core EU institutions. This particularly applies to the ECB and Eurozone group, bound together by a single currency.

The concluding part of the volume focuses entirely on the ramifications of the crisis in Europe, the EU, and its member states. The interviewees range from fearful to hopeful. European coordination and intervention may have mitigated the initial blow of the crisis; however, at the same time, the crisis did reveal a fair number of shortcomings in the EU edifice. Moreover, the crisis could easily delay European cooperation and solidarity, acutely required to address the aftermath of the crisis.

Loukas Tsoukalis's contribution identifies clear deficits in European economic governance. He also draws attention to the incipient crisis predicament in Europe's newest member states. He concludes by delineating the contours of a new European contract in the face of the crisis.

Fritz Scharpf asserts that Europe has a deeply ingrained neo-liberal bias that impedes an effective and legitimate European response to the crisis. Whether Europe can indeed pull itself up by its bootstraps depends ultimately on whether the European Union is able to broaden the current narrow trajectory of European integration as a liberalisation project.

A European political economic strategy was already in place before the crisis. Since the year 2000, the Lisbon Agenda was Europe's roadmap towards a globally competitive economy. Maria João Rodrigues, who was heavily involved in the development of the Lisbon Agenda over the past decade, reviews the successes and failures of the Lisbon Agenda while also suggesting new policy departures.

The final section concludes with two interviewees who have both played a vital role in shaping the European Union as we know it. Former Chancellor of the Federal Republic of Germany, Helmut Schmidt, emphasises the extent to which Europe's problems are essentially political rather than institutional. Advancing the European project is first and foremost an issue of political leadership and vision, something, severely lacking in present-day Europe, Schmidt argues. Former president of the European Commission, Jacques Delors, adds that the spirit of cooperation seems to have subsided in the EU of 27 member states, which can largely be attributed to the inevitable historical sequence of eastward enlargement overtaking policy deepening. However, Delors ends on a positive note, concluding that the crisis presents unprecedented opportunities to formulate new indications of national, European and global well-being.

A New European Contract

Loukas Tsoukalis

PROFESSOR OF EUROPEAN ECONOMIC ORGANISATION,

UNIVERSITY OF ATHENS

"Over the course of the current crisis, I have often been reminded of the ideas of my mentor in International Political Economy: Susan Strange. In 1986, she published a book titled Casino Capitalism *in which she described the main features of a financial system that had gone out of control. They were unorthodox views at the time; indeed, until the big crisis hit us, very few people were prepared to listen to such views. Economic orthodoxy was extremely intolerant of any kind of heresy.*

"I was never a believer in unregulated financial markets and always took a critical stance towards the kind of deregulation we have experienced for more than 20 years. During that time, the international economic system was piloted by an ideology made in the USA, to which the British contributed a fair bit. It would be a mistake, however, to point to these two countries as the sole culprits. Continental European countries may have been sceptical or hesitant at first, but when the music started playing, they allowed their banks to dance to the prevailing tune. Never did they set the tune themselves.

"Financial markets that ran amok, while recycling the huge current account surpluses of China and others, were things that should have worried all those paid to worry about the stability of the financial system. Yet, the overwhelming majority of financial observers were carried away by the prevailing euphoria. True, dissenting voices became louder as more people began to realise the extent of the problem in the US subprime market; but it was too late then."

A TRIPLE FAILURE

The financial crisis that erupted in 2007 and quickly developed into a full-scale economic crisis has laid bare three colossal failures: the failure of the economics profession, the failure of markets and the failure of politics. Of course a failing market is in itself nothing spectacularly new, but it has been forgotten that booms and busts appear to be an inherent feature of financial markets. For years, the economics profession was dominated by hypotheses of efficient markets, rational choice and perfect information. These were the key elements of an economic theory that purported to explain the functioning of our economic system, and the financial system in particular. Deregulation and state abstinence followed naturally.

During the last two decades and more, economics was the discipline that attracted some of the best minds from all over the world. Economists produced ever more sophisticated models of market behaviour, exported their models to the rest of the social sciences, and also managed to convince many members of the political class and the media of the truth they propagated. They set the terms of the public debate and showed little tolerance for dissenting voices. It is staggering how in a pluralistic system, one intellectual fashion can push aside all others.

It is staggering how in a pluralistic system, one intellectual fashion can push aside all others.

At the political level, the failure is no less spectacular. The neo-liberal ideology, especially as applied to financial markets, became the official orthodoxy, and a large part of the political class in our Western democracies bought into it, admittedly more so in the Anglo-American world than in other countries. Politicians simply followed the prevailing spirit of the times. Keynes had already explained rather convincingly how politicians become slaves of defunct economists. Alas, the problem goes deeper and should be a cause for concern regarding the functioning of our democratic systems. Liberalisation and deregulation led to large (albeit temporary) profits in the financial sector, which grew in size and wealth, consequently also in lobbying power. In simple words, money bought influence, which in turn helped to strengthen and perpetuate the prevailing ideology. Politics, in some countries, was thus taken hostage by financial interests. It is the combination of failures in economics, politics, and markets that makes this crisis so extraordinary.

EUROPE'S CRISIS OF ECONOMIC GOVERNANCE

Europe as a whole did not have large current account imbalances vis-à-vis the rest of the world – not like the United States which acted as consumer of last resort, largely through borrowing. Of course, individual European countries did run large surpluses or deficits, but these mostly cancelled each other out. Once the financial crisis broke out however, it became clear that many European banks were highly leveraged. Moreover, since they had bought large quantities of securitised

US mortgages and other toxic assets, it was not difficult for a crisis that had begun in the US to contaminate Europe. Presumably, regulatory authorities had been looking the other way for so long – or simply had not realised what was going on. If British regulators were acting in a manner consistent with the prevailing ideology and official policy, what exactly were German – and other – regulators doing, if anything at all?

Although the crisis has hit the whole of Europe, individual countries have been affected in different ways. Ireland and Spain, for example, struggle with the dire consequences of a housing bubble that has burst. Germany, on the other hand, being Europe's biggest exporter, has been affected more than others from the decline in global demand. Some of the new member states face different predicaments: they are struggling to survive with very high levels of private debt denominated in foreign currencies and the withdrawal of foreign funds. The crisis is surely a European problem that needs to be tackled collectively, but there are also many different national problems that tempt policymakers to *sauve qui peut* responses. European coordination and solidarity in the face of the crisis are therefore far from automatic or spontaneous.

Luckily, Europe soon found itself near the precipice, and as they realised what was at stake in terms of the survival of the single market and the euro, it stepped back. The coordination reflex then took over, and the worst was avoided. This is the good news in the midst of a deep crisis that has brought negative growth rates almost everywhere in Europe – some countries are in fact experiencing reductions in output of around 20% over the course of 2009. We have not yet hit rock bottom: unemployment effects normally follow with a time lag. This could result in more protectionism, as unemployment rises and politicians begin to feel the pressure at home. Already, state-administered aids are often riddled with protectionist specifications. Luckily, the Commission is putting up a real fight to preserve the single market, and with considerable success until now.

The European Central Bank as well has gained respect and admiration for the way it has handled the crisis. Although initially slow to respond, it subsequently rose to the challenge, providing much needed liquidity to cash-strapped banks, with a presence that extends beyond the euro area. In addition, the single currency has proven its usefulness and resilience in times of crisis; it is the euro that made the crucial difference for the more vulnerable members, such as Ireland and Greece, providing them with an effective shield against speculative attacks.

The bad news is that European governance structures have proven to be unfit for their purpose. They do not match the level of integration reached by markets. This is particularly true with respect to the monetary union. The system set up by the Treaty of Maastricht is both weak and unbalanced. Admittedly, that was all that was politically feasible at the time, and perhaps also adequate under fair weather conditions. But no longer. A currency union with loose fiscal coordination and a weak political base defies the historical laws of gravity. The ECB has undoubtedly played a very important role, but it is not enough. Questions of banking supervision and regulation in an integrated market now figure prominently on the agenda, and so should broader questions of economic governance.

Raising the issue of further fiscal and political-economic integration immediately precipitates the following question: What would a more effective system of European economic governance look like? Immediately, more specific questions follow. How will Europe go about trying to reconcile economic necessity with political feasibility? Can national governments realistically be expected to submit themselves to constraints imposed by European institutions with respect to budgetary policy, especially if those constraints were to be adopted by majority decision? In short, the question is whether Europe is politically ready for the fiscal (and other) consequences of monetary union. Such questions form the starting point for a new episode of European integration.

A necessary, though insufficient, condition for more effective economic governance of the euro area will be the convergence of perceptions and interests of the two main actors, namely Germany and France, on a wide range of issues, from fiscal reflation to the role of common institutions for the management of the euro. Other countries, such as the Netherlands, can play an important role as catalysts. These puzzles surrounding further integration are, in fact, a repetition of a familiar story. The entire process of European integration so far has been a succession of dynamic disequilibria. Europe has moved forward constantly by repairing deficiencies in its architecture, which in turn cause their own problems and over time prove insufficient. This is by no means an automatic process, as we have learned from the experience of the last 60 years of European integration. The crisis provides a big opportunity to move forward; the euro can be indeed a major force of integration.

THE PREDICAMENT OF NEW EUROPEAN MEMBER STATES

The crisis has highlighted the strengths and vulnerabilities of the growth strategy adopted by the new member states of the EU. For years, the new members enjoyed high rates of economic growth, accompanied by a radical reorientation of trade and investment patterns. Membership in the EU served as a strong external anchor for domestic reforms and for boosting their credibility in relation to foreign investors and creditors. Economic success reinforced their belief in free markets, which sometimes verged on market fundamentalism among those who had long suffered under the Soviet system. Lecturing on the virtues of free markets by politicians from new member states, who had hardly any good words to say about the inflexible and costly (as they perceived them) social models of 'old Europe', was not that uncommon in European Councils in the years preceding the crisis.

The bad news is that European governance structures have proven to be unfit for their purpose.

Things are different now. Some of the new member states are experiencing a dramatic decline in output as asset bubbles, previously financed through foreign borrowing, burst; foreign funds are being withdrawn, and demand for exports is sinking. Old beliefs are hence shattered as the economic situation deteriorates rapidly, with social and political consequences that are only now beginning to unfold. Many of the new member states had thought that with free and efficient markets it made no difference whether your banks were controlled by Estonians, Swedes, or Martians, as long as they behave as rational economic actors. But when foreign governments were forced to intervene in order to save banks at home, subsidiaries in the new member states risked a disproportionately large drain on funds. After all, when it comes to bailouts, taxpayer money dictates the priorities of a bank. The worst has luckily been avoided so far, while people have begun to learn hard lessons of *Realpolitik* in the midst of the economic crisis.

In cooperation with international institutions, the EU will need to do more in support of its more vulnerable members, as well as other European countries on the outer periphery. The stakes will become very high indeed, especially if economic recovery proves slow and weak. Social and political instability could easily follow in some of the new member states, risking a reversal of progress that had been so copiously achieved during the transition. In particular, in countries with high rates of unemployment, continuation of current trends could lead to major social and political instability. All this said, the economic reality varies significantly from one country to another. The economic situation in Poland is very different from that in Hungary or Bulgaria, the Czechs have been spared the kind of economic ordeal that the Baltics are currently going through. There is, in short, no common story for the 12 new member states, and the way the economic and financial crisis has affected them.

THE LIMITS OF EUROPEAN INTEGRATION

The predicaments outlined above can enforce a more inclusive and comprehensive European contract. Taxation is likely to figure more prominently on the agenda, despite objections by certain member states. As public debts are growing and national states are forced to seek new sources of funding more actively, taxation can no longer remain out of bounds in the context of the single market and the single currency. The elimination of economic borders and the growing mobility of goods, services, people and capital have led to stronger competition among national exchequers, with tax rates being pushed downwards in the process. It is particularly true for capital, the most mobile resource of all. This does not, of course, provide Brussels with a *carte blanche* to dictate tax rates on capital – we are very far from that. The target we should be aiming for is a European agreement on minimum tax rates.

In cooperation with international institutions, the EU will need to do more in support of its more vulnerable members.

A new European contract should also include a more comprehensive social dimension. As the division between winners and losers within countries is becoming more pronounced, Europe can no longer remain essentially the liberalisation project it has been thus far. This said, social and welfare policies will continue to be among the main prerogatives of the nation-state. This is inevitable, as diversity within the 27 European member states is indeed very wide. Levels of economic and social development, for instance, differ enormously, as do institutions and national preferences. This diversity sets narrow limits on what can be done jointly at the European level. The role of the EU lies in delivering complementary measures to those adopted by member states. The European globalisation adjustment fund is a good example of a common instrument aimed at those who stand to lose from international competition. But this should be more than a symbolic gesture, as it has been so far. A more direct link should also be established with economic reform and the Lisbon agenda.

In addition, a new European contract should include policies on energy and climate change in a combined package. Experience teaches us that this is easier said than done, though. Energy is directly linked to high politics, and European institutions have never felt very comfortable in that game. Difficult decisions will need to be taken, and some will be costly, especially when it comes to measures to deal with global warming. On the other hand, a European agreement on energy will have to include the creation of a true internal market, solidarity among members and a common external policy that aims to reap the benefits of size and unity. Individual members need to be persuaded that a European policy will deliver better results for them; preaching will simply not do.

This is, of course, far from a comprehensive list of items that should form part of a new European contract. The crisis may act as a catalyst: the need to safeguard the single market, and even more so the euro, in a very different, and indeed adverse, economic environment is likely to shape the European agenda in the months and years to come. The prospects are not necessarily bright. Europe may have indeed reached the limits of its integration potential. A partial unravelling of its *acquis* cannot be excluded, even though the costs of such an unravelling would be high. It is also possible that the euro will prove to be the most powerful force keeping European countries together – and not necessarily all of them.

Europe's Neo-liberal Bias

Fritz Scharpf

DIRECTOR EMERITUS,

MAX PLANCK INSTITUTE FOR THE STUDY OF SOCIETIES

"I first began to worry about the financial sector when, in early 2007, I learned that it was now common for banks to rely entirely on rating agencies, rather than on personal judgment, when assessing credit risks, and that these ratings were automatically generated by mathematical models analysing performance over the preceding five years. Hence, when it became known that the American housing market was in trouble, I expected problems in the American banking system, but I was not aware of the extent to which these risks had been diffused throughout the global financial system."

BEYOND ECONOMIC AUTARKY

Policy responses to the current economic crisis have clearly benefitted from lessons learned from the past. In contrast to the crisis of the 1970s, the present one had its origin in the financial system, rather than in the real economy. Whereas the financial crisis of the early 1930s was driven into a worldwide depression by government policies of fiscal and monetary retrenchment, modern governments have generally adopted policies of monetary and fiscal reflation, and they have intervened directly to bail out faltering banks and to save important industrial firms. As a consequence, the economic decline is unlikely to be as deep as it was in the Great Depression.

It is doubtful whether the experience of the 1930s will provide much guidance for present policymakers. It suggests that recovery from the Great Depression was not achieved through international coordination, but through a radical re-nationalisation of economic policy. All countries imposed rigid controls on capital movement and currency exchange, and regulated their international trade. Nazi Germany implemented a regime of near-total autarky, and others, including Sweden, the United Kingdom, and the United States, adopted highly protectionist barriers to trade. As a consequence, the capitalist world market disintegrated, and it was only slowly re-created under the Bretton Woods regime and through a series of GATT negotiations in the post-war decades. During this period of embedded liberalism, stability-oriented (Keynesian) macro-economic policies, growth-oriented industrial policies, and egalitarian welfare-state policies could be developed and effectively implemented within the controlled boundaries of the nation-state.

With the economic shocks of the 1970s, this system began to erode. Markets became increasingly open, and by the 1990s, nearly all countries had ceased to regulate capital movements. Moreover, with the fall of the Iron Curtain, Eastern Europe and China, with their skilled and low-paid labour forces, joined the world market, providing new investment opportunities and greatly intensified competition in the markets for goods and services. Economically, globalisation was very successful, but in the advanced economies it also challenged the social cohesion that had been achieved in the period of embedded liberalism.

> *Compared to the 1930s, it is clear that international economic interdependence has progressed too far to make protectionism – let alone autarky – a viable option.*

What lessons can be learned from this experience? Compared to the 1930s, it is clear that international economic interdependence has progressed too far to make protectionism – let alone autarky – a viable option. At the same time, however, the present crisis demonstrates the extreme vulnerability of a world economy without national boundaries and with completely deregulated capital markets. Although the economic crisis is a global problem requiring globally coordinated solutions, the internationally harmonised regulatory standards need to be adopted and effectively implemented by nation-states. However, the regulatory efforts of individual states are easily avoided by capital flight, and they are likely to be undermined by regulatory competition among the states themselves. In other words, even internationally coordinated solutions depend for their effectiveness on the re-establishment of economic boundaries that would allow some control over capital movements and some re-embedding of capital markets. This is true for the global economy as well as for the European Union.

THE LIBERALISING TRAJECTORY OF THE EUROPEAN UNION

Compared to the economic pressures of globalising markets, the EU has been a much stronger liberalising force in its member states. This is due to fact that European law has progressively enforced negative integration and deregulation, and these rules are virtually irreversible even if political preferences, economic conditions, or social needs should change. Both the liberalising tendency and the irreversibility of European law are caused by two basic institutional conditions. On the one hand, the European Court of Justice (ECJ) has assumed responsibility for promoting European integration through its interpretation of the treaties. On the other hand, the high consensus requirements of political decisions make it nearly impossible for policymakers to correct decisions made by the ECJ.

In the Treaty of Rome, the member states agreed to create a common European market. Originally, however, this was understood as a political commitment, whose realisation was negotiated at every juncture by politicians. Yet in the crisis of the 1970s, political agreement on further integration became more difficult, whereas the ECJ was now able to remove national barriers to trade by re-interpreting the Treaty commitments as directly enforceable 'economic liberties' of individuals and firms. This 'Integration through Law' was widely welcomed by 'good Europeans' in all political camps. It also had a powerful liberal bias which was in line with the neo-liberal intellectual climate of the 1980s.

But the ECJ's reasoning is structural, rather than ideological. Given its reliance on the enforcement of individual rights, the Court's decisions can only remove national regulations. The effect is negative integration and deregulation. Since only private parties with a strong interest in removing national regulations can reach the Court through the referral procedures, the Court is continuously faced with demands to extend the definitions of Treaty-based individual rights (including non-economic rights of non-discrimination). By contrast, the interests of those groups that benefit from existing national laws and institutions cannot get a hearing before the Court. Thus, the values of democratic self-determination in the national political community are lost in the process of 'Integration through Law'.

At the same time, the decisions of the ECJ are more immune to political corrections than the decisions of any national constitutional court. If they are based on an interpretation of the treaties, they can only be reversed by an amendment that must be adopted unanimously and ratified by all 27 member states. The obstacles are not much lower when the decision is based on an interpretation of European legislation; in these cases, correction requires an initiative by the Commission, qualified majorities in the Council, and an absolute majority in the European Parliament. For the same reasons, attempts to replace the national regimes that were deregulated by the Court through European legislation are easily blocked by member states that benefit from regulatory and tax competition. As a consequence, European legislation will forever have a liberalising bias.

The fiscal response to the economic crisis was weaker in Europe than it was in the US. This was the result of both positive and negative characteristics of the EU and its member states. On the positive side, member states in Continental Europe and Scandinavia have much more comprehensive automatic stabilisers than does the US or even the UK. These mitigated the decline of aggregate demand. At the same time, available instruments of labour market policy could be used to prevent or delay the rise of unemployment, and existing welfare-state institutions could provide a degree of protection for individuals and families. In other words, anticipated political pressures may have appeared less dramatic in Europe than in the United States.

However, the more limited macro-economic response in Europe was also the result of institutional deficiencies. In spite of the progress of European economic integration, the response to the global crisis was left to EU member states. But many member states simply did not have the resources to implement extensive recovery packages, as they were already too deeply in debt. One reason is that the European Monetary Union has severely reduced the capacity of its member states for macro-economic management. Of its four main instruments – monetary policy, exchange-rate policy, fiscal policy and wage policy – the first two have been taken over by the European Central Bank (ECB). They are, of course, exercised without regard to the specific economic conditions of an individual member state. At the same time, national fiscal policy is constrained by the deficit rules of the stability pact. Finally, countries differ greatly with regard to the institutional capacity of unions to achieve wage settings that do not violate macro-economic constraints. Where that capacity was lacking, member states were in trouble even before they were hit by the international crisis.

European legislation will forever have a liberalising bias.

However, while some countries were simply unable to resort to fiscal reflation in response to the crisis, all of them also faced a severe coordination problem. Given the global scope of the crisis, all European countries could be described as small open economies. Even relatively larger states – such as Germany and France – had reason to fear that the positive effects of national stimulus packages might end up far from home, and thus they tried to design programs that maximised the chances of local effectiveness, rather than focusing on the speedy effect of increasing global – or at least Europe-wide – aggregate demand. In other words, the crisis has demonstrated a fundamental deficiency of the European Monetary

Union. Its institutional machinery for macro-economic management is asymmetrically designed to serve only the purposes of price stability and fiscal sustainability. The problems it is meant to guard against are those of the inflationary pressures of the 1970s and early 1980s, whereas the problems of a deflationary crisis have been totally ignored. As a result, the Monetary Union lacks the institutional infrastructure, the policy concepts, and the procedural routines that would have been necessary to achieve the co-ordinated monetary and fiscal reflation of European economies that might have had a strong impact on the worldwide crisis.

THE CASE OF INSTITUTIONAL REFORM

Regardless of the policies implemented, all EU states will emerge from the current crisis with enormously increased public debt. Because the EU treaties ruled out the possibility of the ECB providing credit to governments, this debt is owed to private capital owners. If it must be repaid through higher taxes on consumption and wages and through cuts in social transfers and social services, the effect will be an unprecedented upward re-distribution, with potentially worrying repercussions for national and European politics.

Although it is too late to be of help in the present crisis, the EU ought to consider reforming its rules for the ECB. In the face of a sudden and massive decline of aggregate demand and fully functional production capacities, the direct financing of effective fiscal regulation through central bank loans would not have inflationary effects. At the same time, it could avoid the negative redistribution effects of budget deficits financed on the capital markets. Hence, the rules prohibiting providing central bank credit to governments ought to be modified. However, loosening the tight constraints that European law imposes on the national taxation of mobile capital is of even more immediate practical importance. The rules protecting free capital movements and the right of establishment against any national impediments have both created opportunities for tax avoidance and tax arbitrage which allow firms and individual capital owners to reduce the 'tax price' of the local infrastructure which they use. At the same time, these rules have created conditions of tax competition among member states, which small economies can win. The losers, however, are forced to shift the tax burden increasingly onto immobile tax bases: consumption, wages, and real estate. Therefore, what would be needed is a relaxation of the rules protecting capital mobility and renewed efforts to overcome incentives to tax competition through harmonised EU rules on capital taxation.

In addition, globalisation has created enormous international imbalances where credit-financed consumption in the United States stimulated the growth of industrial exports from China, Japan, and Europe, whose surpluses were then recycled back to America. After the crisis, this relationship cannot be re-established. If the United States is not able to play the role of the universal consumer any longer, China as well as European export-oriented economies will no longer be able to rely mainly on industrial exports to drive their economies. In Europe, this will mean that domestic employment will need to be shifted to services that are locally produced and locally consumed. Here, the potential growth industries will be health care, child care, care for the aged and, above all, education and training. On the face of it, there isn't much that the EU can do to directly promote this necessary transformation. Nevertheless, it could assist in learning processes through its 'Open Method of Coordination' and the Lisbon Process. It could also target structural and cohesion funds to support the growth of these services (rather than focusing on the construction of luxurious highways in depopulated rural areas of old and new accession states). Moreover, European law constraints on the organisation of social and infrastructure services in member states ought to be removed.

What matters most is that European politics must assert the power to break the legal stranglehold of outdated and dangerous neo-liberal dogmas.

This last point suggests that more far-reaching and challenging institutional reforms will be essential for the future viability of the EU. These reforms must correct the fundamental institutional asymmetries in EU governance that have favoured the enactment of neo-liberal ideals and continue to protect them against political challenge. The economic crisis brought to light the vulnerability of a regime of totally liberalised markets. This realisation has created a window of political opportunity in which it may be possible for European leaders to achieve the consensus necessary for reforming the fundamentals of the system. Specifically, it would be necessary to establish political limits on 'Integration through Law' and on the ECJ's power to enforce ever-wider definitions of economic liberties that constrain the policy choices of member states and of European legislation alike.

Since substantive Treaty amendments to protect national autonomy have proven ineffective in the past, and since European legislation that tried to achieve similar purposes has been reinterpreted to conform to the Court's most liberal definition of Treaty-based liberties, it follows that a procedural solution is required. One possibility would be to allow member governments to appeal to the judgment of their peers in the European Council when they see their autonomy violated by ECJ decisions that stretch the intended meaning of Treaty clauses or of European legislation. If supported by a majority of the Council, the decisions would be affirmed. If not, the challenged national solution would be allowed to continue.

Perhaps better solutions could be found. What matters most is that European politics must assert the power to break the legal stranglehold of outdated and dangerous neo-liberal dogmas. 'Integration through Law' may have been a useful stratagem to bypass political obstacles in the early phase of European integration. In the meantime, economic integration has attained a degree of perfectionism that far exceeds the ambitions of established federations like the United States, Canada or Switzerland. At the same time, judicial legislation has continued to expand without political constraints, and its consolidated *acquis* is suffocating the processes of democratic self-determination at national and European levels. This is a dangerous state of affairs, which ought to be corrected.

Beyond Lisbon

Maria João Rodrigues

PROFESSOR OF EUROPEAN ECONOMIC POLICIES,

INSTITUTE FOR STRATEGIC AND INTERNATIONAL STUDIES, LISBON

"I first had strong concerns about a pending economic crisis in 2007 when I was advisor to the Portuguese presidency of the European Union. Within my network of experts on European policy matters, concerns about global economic imbalances, in particular between the American and Chinese economy, were widely shared. Then all of a sudden we saw the rising problems in the financial markets around toxic assets, for which we prepared the European Council.

"Although within the Economic and Financial Council (which includes all economics and finance ministers of the European member states) some were very worried about these emerging trends; there seemed to exist a division of opinions. Some of its members were convinced this was a fleeting occurrence, that it would be overcome very soon; therefore, we were to avoid dramatising it. Others claimed that the problems ran deeper and that measures had to be taken. Little result came from the Council, however; the only adopted proposal was the roadmap designed by Ecofin, which consisted of some steps to increase the monitoring system. It does not amount to much compared to the type of measures Ecofin or the G20 are discussing today."

CRISIS REVIEW AND RESPONSE

As is becoming increasingly clear, the current crisis is a systemic crisis much like the crisis of the 1930s. Its origins lie in a particular breed of short-term capitalism based on shareholder value. This yardstick became dominant in all key areas of economic decision-making, from financial decisions to creating jobs. Although this analysis particularly applies to the so-called Anglo-Saxon type of capitalism, a similar trend could be identified in Continental, Southern, and Nordic models.

A systemic crisis demands a sustainable, systematic response, which means both direct and structural reforms. These reforms should not only apply to the financial system or to corporate governance, but also to areas that are traditionally not associated with this crisis, such as public services, and the social protection and education systems; in other words, a larger agenda for reform is necessary.

We could seize upon the crisis as an opportunity of creative destruction, to create new capacities to invest in new areas, new companies, and new jobs and in such a way that they become more sustainable for the future.

FINANCIAL

It is clear that Europe is responding at a slower pace and less aggressively than the US, which could bring one to say Europe is behind in formulating an adequate response. However, Anglo-Saxon capitalism demands a quicker and tougher response. First, these countries need to control the turmoil in their financial and banking system. Secondly, they require a stronger stimulus package to counteract the recession.

We could seize upon the crisis as an opportunity of creative destruction.

Even though Anglo-Saxon economies suffered a harder initial blow, the European continent is facing a dreaded situation of negative growth at -4% on average. European countries have room to maneuver in fiscal terms and therefore could supplement any stabilisation that may occur by at least 2%. Unfortunately, not all member states that have this option are choosing to do so.

A fiscal policy aimed at supplementing stabilisation would be a sound way to, first, restore bank lending, as this is at the heart of recovery. Banks should not only be supported by an approach that is negative to the taxpayer, (such as government guarantees) but also be subject to requirements of greater transparency. The aim would be to lend support to banks conditional on their readiness to lend again to business and people and their willingness to volunteer transparency on the pain of intervention by public authorities. Structural reforms and change should be the second priority of these fiscal packages, or else we may miss a unique opportunity afforded by these extraordinary fiscal efforts – such as an intelligent economy built on the recovery of public and private investments.

In turn, a more intelligent economy allows us to focus on completing the necessary efforts in the social infrastructure considering the very dynamics of the crisis, which is now developing into a social crisis. A final argument for a comprehensive response can be found in the fact that the crisis has radically altered socio-economic conditions companies and jobs which would have been perfectly viable under previous conditions now run the risk of being included in the list of economic fatalities.

A new policy mix should also address the political dilemma regarding the legitimacy of both national politicians and the European Union. It is possible for politicians to favour both safeguarding and creating viable jobs, despite accusations of protectionist policies. A possible measure is to utilise the internal flexicurity instruments such as time-sharing, work-in-training and wage moderation. Additionally, in the policy mix for employment a priority should be included to foster future job creation. Meanwhile, the monitoring of re-structuring should be adapted to ensure layoffs will be a solution of last recourse although, admittedly, European companies by and large are taking a quite responsible approach thus far.

LABOUR

The European Union can create more and better jobs, to begin with, in all sectors implicating a greener economy. This will have strong implications for the transport system, housing system and urban life. The IT sector is another area with great potential; the information revolutions are far from complete. A third example is business support to Small and Medium Sized Enterprises, this sector holds huge job potential particularly in personal services such as those in the health sector and services catering to the ageing population. Meanwhile, Europe can always play an important role in creating industries which will increase competitiveness across the board.

With due regard for the German economy, Europe, and China for that matter, may have to dial down the export expectations as the United States is no longer the consumer it once was. Still, we may ask whether there is a future for manufacturing in Europe. The car industry, for example, is quickly going to shift towards greener, high-quality products, supported by good customer service. Europe has the capacity and labour force to compete with Japan, the United States and China in this area.

In addition to creating and safeguarding jobs, protecting those people in precarious jobs or who are possibly facing unemployment, it is imperative to make sure these workers are not discriminated against in access to social protection. The current priorities adopted by the EU, such as active integration into the labor market, ensuring access to public services and utilising minimum income schemes, will be put to the test when we encounter extreme situations of social exclusion and poverty.

One idea is to use the Social Fund to introduce minimum income protection, particularly in the new and more vulnerable European member states, assuming older member states will not need them. This idea has elicited a debate on whether such a broad understanding and widespread cohesion is a realistic target for Europe. This debate is indicative of a basic dilemma, namely, do we move forward, furthering European integration in response to this crisis; or do we risk the crisis undermining European integration?

We have reached a very high level of interdependency in our economies. This implies that national policies no longer suffice to respond to a crisis such as this one, and must be complemented by stronger European policies. This is most apparent when it comes to financial supervision. The same applies to fiscal policies, because the impact of a fiscal stimulus reaches further than the nation-state if this is coordinated at a European level, and even more if it is coordinated in adherence to the same key priorities.

A new challenge is the role of industrial policies, because now we will have many governments trying to protect their companies and their jobs by providing state aids. This can challenge the single market as a whole as it can introduce a situation of unfair competition. State aids should comply with a clear common framework, while complemented by a European industrial policy. Rather than a protectionist industrial policy heavily reliant on old concepts, one could think of an active policy to support new activities, replacing or updating elements in each sector. Perhaps similar to the innovation policy, the framework would be conducive to conditions for companies to innovate and with obvious connections to research and education.

So far this is not the case, and what is at stake is not only the completion of the single market, but also the support required for European companies to become and remain competitive in global markets. Some decades ago, the main purpose of competition policy was to destroy barriers. However, now we should focus on another problem we are experiencing, which is the competition regarding our global counterparts. A merger of European companies could enhance their global competitiveness.

In the face of the crisis, the European financial instruments appeared limited. Nevertheless, there is an effort to speed up the structural funds to benefit areas beyond the realm of the EIB. However, the new instruments developed by the European Investment Bank are likewise limited by its lack of social capital. An alternative option is to speed up the community programs in regards to, for instance, competitiveness, innovation and employment, but there is still little money as the European budget is just around 1% of the EU GDP. Therefore, it became relevant to discuss new financial developments such as Eurobonds.

Perhaps they could improve the credibility of the proposal, just one of the many hurdles, in order to make it more acceptable. Eurobonds should be a possibility available to all member states. Additionally, Eurobonds should be used not to bail out the debts of the past but to finance investment programs for the future. Otherwise we will have a moral hazard in this instrument, because some member states would be paying for the debt of others. Therefore, the fiscal responsibility of an individual member state should be minimised, which would be ensured if the member states' budgets included guarantees. Ideally, a European agency would be charged with issuing the Eurobonds and reckoning with the national debt management structures.

TAKING STOCK OF THE LISBON AGENDA: FAILURES AND SUCCESSES

The crisis detracts from the targets of the Lisbon Agenda as formulated in 2000. The crisis therefore offers a crucial moment of pause to take stock of what has been achieved so far and to see how the agenda can be revisited in the face of the crisis. A challenge for Europe is designing these instruments that create these dynamic dimensions. In this light, it is interesting to revisit the Lisbon Agenda. An updated Lisbon Agenda can strike a new balance between competition, capacity building and sustainability and offset the neo-liberal interpretation that has dominated the process of European integration so far.

We are likely approaching a winning opportunity to launch these instruments, as the international financial markets are looking for alternatives to American bonds. The Chinese are buying gold to avoid being too reliant on American bonds, and they are questioning the role of the dollar as the reserve currency. In such a situation, offering a new instrument would be a timely and natural development of the Eurozone. The Eurozone is currently credible and sound enough to take this kind of step forward.

This is not the time for business as usual. There are choices to be made.

When this idea was first introduced, only a minority supported the idea of Eurobonds; now this has changed as more governments are supporting the idea, as well as many in the Commission. Eurobonds provide an excellent example of how European solidarity should tackle this crisis; otherwise we risk a huge setback prohibiting us from moving forward. This is not the time for business as usual. There are choices to be made to prevent forfeiting opportunities arising out of this crisis. One could, arguably, kill two birds with one stone: a sound financial instrument which will also forge European solidarity.

When the Lisbon Agenda was first conceptualised, we were facing intellectual debates where the central discussion was still between a neo-classical and a post-Keynesian school of economics. Some thought it would be important to overcome this dilemma by also looking at the underlying growth process, and that the discussion regarding macro-economic management was not the whole story; that this was a debate that needed to be overcome, especially in order to foster sustainable growth. We needed to look at the structural factors which were perhaps impeding growth and thereby identify the ones underpinning growth while emphasising the role of knowledge, which would ideally be accompanied by an institutional transformation regarding the transition to a knowledge-intensive economy.

With the new growth theories as a point of departure, we had to acknowledge their implications for economic and social policies. The aim was, first, to speed up the transition to an economy that would increase competitiveness on the one hand, but also social cohesion on the other, in order to overcome this traditional dilemma. The second priority concerned reforming the welfare states in Europe with developmental welfare systems. A third priority, which could complete the classical European agenda, was to create conditions for companies to compete and complete the single market agenda. Finally, the fourth priority was to have macro-economic policies able to support this structural change. That is why the content of public expenditure and the criteria for taxes matter so much. Finally, a fifth priority of increasing importance was added regarding the environment. Therefore, we should underline that our approach was combining the concerns with growth and innovation with the more recent concern with sustainability.

The crisis arguably led to a new theoretical synthesis between a comeback of Keynesian economics, for example the fiscal stimulus, combined with the requirement that we connect Keynesian theories to the other schools which emphasise the role of structural change. Perhaps this means emphasising the role of new technologies, but above all, of structural reforms and institutional transformation. Different national models can converge into a meta-model, which is suggested by the Lisbon strategy. Meanwhile, financial markets and corporate governance require a certain amount of re-regulation. The second remark to be made about the Lisbon Agenda is not to assume that the implementation of the Lisbon strategy was only to be based on the open method of coordination. From the outset, the implementation of the Agenda was to use all the available instruments: notably, community law, financial instruments, community programs and social dialogue.

Achievements thus far include the creation of a new strategic consensus in Europe, which is shared considerably by the main civil society stakeholders. A second achievement is that it was possible to launch a partial process of coordination of economic and social national policies, many of which were considered policies of national sovereignty. The third achievement was the re-orientation on some of these policies by some member states. The information society, however, clashes with social protectionism, as demonstrated in parliament policy, where they risk less research and innovation. Correspondingly, indicators revealed an average growth rate in Europe of 3% before the crisis, and net job creation was around 14 million, quite close to the 20 million target, including an increase in female employment. Of course, the level of achievement varied across the member states. Meanwhile, there was a new approach to policymaking, based on management of and learning by objectives.

The Lisbon Agenda intended to combine economic and social development. Even though we are far from that, Europe is still the only continent in the world which is the closest to these goals.

However, the central innovation and life-long learning policies were developing too slowly and differed among member states. It took a long time to understand what innovation policy was. There was a considerable amount of resistance to life-long learning trajectories. This requires radical change on the governance side in order to overcome a low level of ownership at either the national or European level.

Meanwhile, the level of commitment of the different Council formations varied as well. Employment policies appeared committed, however sometimes without a cohesive process of implementation. Other crucial Council formations were ineffective, such as the Competitiveness Council and the Education Council. Finally, inadequate communication played a large part in the failure of these policies; the biggest failure has been communicating about Europe in general.

Bear in mind that the Lisbon process went through different phases. At first, there was a strategy that was turned into an agenda, an operational program composed of hundreds of measures. Afterwards, this was also adopted by the new and future member states. Then a debate followed on how to connect the Lisbon strategy with the new European Treaty. A crucial discussion ensued on how to strengthen the financial instruments to implement the strategy which, by the way, had a rather disappointing outcome. Consequently, a debate was initiated regarding governance mechanisms and the need to launch national reform programs. Hence, the discussion turned to the external dimension of the EU, which was when other countries started to analyze the Lisbon Agenda. The Chinese, Russian and Indian governments are very aware of this European strategy, which allows for a very interesting set of interactions. Finally, energy and climate change were more explicitly acknowledged in these discussions and became an important focus of policy development.

The strategic goal of the Lisbon Agenda was not to create the most competitive economy in the world. It was, in fact, heavily influenced by the Nordic model, a long-term strategy which aimed to combine a high level of competitiveness with sustainable growth, more and better jobs, social cohesion and respect for the environment. In sum, the Lisbon Agenda intended to combine economic and social development. Even though we are far from that, Europe is still the only continent in the world which is the closest to these goals. This strategy becomes particularly relevant if one looks at the American model and recalls Obama's recent announcements regarding the health system and the American welfare system in general, and the cost of a greener economy. Likewise, in China they are announcing a more comprehensive social system especially focused on health care. In a sense, we are witnessing a unique historical opportunity to have a convergence of economic and social models. Admittedly, the differences will always remain, but still we can expect a certain convergence towards more balance in these continents.

It is interesting to see where Europe may serve as a role model for these countries. Europe's macro-economic fundamentals were stronger prior to the crisis, and the structure of the industrial specialisation is more balanced and diversified, except for the UK. The social model is the legacy of a long tradition of the welfare state in Europe and includes the role of public services, which arguably makes Europe better equipped to combat a crisis.

However, in view of Europe's ambivalent attitude towards the Lisbon Agenda and the prerequisite of consensus, European integration, or the lack thereof, may destabilise Europe and cause a serious setback. Therefore, Europe requires a stronger governance framework and stronger political leadership. So far several scenarios are imaginable; the worst-case scenario is a fragmentation of Europe, due to entrenchment and protectionist reactions by many member states. This would increase social tension and undermine the process of European integration. The best-case scenario is where a coordinated response to the crisis produces stronger European integration, as mentioned above. However, we cannot exclude a third scenario, which is a patchwork of other solutions; some member states bailing out other member states, some companies investing in other companies, but in an uncoordinated manner. In fact, these three scenarios are now taking place. The question is which should be the dominant one.

It is possible to discern two political agendas in these scenarios. One is a relatively new agenda arguing that we should now have a certain fiscal system to avoid an immediate catastrophe. This is limited insofar as it will burden future generations, which certainly warrants revisiting liberal inspired reforms. Another, unavoidable agenda is in favour of a stronger fiscal stimulus, which should be used for a deeper transformational process of our economies and societies.

As for an international agenda, it is true that the original idea of liberalism was to open up world economies at a pace deemed suitable by national economies to ensure political support. Welfare states had to reconcile external adjustment and domestic compensation, therefore not inward-looking but pursuing an international agenda. As the popularity of liberalism as well as neo-liberalism declines, the Lisbon Agenda does offer a political compromise between opening and deepening the single market. However, this process should be happening by strengthening the welfare system, combined with a special approach enabling people to deal with change, the political compromise.

In any case, this implies the assumption that standards could improve along with strengthening competitiveness, quite basic assumptions of the European model. However, an agenda like that cannot have success in Europe alone. It is in Europe's interest to have a certain international convergence in spite of the differences between these different models. Consequently, an interesting question arises, namely: can we converge in spite of our differences and on an international level? Once again, the crisis brings forth new scenarios of opportunity. Either we can have scenarios of protectionism, leading to a downward competition between capitalist systems, or the best-case scenario, to build a global governance framework to ensure an upward competition.

Nevertheless, it remains crucial to reform global governance in order to achieve such a framework for others to compete in an upward direction. Looking at the current agenda of the G20, I think that we have important elements of this framework already on the table, dealing with regulations of financial markets and coordinating the recovery plans, as well as aiming at providing new financial instruments to developing countries. A larger agenda for the next G20 summit can be expected, because we are bound to have the issue of trade and how to avoid protectionism, and also certainly the issue of climate change in the run-up to the Copenhagen summit. If you consider that, the main components of a new global deal may be on the table in September 2009.

It is no easy feat to negotiate a Global New Deal as a lasting solution to today's current crisis. It is important to pay due regard to sequence. Even though the G20 is not the end of the story, as representativeness and UN endorsement are crucial, the most effective sequence should start with coordinating recovery, activating banks and regulating the financial system, and conclude with an agreement on trade. Within this framework, the issue of climate change and agreement on the adoption of the decent work agenda must come up as well, but not as a starting point, as these issues are more antagonising than urgent. Meanwhile, this sequence should be accompanied by a major rebalancing of power between the main actors to ensure credibility. It is not realistic to ask Brazil or China to increase financial contributions to the IMF if they are not given more power on the board. This does indeed imply that European countries may have to give up seats as well.

The Quest for Vision

Helmut Schmidt

FORMER CHANCELLOR

OF THE FEDERAL REPUBLIC OF GERMANY

"The crisis hardly struck me as a surprise: for over a decade I had been writing articles warning of the weaknesses in the international financial markets. I had been trying to draw attention to the dangers of using derivatives as financial instruments and had written a great deal on predatory capitalism. To me, it was clear that the dangers in the financial markets were growing. But few seemed willing to take such warnings to heart.

"Looking back, we have missed an important window of opportunity: the spectacular failure in 1998 of the prototypical American hedge fund and brainchild of Robert C. Merton, Long Term Capital Management Fund (LTCM). Its collapse was followed by a massive bailout, following the too-big-to-fail logic which features so prominently during this crisis. It was at that moment that many more people began questioning the stability of the financial sector. This triggered fierce debate, including one between Alan Greenspan, William J. McDonough, then respectively chairman of the Federal Reserve and President of the Federal Reserve Bank of New York, and myself. They advocated bailing out the LTCM fund, claiming that given its size, allowing it to fail would trigger a domino effect of failing funds, firm, and banks. Although I understood this risk, I argued that it would be better to let this organisation fail and serve as a warning to other companies of the dangers of excessive risk-taking.

"The bailout set the trend of saving financial firms to prevent a chain reaction. Although a successful strategy for preventing economic damage, the logic of bailouts masked the fundamental instabilities of the financial system. And so the financial industry was effectively sheltered from the consequences of their own risk-taking for an entire decade. This logic finally broke down with the decision to let Lehman Brothers collapse in 2008. This indeed triggered a global financial crisis, but on a far grander scale than the collapse of LTMC could possibly have caused a decade ago. Had they allowed it to collapse, the current crisis could have been prevented at the cost of relatively marginal economic costs. The Federal Reserve missed the opportunity to eradicate systemic weaknesses before they became ingrained."

The economic crisis brought to light the dangerous extent to which national economies have become globally interwoven. This far-reaching interdependence not only caused the economic crisis to spread quickly across the globe, but will simultaneously be one of the biggest hurdles during the crisis recovery period.

Large and small countries alike are profoundly dependent on world markets for their economic survival. Germany epitomises this reality; in 2007, exports as a percentage of GDP were up to nearly half of all domestic production. Although the majority of this was exported within the European Union, a large share also went outside of the Union, further increasing Germany's vulnerability to markets over which it can exercise little control. Germany is certainly not alone in this regard. Many other countries, the Netherlands included, have become equally export-dependent.

The spirit of internationalism and the motivation to tackle global problems are very thin.

Even the largest economic powers have not been immune to a creeping dependency on international markets. As well as being heavily reliant on imported foreign oil, the United States depends on foreign credit for its growth and consumption. Both of these requirements make it extremely vulnerable to what happens elsewhere. Foreign creditors such as China and other countries in East Asia have grown increasingly essential to the survival of the US system. The US debt to China puts them in an extremely dangerous position. If an antagonistic government came to power in Beijing and put China's American government bonds on the market, the US may never be able to recover. This is a point often forgotten in analyses of the crisis, that politics and economics are inseparably linked. Relations between superpowers such as the US and China are never solely economic.

In turn, China itself is also addicted to foreign markets. This has been made painfully clear since the present crisis, as up to 30 million Chinese workers have lost their jobs. While China's national policies may have played some role in this, it was primarily the result of their reliance on exporting companies for employment. The manifest outcome of this interdependence is that every country has become devastatingly susceptible to even minor fluctuations in global markets. Ideally, this realisation would lead to increased economic cooperation between countries, but this has hardly been the case. Yes, there have been outward shows of unity and coordination – for example in the G20 meetings – but these have not translated into real cooperation. Instead, leaders returning from summit meetings go back to their day-to-day operations, focusing exclusively on further-ing their national interests. The spirit of internationalism and the motivation to tackle global problems are very thin.

One of the principal reasons for this lack of cooperation has been the absence of any theoretical framework to guide it. In that respect, the past also offers little guidance. Of course, the current economic crisis has much in common with the crisis of the 1930s, but the interdependencies of the international economic sys-tem makes today's crisis fundamentally different. The 1930s was a crisis for the West only; it did not spread globally because countries were not as dependent on each other. Because of their relatively greater national autonomy in the 1930s, countries were able to put into place their Keynesian recovery plans. The way the United States and Germany quite effectively rekindled their economies would be impossible under today's circumstances. Roosevelt's policies worked on the premises of relatively closed national economies. In today's globally entangled economic systems, the rules of crisis management are fundamentally different, and people struggle blindly to create these new rules.

The only theory we have at hand at the moment is one that has crowded out all others over the past decades: the idea of free trade. Although this has been ap-plied diligently in the European Free Trade zone, the North American Free Trade area, and Mercosur, the theory is fundamentally unsatisfactory. There are no rules for monetary transactions or movements of capital. Free trade is a very, very narrow doctrine and certainly cannot explain how the collapse of a handful of rotten banks in the US brought down the Southeast Asian economies, halfway around the world. We have no theory to grasp such events, let alone manage or prevent them. Nor do we have any firm idea what types of institutions our global economy requires in order to avoid them. Even the highest-level Nobel Prize winning economists over the past few decades have produced no satisfactory work in this regard. Most of what they write is superfluous, full of mathematical formulas and modelling, leaving no room for the key ingredient of human psy-chology and emotionality.

Admittedly, free trade and global economic interdependence may have caused marvels of economic growth, but they have left the global economy exceedingly vulnerable, as economic integration has lurched ahead with no theory to guide it. The economic crisis has led people to slow down and think about these funda-mental problems.

SHORTCOMINGS OF THE EU

Being part of the entangled global world, Europe faces all of the problems men-tioned above. Its biggest concerns and problems are, however, entirely of its own making. Although they were not generated by the economic crisis, these self-inflicted shortcomings will make it very difficult to implement effective recovery measures.

The unanimity requirement of the European Union is the most serious of its predicaments.

The unanimity requirement of the European Union is the most serious of its predicaments. Ever since the European project was conceived in 1952 as a union of coal and steel, unanimity has been idolised. Right through the Treaties of Rome and Maastricht, which eventually expanded the Union to its current size, this requirement was upheld against practical wisdom. In this way, the European Union has emasculated itself, rendering effective action next to impossible. As a consequence, the Union as an institution can focus its actions only on changing minor bureaucratic rules. Thirty years ago Henry Kissinger complained that he didn't know what phone number to call to talk to 'Europe'. Today, this problem is still present, and even exacerbated: with 27 members, Europe has 27 voices, and 27 phone numbers for Kissinger's successors to call. Even with the Lisbon Treaty, unanimity will still be required in 72 different policy areas.

It follows that the European Council is a deeply flawed institution. In a situation in which each of the 27 Council members have equal voting rights and the right to veto, striking power is sorely lacking. In addition, they are nominated rather than elected, with the result that the Council is generally filled with unaccountable diplomats rather than with popularly engaged politicians. This is highly problematic. As the legislative branch of the EU, the European Council is the only body able to initiate action, it lacks legitimacy and the capacity to do so. The European Parliament (EP), on the other hand, is a democratically elected representation, yet they have no power to appoint Council members or to control their actions. It is an institutional deadlock. Given the weaknesses of the European Council and the EP, in order to effectively address a problem like the current economic crisis, Europe would do well to create a new institution such as a European Economic Government to help govern the economy of the Eurozone.

The only element of the EU that is working successfully is the European Central Bank (ECB), albeit purely by grace of the fact that politicians are unable to talk their way into its operations. The ECB is unique among central banks in that it covers 15 countries that all share a single currency, yet it is fully independent of politics. This is not the case anywhere else in the world. In the US, Canada, Japan, or China, central banks are politically accountable. Of course, this is a very jeopardous construction. Although the current structure prevents the Bank from being hijacked by political interests, the success of the ECB depends almost exclusively on the capacities of its directors. To date we have been lucky; directors such as Wim Duisenberg and Jean-Claude Trichet have simply done a very good job, issuing nearly flawless monetary policy.

EUROPE: WHERE TO?

At the moment, the question Europe, quo vadis? is certainly highly relevant. In the post-crisis period, we heard many voices that claim crude capitalism has failed. Another popular credo is that welfare state economies have historically earned their spurs and therefore should be reconsidered as the most viable model. In fact, this is a rather simplistic interpretation of our current condition. 'Welfare state economy' is a term that does not provide a radical alternative for the capitalist modus that has brought us the crisis.

In reality, welfare state countries such as the Netherlands, Germany, and France utilise an economic structure that is generally three-tiered. First, the private sector, including manufacturing and industry, in principle operates well and along the lines of an open market in which actors are primarily profit-driven. At the other end of the spectrum stands the tier of covering the terrain of social expenditures. This includes people living on state pensions, social security, and parent or child benefits. This sector is significant. In Germany, for example, for every 100 employed Germans, 25 live on pensions that are partially state-funded. Add to this the share of the population fully dependent on social benefits. It is a sector that, in effect, is separated from the market economy. In between these two areas lies the third: the public corridor. This covers government production and employment and includes public works (such as waterworks in the Netherlands or the German motorways) as well as educational facilities such as schools and universities. It works similarly to the private sector, except that the state, rather than private buyers, commissions the projects. Thus, these economies are neither crude capitalist nor pure welfare states. The social sector, which was largely set up in the second half of the 20th century expressing Europe's social orientation, is certainly not capitalist. Through it, these countries sustain peace and survive politically by providing directly for their citizens. They are certainly not the profit-driven machines like the City of London or Wall Street in New York, which people imagine when they think of capitalism.

Yet welfare state countries are extremely dependent on capitalist market systems because of the importance of their private sector. Just as in the rest of the world, this sector has become increasingly globalised, making these countries heavily dependent on imports and exports. Although European countries with colonial pasts are accustomed to this model, many are undergoing dangerously rapid transitions. When I was in office, Germany's exports were at 22% of GDP, but by 2007, they had ballooned to 47% of GDP. It is therefore idealistic to claim that welfare state systems have triumphed over crude capitalism, as welfare states are simply heavily dependent on capitalist systems. Fixing the economy is therefore not a matter of choosing the right model, but starts with recognising the hybridity of our modern European welfare states. This recognition warrants no other conclusion but that institutional regime change has to be effective at the level of the global free market as well as at the level of the welfare state and the corridor in between.

LACK OF LEADERSHIP

The most harrowing obstacle to post-crisis recovery is lack of leadership – a worrying deficit both in Europe and for the global community. Europe suffers from a lack of grand ideas and – perhaps even more detrimentally – a lack of visionary protagonists who further the European project. We are hard pressed to find equivalents of people like Churchill and De Gaulle today. Traditionally, the European cart was pulled by a Franco-German axis, in which France proved to be the most consistent and crucial engine propelling European integration. This role was personified by iconic figures such as Jean Monnet, Robert Schumann, Giscard d'Estaing and Jacques Delors. The heirs to the European project, unfortunately, have little of the drive to act in concert that characterised their predecessors. European leaders of today are primarily concerned with national interests, a problem that is heightened in times when global circumstances so ardently call for an internationally orchestrated response.

The structural flaws of the EU make this deficit even more acute, as it is nearly impossible for leadership to fully take wing in a context of 27 member states competing for influence within the framework of the European institutions. When the Union was more limited, even smaller countries like the Netherlands could be significant agents of change. In addition, since the fall of the Soviet Union, Europe has lost its common enemy and its sense of purpose in unifying the EU. Previously, countries had stuck together also out of fear, but now this force is gone.

At the same time as Europe suffers from a leadership crisis, the international community faces perhaps an even greater deficit of leadership. In the context of the economic crisis, there is an urgent need for management of the globalisation process in order to achieve recovery. The US is no longer positioned to lead alone, and although joint leadership between the US and China might be ideal, their distrust of one another is so deep that such an alliance is unlikely to emerge. Until Bush, the US saw the Chinese as communists and distrusted them on this basis. Those preconceptions wear away only slowly. The Chinese, in turn, are surrounded geographically by the US military – in South Korea, Japan, Kazakhstan, Uzbekistan, the Pacific, India, and the Indian Ocean. The recent US operations in Afghanistan and Pakistan and its threats against Iran will intensify this distrust.

> *Europe suffers from a lack of grand ideas and – perhaps even more detrimentally – a lack of visionary protagonists who further the European project.*

There are two regions that may be able to step forward by 2050 and assume some sort of leading role. First, India, with its booming economy and highly educated population, may emerge as an important international power. Second, Muslim countries, although currently under weak and divided leadership, may be able to unify themselves into a coalition with a global leadership capacity. They control the bulk of the world's oil, yet have historically been treated appallingly by Western countries, specifically by the US. Because the strongest leadership in many of these countries is often religious, it is feasible that religious leadership could unify them.

On a global scale, little leadership can be expected from the EU. Even in response to the economic crisis, they have not found the unity to overcome their numerous institutionalised hurdles to effective action. They are too bogged down in their own problems to lead internationally. At this critical juncture, however, the need for new ideas and new directions stands undiminished internationally. The economic crisis has demonstrated the interconnectedness and vulnerabilities of the globalised economy in a way never before imagined. This interdependent global economy must be complemented with a leadership body capable of commanding the legitimacy to influence it. If Europe is to make a step towards commanding part of that role, it first has to overcome its internal problems. This requires a willingness to see the crisis as an opportunity for structural reforms and, above all else, the courage and capability to translate this into a new European concept.

Rekindling the Spirit of Cooperation

Jacques Delors

FORMER PRESIDENT OF
THE EUROPEAN COMMISSION

"I had voiced my recurrent concerns about pre-existing economic instabilities long before the fall of Lehman Brothers triggered the current economic crisis. These concerns began at the end of my presidency of the European Commission in 1995. In various meetings, bankers and other partisans of economic innovation explained to me that an increase in share prices meant the creation of additional wealth. This puzzled me, as it seemed to be a fictitious way of measuring increased wealth. The mirage could only be upheld with clever strategic tricks, for example, companies would reduce their numbers of shares so as to lower the dividends. For me, this was a sign that finance dominated the economy. It was also an indication of how different the growth of the past decades had been from the growth Europe experienced during les trente glorieuses, *which was based on real economic growth. I expressed this concern in the 1993 White Paper to the European Commission, entitled "Growth, Competitiveness and Employment", which was accepted by the Commission but did not prompt a close scrutiny of the economic facts.*

"A second economic factor that puzzled me were the incredible rates of revenue generated in the financial industry each year. Even after the dot-com bubble burst at the end of the 1990s, which should – in theory – have affected revenues, the financial industry continued to measure annual growth rates of up to 15 percent. This was, of course, nearly impossible, as even those involved in this industry were forced to admit. Nevertheless, these rates were taken at face value by many and became false indicators of economic vitality.

"Once I had fully grasped these two structural irregularities, they prompted me to critique principles underlying the Washington Consensus. Of course, in my role as president of the European Commission, I also advocated competition and the free flow of financial traffic, as was illustrated by my endeavours to create a single European market. However, in pursuing this goal, I had foreseen very different outcomes than the unconditional embrace of free trade and deregulation that in fact emerged. This development illustrates a proverb from the political sciences: "Power devoid of regulation leads to abuse." This aptly captures what happened when the powerful instrument of breaking down trade

barriers and deregulating markets was stripped of any form of control and turned into an unquestionable maxim.

"Whether Europe will emerge from the crisis very much depends on cooperation between member states on both economic and financial issues. I have always pledged for a true balance, inside the EMU, between the monetary side (the independent ECB) and the economic side (by a real coordination of national macro-economic policies). However, the spirit of open discussion and cooperation was rarely dominant in the Council of the Finance Ministers. This explains the fragmentation of the European reaction to the current crisis."

FROM GROWTH TO THE CREATION OF VALUE

The roots of the crisis lie in a global paradigm shift in political economy which began in the early 1980s. This shift is expressed by three macro-economic changes. First, the traditional link between salary and productivity was broken. Up until the 1970s, the financial reward for work was based on real output. However, with the advent of neo-liberal economic principles, these factors were no longer necessarily linked. It should be noted that this trend was often politically encouraged; many countries established policies of reducing the cost of labour. The effects of severing the link between salary and real output is most prominently visible in the financial sector, where the creation of inflated value by clever manipulation of new assets was rewarded with huge bonuses.

The welfare state has been a useful counter-force to the crisis.

This trend was paired with a shift towards new growth drivers: the innovations in the financial industries and in real estate business. The ability to generate almost limitless wealth in these sectors was not explained by any notable economic theory. Nevertheless, over time the practices became accepted in the writings of influential economists. From there, it was further legitimised, as these growth drivers were incorporated into conjectural analyses.

The third macro-economic shift is constituted by accommodating monetary policy and deregulation, which heightened the effects of the aforementioned trends. Normally, these three factors combined would eventually have proven unsustainable. However, an endogenous phenomenon gave them an extra lease on life, as a sudden increase in oil prices and the prices of other raw materials drove up both demand as well as speculation. This prompted yet another cycle of inflated profit-seeking. Given their radical effects in perpetuating this economic binge, the exact effects of the change in the price of oil and raw materials warrant further investigation.

This economic regime had various adverse effects. The gains that were possible under this regime were exploited to the fullest extent on both sides of the Atlantic. Most notoriously in the United States and the United Kingdom, but countries such as Ireland and Spain also reaped the short-term gains, leading to massive housing bubbles that recently have come to haunt them. At the same time, the astounding GDP growth measured during this period actually mostly benefited the higher income tiers.

The economic crisis compounds problems of European integration.

There are, luckily, also reasons for optimism. What immediately becomes apparent is that the welfare state (which was created before the war in Nordic states, but post-war in much of the rest of Europe) has been a useful counter-force to the crisis. Despite the fact that centrist and right-wing governments presently control many European states, this historical by-product of European social democratic governments remains strong and has saved Europe from further catastrophe in the wake of the crisis.

A LACK OF SPIRIT OF COOPERATION

The European project has always been driven by two central ideas. The first was the idea of reconciliation. After the war, it became imperative to bring European nations back together, and specifically to promise future generations of Germans that they would eventually be re-integrated into the European framework. These motivations were important drivers of the European project in the beginning. However, with the passage of time and the influence of new generations, this initially pressing imperative has naturally declined in importance. The second factor, however, has continued to remain relevant; Europe, at many points in time, has been faced with a choice between downfall and survival. European integration was a means for the individual European countries to remain competitive with the various global economic and technological innovations over the past 40 years, most of which have originated outside of Europe.

Although these two historical driving forces of European integration differ radically, they were underpinned by the same spirit of cooperation and solidarity. Within this framework of cooperation and solidarity, competition between European states – joined together by a single market – is the final premise of European dynamics. Europe functions best on the basis of this tripartite structure: competition which stimulates, cooperation which reinforces, and solidarity that unites. Presently, however, cooperation and solidarity are sorely lacking, and as a result, competition is all that remains.

This implies that, in retrospect, European integration has not played out as was hoped. Among the protagonists of the European integration, the hope was widely shared that economic and monetary union would be conducive to cooperation and solidarity. It was hoped that economic and monetary cooperation would naturally be followed by social dialogue. Unfortunately, this latter stage never emerged. From this perspective, the European Union has not been a success.

The economic crisis now compounds these problems of European integration. Once again, this juncture brings Europe to a choice between downfall and survival. In order for the outcome to be survival, cooperative and unified anti-crisis measures must be undertaken. Take, for example, the measures to aid Europe's struggling automobile industry. Ideally, member states should have ensured that car premiums were the same across borders, but even such minimal cooperation seems unattainable. In addition, the crisis should be used as an opportunity to enhance cooperation and cohesion between the European finance ministers, but they too seem reluctant.

Europe functions best on the basis of this tripartite structure: competition which stimulates, cooperation which reinforces, and solidarity that unites.

The crisis, in fact, reveals another limitation of European integration: the emphasis on the technocratic over the political. The challenges the crisis brings cannot be met with the purely technical instruments provided by Europe's institutions. Enhancing the political dimension is direly needed. This calls for an increasing the role for the European Parliament, and an important role for the general affairs council in close cooperation with the European Commission. That means that the Commission's right of initiative must be respected and enhanced.

This imbalance between technocracy and politics is the result of maintenance long overdue. To use a blunt analogy: Europe is like a car with splendid design, but once the hood is lifted it is revealed that the motor does not work. Many had expected that a political Europe would automatically follow an economic and monetary Europe, but such a process cannot occur by itself. A politicisation of Europe is something that requires inspired and visionary politicians that believe in the benefits of an integrated Europe. Alas, such foremen seem presently in short supply.

This said, it would be wrong to attribute Europe's shortcomings solely to a lack of leadership. Public opinion is no longer favourable towards Europe, and the number of people who consider themselves 'European' is dwindling. To a large extent this is due to the fact that Europe has not taken the time to redefine itself as it grew larger. In other words, Europe has gone through a process of enlargement without deepening. This lack of a pronounced identity has, for many citizens, made Europe a rather frightening entity. Looking back, Europe squandered many opportunities to redefine itself, choosing instead to plunge forward into the next round of enlargements – with the accession of Britain, the former Mediterranean dictatorships, and finally the countries previously behind the Iron Curtain.

This does not mean that Europe completely lacks substance and identity. In fact, Europe is one of the few places in the world that has created a set of adequate institutions in answer to the processes of globalisation. It has a sophisticated combination of both nation-states and supranational institutions to deal with these challenges. Indeed, it is telling that, for example, southeast Asian countries and MERCOSUR look to Europe as an institutional model. Yet this comparative advantage could certainly be communicated more vividly to the European public. It is a pity how little Europe has managed to rally its assets in the face of the current crisis.

THINKING BEYOND GDP

For Europe to maintain its status in a globalising world, there are a plethora of challenges that must be met. First of all is the task of redefining the indicators that are used to judge the quality of society. The crisis has made it clear that the focus on GDP and added value is not sufficient. This does not mean that the indicator of GDP should be discarded as a whole, but that it should be supplemented with social indicators and stock statistics on capital, wealth, and the environment. Embracing these different indicators would imply a move towards economy of lower growth and smaller salaries, which would nevertheless be presented and perceived as successful, because of its wealth in other areas such as the environment and leisure. While such a shift may be desirable even for its own sake, it may also have become unavoidable. The great burden of public debt and shifts in the global allocation of labour may make a shift to a more sober economy the only alternative.

The problem of public debt – the inevitable consequence of the crisis – is augmented because of demographic pressures. Between 2007 and 2030, the European Union will see its working population decrease by at least 20 million people, while the number of Europeans aged 65 and over will increase by 40 million. These demographic upheavals are likely to severely hamper growth from reaching its pre-crisis levels. In addition, this will further complicate European cooperation and solidarity as each country will experience slightly different consequences of this demographic shift. Also, the unwinding of public debt puts cooperation under further pressure. With, for instance, Germany adopting a more rapid debt-reduction program than the others, tension within the economic and monetary union is increased. Europe runs the risk of experiencing a rift between those countries that will just 'let go' and those who practice more budgetary restraint.

In order to meet these challenges, Europe must go beyond mere monetary and economic union. Despite hopeful claims to the contrary, this much needed politicisation should not be expected to come solely from Germany and France. The idea that these two countries can single-handedly lead Europe to lift itself by its own bootstraps is, quite simply, irrational. Specifically, the early member states should step up to share this leadership role, most notably the Benelux countries. While this may, on the surface, appear to be euro-nostalgia, in fact it may be the only way to revitalise the European vision.

Towards a New Agenda

Ben Knapen

We predict the future every day; we have no choice. We often get it wrong, but wrong predictions are also part and parcel of expectations. In fact, some predictions have been so spectacularly wrong that they actually brought the unfortunate writer eternal fame: British economist and politician Norman Angell was the author of *The Great Illusion*. He argued that worldwide economic integration had made war futile, counterproductive, and outdated – something of the past that mankind had overcome. Published in 1910, this book was a huge success, and ironically became even more successful after the Great War.

But financial and economic crises have a logic all of their own. If pundits predict a crisis, it does not happen. Instead, heeding these warnings, consumers, manufacturers and public authorities anticipate and respond. In so doing they break the chain of events leading to a crisis. The foundations shift, and the prophecy becomes self-defeating. Therefore, only the luminaries who go against the current to predict such crises are remembered. The Nouriel Roubinis of this world deserve all the credit they get, yet their number must necessarily be very limited; they are a few lone stars in an otherwise dark sky.

However, this is not to say that nobody saw it coming. Take, for instance, the doorman at the HeyJo club in Jermyn Street in London, who knew something was amiss as far back as 2005. In this well-known club frequented by young bankers, you did not have to be a Roman Abramovich at that time to casually knock back a few bottles of champagne costing 20,000 pounds apiece. It became a common occurrence on every payday. The doorman concluded in 2005 that this could not last. How much weight does a doorman's opinion carry in the world of shares, futures, and derivatives? Too little, as we now know.

But it nags. The public would like to have managers, experts and researchers it can trust and rely upon. In turn, these professionals ask the public to have confidence in their position and expertise. Recently, however, the basis for such confidence has come under question. All the contributors to this book noticed some of the early warning signals, but responded to them in different ways. The imbalances in the world had been recognised and analyzed years ago, and most agreed and were fully aware that they were untenable in the long term. Recognising symptoms, though, is different than diagnosing a crisis. Perhaps the feelings of bankers are best summed up by Stephen Roach, Chairman of Morgan Stanley Asia. He told us that he did indeed feel that something was seriously wrong: the data displayed increasing, worrisome imbalances. Yet things continued to progress smoothly. So, from time to time a little doubt crept in. Is my analysis correct? Did I miss something? Every time, Roach came back to the same conclusion that something was indeed very seriously wrong. But self-doubt, however small, always undermines your choice of words, and determination, when warning the broader public about things to come.

Looking at it from a slightly different perspective, commentators have noted that people were too eager to drink the 'Kool-Aid of success'. It was uncomfortable to be a non-believer in the recent market miracles, and as a result, dissident views were not likely to be heeded or brought to the fore. The success of unfettered markets and the strength of their ideological underpinnings blinded academics and policymakers alike. With the crisis, these blindfolds were violently removed.

WHAT DO WE SEE NOW?

If nothing else, economists will be going through a long period of sobering up. The theory of efficient markets operated by rational actors was the dominant intellectual economic paradigm from the early 1980s onward. It led to a refinement of macro-economic models and gave economics the aura and authority of an exact science. It yielded a spectacular series of Nobel Prize winners who performed pioneering work in the mathematisation of economic behaviour.

The crisis has disposed of this dogma. Human behaviour, informational inconsistencies, and irrationality must be reintroduced to economic thinking. The discipline of economics will have to shed its 'hard science' pretentions and accept its role in the 'social sciences'. It will have to become more modest, too. This is easier said than done – an entire generation has been brought up to believe in the concept of the efficient market. Institutions will continue to cling to this concept, and a paradigm shift will be more difficult than recent revelations would justify, especially since alternative constructs are not readily available.

The excesses of deregulation have hit society hard. Public institutions and authorities matter; in fact, they have proven to be indispensable. Nobody expects the demise of the free market system, but we are witnessing the passing of the neo-liberal ideology that went along with it – at least insofar as that ideology can be defined as a system of beliefs that steers towards a desired credible outcome. This ideology elevated the free market to the status of an ultimate goal and an enlightened ideal, rather than one of many possible *means* by which society can increase its prosperity and well-being. The crisis seems to have debunked this ideology: the free market is now seen as a means rather than an end. Re-establishing the rules of the game and the relationship between the market and the public authorities has returned to the top of the political agenda. Even free market zealots have been forced to concede that, if not government, then at least governance has a role to play in the economy.

Nevertheless, recent state interventions have been characterised by great uncertainty. Although politicians appear resolute in their statements, there is little popular enthusiasm backing up this new activism. Legitimacy for state intervention in a post-modern intellectual world is hard to come by, at least in the Western world. In America, anti-etatism is part of the national identity. In Europe, national governments are constrained by interdependencies, which restrict their room for manoeuvre and undermine their authority. To date, this has left Europe lacking the self-confidence it requires to implement new, sustainable arrangements.

This lack of self-confidence is not new, but has been a longstanding and nagging question. The populations of the Western world have long been uneasy about globalisation and the emergence of Asia. While those at the top always used to welcome these developments as win-win situations, large sections of the middle class feel more and more uncomfortable about the prospect of worldwide competition, outsourcing, the pressures on wages, and, in the case of Western Europe, on the welfare systems. In this regard, the financial crisis may also be considered a wake-up call for everyone; the seat of economic vitality is shifting from West to East, and everyone will have to deal with it in one way or the other. Despite the setbacks incurred by countries such as China and India since the crisis, they are emerging relatively stronger from this drastic readjustment of global weight and influence. The West still has a technological lead, but the global factory of China is rapidly catching up, and a country such as Germany has every reason to be worried by this development. Larger, more powerful competitors are now beginning to challenge its traditional post-war dominance in industrial innovation. Kuwaiti sheiks who bought share packages in Daimler-Benz 25 years ago were considered an exotic curiosity; the mere suggestion in the spring of 2009 that Chinese investors might consider taking over Opel was considered a downright threat.

In addition, the position of the dollar as the global reserve currency is likely to be called into question as US political, financial, and industrial hegemony begins to slip. It won't happen overnight, but we may be witnessing a gradual transition. However, it remains to be seen what currency will supplant the dollar. The supporters of global governance are advocating the development of a new IMF reserve currency, but the expansion of global governance in itself is equally contested. Moreover, the ownership of a global reserve currency holds considerable advantages. America has benefitted from this for decades, and China may discover similar benefits in the long run.

Prospects are also coloured by the uncertainty in discerning new potential growth drivers. The economic crisis of the late nineteenth century was left behind because of growth generated by electrification and industrialisation. Following World War II, a new middle class emerged, and growth was driven by durable consumer goods. The fallout from the crisis in the 1970s and 1980s was cushioned by growth generated by the ICT revolution. Where will the next growth impulse come from? The expansion of the Chinese middle class may lead to increased global demand, and improved education and training in the US may raise the productivity and prospects of the lower-middle class. But these changes are probably insufficient. Despite a host of new ideas and technologies, the source of the next great boost to demand remains unrevealed. People hope that a Green New Deal or developments in biogenetic technology will provide breakthroughs, but the appeal of these idealistic possibilities cannot overshadow the fact that growth drivers significant enough to counteract the current recession have yet to be found.

The crisis may bring about a certain degree of de-globalisation. Many experts predict a re-nationalisation of the financial sector. Banks will be placed under the stricter supervision of national authorities, backed up by the power of the national government and the taxpayer. The reduced investments that would ensue would be a justifiable price to pay for greater financial stability, some argue. That is what we are witnessing now. It remains questionable to what extent states will be able and will go forward with re-embedding other parts of the economy nationally. The fact that the economy is deeply interlinked with technology and cultural globalisation makes economic processes very resistant to governmental attempts to reform the system on a national level these days.

Governments need operational authority and the power to address the social consequences of the crisis. Many experts in this volume refer to the increasing inequality manifested both at the national and the global levels. Within states, certain groups are disproportionately affected, such as people with limited pension resources, the young, the unemployed, those with high mortgages, and young entrepreneurs with few financial safeguards. Internationally, those affected include poor countries with limited export varieties and those with an emerging middle class. Unemployment in urban areas will push many into poverty, including large sectors of the population that only recently migrated away from rural life and became dependent on wage income.

These inequalities force national governments to act, and globally, they call for even more profound measures. Development economist Nancy Birdsall argues for nothing less than a new global social contract. The economic crisis exposed the misconception that globalisation is synonymous with global deregulation. In fact, global governance is vital to globalisation, yet it also poses the greatest challenge. One may argue that G20 meetings illustrate the fact that there is at least a beginning of an awareness of the need to devise a legitimate global governance mechanism. Realistically, organisations such as the Bank for International Settlements, the IMF, and possibly the World Bank should play a vital role in such a process. Creating legitimate global governance will also require – though this will be far more difficult – an acknowledgement by Western countries that the world has changed and that emerging countries must be included. Only with emerging countries on board as full partners can an authoritative and effective system of global governance be created that clearly defines the global playing field. The question of whether the globalisation wave of the past two decades will continue to progress into the future or recede into the past will depend primarily on the skills of the world's most important governments. They must overcome their vested interests and readjust all of the post-war systems of global governance – from Bretton Woods to the UN Security Council – to represent the changed equations of wealth and power in the world.

History teaches that such changes are hardest for receding hegemons. For them, these changes involve a long and bitter farewell to privilege, status, and power. The process also poses real challenges for emerging countries. While they all agree on the need to reconstruct multilateral organisations, emerging countries still have no plan for how to cope with or how to implement these new global responsibilities. How can these changes be achieved effectively in order to reflect the new dynamics of international relationships? How can old and new parties play a role in this process? Examples of smooth transitions are rare in history. At this stage of the proceedings, experts advocate vision and statesmanship. While it is hard to disagree with such prescriptions, asking for leadership and vision usually masks underlying uncertainties. Currently, only some vague outlines of an intellectual framework for such a change are slowly beginning to emerge, and they are occasionally supplemented by a brilliant idea or two. More than this has not been forthcoming.

WHERE DOES ALL THIS LEAVE EUROPE?

This volume is devoted to a diagnosis of the crisis and initial steps towards searching for an institutional response. The United States is a prominent force in this respect, both materially and institutionally. This applies far less to Europe. Even though in Europe's economy, demography, and market size outstrip everyone else in the world, Europe exists only in part as an institution. In global organisations, it usually acts in a fragmented manner. When the recession took hold, Europe had already been engaged in its own institutional crisis for some time, and many claim that it was more than that – that it was a real and fundamental identity crisis. Dreams of a single Europe were gone, the European Union had become too large to generate mutual solidarity among its members, and the many member states were actually divided on a host of subjects or were no longer prepared to impart any more sovereignty. Where does Europe stand now following its experience with a serious financial crisis?

There has been a bright side. The European Union proved to be a blessing at the height of the financial crisis. The euro had a calming influence, and the consultation mechanisms worked. Agreements were reached when they were necessary. Leaders and officials sat together, improvised, and achieved admirable results in the days of the emergencies.

It has also become quite clear where the system has its shortcomings and needs improvement. The European Central Bank needs greater supervisory powers. Furthermore, the monetary union may not be able to flourish in the long run without European taxes and debt instruments, making a European Economic Government an additional imperative.

Going even a step further, it could be concluded that Europe needs a new social contract. The Lisbon agenda is too much of a globalisation agenda, and 'Brussels' has been forced into the role of custodian of the free market, appearing as a representative of an ideology rather than a mechanism to enhance social and economic values.

At the same time, these desiderata have an air of weariness about them. People are increasingly distrusting of Europe, and national politicians are following their wary lead. In the words of Dominique Moïsi, the European project is said to have only half-hearted pragmatic supporters and fervent opponents, and both consider 'Brussels' to be a sort of bureaucratic no-man's land.

Europe is afflicted by the destructive myth of *Les Trente Glorieuses*: the 30 post-war years in which towns and villages were rebuilt, people worked hard, families stayed together, and social stability and security could be created. The growth figures were comparable to those of modern-day Asia, and there was a demographic vitality – the word 'ageing' never came up.

Of course, this image of that period is myth. Not because these images are all wrong, but because it is now being conceptualised in a framework of familiarity, cosiness and happiness that does not do justice to the burdens of those days. The hardships have been glossed over, and all that remains is the image of a lost golden age. Nevertheless, the myth of *Les Trentes Glorieuses* is very much alive. It is rhetorically positioned in stark contrast to the present, which for many years has been characterised by what Mark Elchardus refers to as a 'culture of discontent', conceptualised by the media and exploited by populists.

Europeans may have benefited greatly from integration – and from globalisation for that matter – but at the same time they also experience it as a threat. The middle class is no longer convinced that the next generation will have a better life than they did, and feel they must walk on eggshells in order to safeguard their prosperity and social security. This sentiment manifests itself in a variety of ways, but there is an overarching trend of clinging to one's own national context, in other words, to the politics of identity.

At the same time, European integration and interdependence, globalisation, and the free market concept have diminished the room for manoeuvre, authority, and legitimacy of national governments – in some member states more than in others, however.

Consequently, anyone envisaging the return of the state in the European Union after the financial crisis must immediately ask: Which state? The nation-state or Brussels? For the time being, the first scenario seems the most likely, as the member states are taking care of their own banks and are breaking up international banks in order to manage these interventions at the national level. However, the jury is still out on whether the wishes of states to handle such matters are in line with their resources and capacities. This too will vary from one member-state to the next.

It is doubtful whether the financial crisis will instigate further European integration. Europe is a project that will be difficult to continue in the face of a pessimistic outlook on the future or a general lack of self-confidence. It is a project that requires a certain amount of self-assurance and conviction. Indeed, there is a commonly shared conviction at the moment that no final goal for the European project – no European ideal – can or should be agreed upon, which illustrates the extent to which the project is currently in keeping with the pessimistic spirit of the times.

Nevertheless, anyone looking from the outside cannot avoid concluding that, as André Sapir put it, Europe is becoming a smaller place in a bigger world. Member states such as France and Great Britain continue to cling to their permanent seats on the United Nations Security Council. Can anyone imagine that this will have any relevance in 2025 if they have not managed to speak on behalf of Europe (or even better, to exchange those two seats for one European seat?) Can anyone imagine the International Monetary Fund still having any relevance if the chairman is still being chosen from one of the European member states?

The financial crisis was still not a wake-up call for Europe. It did, however, show that the notion of mutual dependency exists and, therefore, that there is a willingness to compromise. The desire for new structures and exciting new initiatives, on the other hand, was proven to be lacking. It still is. Shifting global centres of gravity and a new generation in Europe may offer a new opportunity – the 'culture of discontent' need not be hereditary. Before this can happen, a new narrative and a new intellectual framework will be needed. This is missing at present, but a few potentially interesting building blocks are coming into sight – let us call them the unreaped rewards of a credit crisis.

Overview of the Interviews

Date and Location	Interviewee	Interviewers
18 May, Brussels	Mark Elchardus	Anton Hemerijck & Ellen van Doorne
25 May, The Hague	André Sapir	Anton Hemerijck & Ellen van Doorne
27 May, Amsterdam	Amy Chua	Ben Knapen & Casper Thomas
28 May, Cologne	Fritz Scharpf	Anton Hemerijck & Casper Thomas
28 May, Brussels	Maria João Rodrigues	Anton Hemerijck & Casper Thomas
4 June, Hamburg	Helmut Schmidt	Ben Knapen & Casper Thomas
6 June, The Hague	David Soskice	Anton Hemerijck & Ellen van Doorne
8 June, Louvain	Paul de Grauwe	Anton Hemerijck & Casper Thomas
15 June, The Hague	Dani Rodrik	Anton Hemerijck & Ellen van Doorne
18 June, London	Tony Atkinson	Anton Hemerijck & Casper Thomas
19 June, London	Anthony Giddens	Anton Hemerijck & Casper Thomas
19 June, London	Willem Buiter	Anton Hemerijck & Casper Thomas
22 June, Madrid	Stephen Roach	Anton Hemerijck & Ben Knapen
24 June, Athens	Loukas Tsoukalis	Anton Hemerijck & Casper Thomas
25 June, Amsterdam	Dominique Moïsi	Ben Knapen & Jessica Serraris
29 June, Cambridge, MA	Suzanne Berger	Anton Hemerijck & Ben Knapen
30 June, Cambridge, MA	Peter A. Hall	Anton Hemerijck & Ben Knapen
1 July, Washington	Amitai Etzioni	Anton Hemerijck & Ben Knapen
1 July, Washington	Nancy Birdsall	Anton Hemerijck
2 July, Cambridge, MA	Charles Maier	Anton Hemerijck & Casper Thomas
3 July, Berkeley	Barry Eichengreen	Anton Hemerijck & Casper Thomas
7 July, Paris	Jean-Paul Fitoussi	Anton Hemerijck & Casper Thomas
10 July, London	Richard Sennett	Anton Hemerijck & Katherine Tennis
2 September, Paris	Jacques Delors	Anton Hemerijck & Casper Thomas

Biographies of the Interviewees

TONY ATKINSON

Sir Tony Atkinson is a Fellow of Nuffield College, Oxford, and currently F. W. Taussig Research Professor at the Department of Economics, Harvard University. Previously he held positions at Cambridge University, the London School of Economics (of which he is an honorary fellow), University College London, and MIT. Meanwhile, Atkinson also holds honorary doctorates from many European universities, has served as president of the European Academic Association, the International Economic Association, the Econometric Society, and the Royal Economic Society, as well as being an honorary member of the American Economic Association.

Atkinson was editor of the *Journal of Public Economics*. He is also a member of the Research Council of the European University Institute in Florence, and of Section 37 of the *Comité National du CNRS* in France, as well as chairman of the Foundation for International Studies in Social Security. He has been a member of the *Conseil d'Analyse Economique*, advising the French Prime Minister from 1997 until 2001.

His most recent work discusses problems of economic inequality and social distribution of income in the European Union, as well as social security and public finance. Atkinson is one of the most authoritative voices on income distribution, having developed an inequality measure, the Atkinson Index, which allows for ascertaining developments in different segments of the distribution of income. His work includes *Income Distribution in OECD Countries* (1995), *Incomes and the Welfare State* (1996), and *Social Indicators: The EU and Social Inclusion* (2002).

SUZANNE BERGER

Suzanne Berger is Raphael Dorman and Helen Starbuck Professor of Political Science at the Massachusetts Institute of Technology, director of the MIT International Science & Technology Initiative, as well as of the MIT-France program, and currently also a member of the Committee of the Minda de Gunzburg Center for European Studies at Harvard University. Berger has served as Vice President of the American Political Science Association and as founding Chair of the Social Science Research Council Joint Committee on Western Europe. She is also the former chair of the Political Science Department at MIT. Berger has been elected to the American Academy of Arts and Sciences and was named a chevalier in France's Légion d'Honneur.

In 2005, Berger completed a five-year study by the MIT Industrial Performance Center, consisting of case studies of more than 500 international companies, analysing failing as well as succeeding practices in the global economy and forging a new line of thought in the debate on globalisation and becoming one of the world's leading academics on the dynamics of economic and political process and globalisation.

Professor Berger's key works are *How We Compete* (2006), *Peasants Against Politics, The French Political System, Dualism and Discontinuity in Industrial Societies* (with Michael Piore), *Organising Interests in Western Europe* (1981), and *National Diversity and Global Capitalism* (1998 with Ronald Dore).

NANCY BIRDSALL

Nancy Birdsall is founder and president of the Center for Global Development. She formerly served as director of the Economic Reform Project at the Carnegie Endowment for International Peace and executive vice-president of the Inter-American Development Bank. At the IDB, Birdsall oversaw the management of a $ 30 billion public and private loan portfolio. Before that, Birdsall was director of policy research at the World Bank. She currently serves on the board of Accion and the Per Jacobsson Foundation, and as special advisor to the administrator of the United Nations Development Program.

Birdsall has written extensively about global development, economic inequality, income distribution, global governance, and global public goods.

Her recent publications include *The White House and the World: A Global Development Agenda for the Next US President* (2008), *Fair Growth: Economic Policies for Latin America's Poor and Middle-Income Majority* (with Augusto De La Torre & Rachel Menezes – 2007), and *The Distributional Impact of Privatisation in Developing Countries* (with John R. Nellis – 2005).

WILLEM BUITER

Willem Buiter is a professor of European Political Economy at the London School of Economics and Economics professor at the University of Amsterdam. Previously, he taught International Macro-economics at Cambridge Univer-sity and held the position of Trippe Professor of International Economics at Yale University. Alongside his teaching positions, Buiter currently serves as a research associate for the Center for Applied Macro-economic Analysis at the Australian National University, a senior research associate of the Financial Markets Group at LSE, as well as an associate editor for the *Journal of Financial Economic Policy.*

Previously, Buiter chaired the Council of Economic Advisors of the Lower House of the Dutch Parliament, was Chief Economist at the European Bank for

Reconstruction and Development, and an external member of the Monetary Policy Committee of the Bank of England. He was a member of the Council of the European Economic Association, the Royal Economic Society and the EMAC Panel of Independent Advisors. Meanwhile, Buiter has also served as a consultant in both public and private financial institutions in Latin America, Asia, and Central and Eastern Europe.

Buiter's books include *Financial Markets and European Monetary Cooperation: The Lessons of the 92-93 ERM Crisis* (with Giancarlo Corsetti & Paolo Pesenti – 1998), *International Macro-economics* (1990), *Principles of Budgetary and Financial Policy* (1990), *Macro-economic Theory and Stabilisation Policy* (1989) *Budgetary Policy, International and Intertemporal Trade in the Global Economy* (1989).

AMY CHUA

Amy Chua is the John M. Duff Jr. Professor of Law at Yale Law School. Prior to teaching at Yale, she was a visiting professor at Duke Law School, Columbia, Stanford, and New York University. Before Chua embarked on a teaching career, she was a corporate law associate at a private firm and clerked for Chief Judge Wald in the Washington, D.C. Court of Appeals. Chua specialises in international business, law and development, ethnic conflict and globalisation.

Chua's most recent book, *Day of Empire: How Hyperpowers Rise to Global Dominance – and Why They Fall* (2007), argues that the success of major empires may depend on their tolerance of minorities. *World on Fire: How Exporting Free Market Democracy Breeds Ethnic Hatred and Global Instability* (2004), a New York Times bestseller, studies ethnic conflicts in various societies caused by disproportionate economic and political influence of so-called 'market dominant minorities' and majority-supported ethno-nationalist movements, fuelled by globalisation and democratisation.

JACQUES DELORS

Jacques Delors was president of the European Commission from 1985 to 1995. Under his presidency, the Economic and Monetary Union was formed and established by the Treaty of Maastricht in 1992. He gave new impetus to the process of European integration by speeding the completion of the Single Market and strengthening the social and political dimension of the European project. He had previously been the French Minister of Finance. In 1996, Jacques Delors founded the research institute Notre Europe and is today its founding president. In May 2000 he was appointed president of the CERC (*Conseil de l'emploi, des Revenues et de la Cohésion Sociale*) until July 2009.

BARRY EICHENGREEN

Barry Eichengreen is George C. Pardee and Helen N. Pardee Professor of Economics and Professor of Political Science at the University of California, Berkeley, where he has taught since 1987. He is a Research Associate of the National Bureau of Economic Research (Cambridge, Massachusetts) and research fellow of the Centre for Economic Policy Research (London, UK). In 1997-98 he was Senior Policy Advisor at the International Monetary Fund. He is a fellow of the American Academy of Arts and Sciences.

Professor Eichengreen is the convener of the Bellagio Group of academics and economic officials, and chair of the Academic Advisory Committee of the Peterson Institute of International Economics. He has held Guggenheim and Fulbright Fellowships and has been a fellow of the Centre for Advanced Study in the Behavioural Sciences and the Institute for Advanced Study. He is a regular monthly columnist for *Project Syndicate.*

He was awarded the Economic History Association's Jonathan R.T. Hughes Prize for Excellence in Teaching in 2002 and the University of California at Berkeley Social Science Division's Distinguished Teaching Award in 2004. He is also the recipient of a *doctor honoris causa* from the American University in Paris.

Eichengreen's recent publications include *The European Economy since 1945: Coordinated Capitalism and Beyond* (2008), *Globalising Capital: A History of the International Monetary System* (2008), and *Global Imbalances and the Lessons of Bretton Woods* (2006). His forthcoming book, *A Tale of Two Depressions,* will build on a recent article he published under the same name with Kevin O'Rourke.

MARK ELCHARDUS

Mark Elchardus is a professor of Sociology at the Free University of Brussels, Belgium, and the director of the research group *Tempus Omnia Revelat* (TOR). His main research interests include cultural sociology, sociology of time, politics, and democracy. He has done research on the modern development of opinions, attitudes, and feelings, including the role played by education, the voluntary sector, and media.

He is widely published, having written over 250 articles, chapters and reports. He is the editor of 13 books and the author of 16. His key works include *De Symbolische Samenleving* (2002) and *De Dramademocratie* (2002).

AMITAI ETZIONI

After receiving his PhD in Sociology from the University of California, Berkeley, Amitai Etzioni served as a professor of Sociology at Columbia University for 20 years, serving part of that time as the Chairman of the department. He was also a guest scholar at the Brookings Institution before serving as a Senior Advisor to the White House on domestic affairs from 1979-1980. In 1980, Etzioni was named the first university professor at George Washington University, where he is the Director of the Institute for Communitarian Policy Studies. He has also recently been awarded the Meister Eckhart Prize by the Identity Foundation, in collaboration with the University of Cologne in Germany.

In the 1990s, Etzioni served as the president of the American Sociological Association and was the founding president of the International Society for the Advancement of Socio-Economics. In 1990, he founded the Communitarian Network, a not-for-profit, non-partisan organisation dedicated to shoring up the moral, social and political foundations of society. Meanwhile he served as editor of *The Responsive Community: Rights and Responsibilities*, the organisation's quarterly journal, from 1991-2004.

Two of his most notable books are *The Active Society* (Free Press, 1968) and *Security First: For a Muscular, Moral Foreign Policy* (Yale University Press, 2007).

JEAN-PAUL FITOUSSI

Jean-Paul Fitoussi is Professor of Economics at the *Institut d'Etudes Politiques*, Paris, and chair of the Scientific Committee there. He is also a professor at Luiss University in Rome. He is currently president of the *Observatoire Francais des Conjonctures Economiques*. Fitoussi is also a board member of the *Fondation Nationale des Sciences Politiques*. Fitoussi publishes regularly in French and foreign media, while also acting as managing editor of the *Revue et Lettre de L'OFCE*, contributing editor of the *International Journal of Development Planning Literature, International Labor Review, Critique Internationale and the Journal of Development and Globalisation* (Berkeley Electronic Press). Fitoussi's research focuses on inflation and unemployment theories, foreign trade, macro-economic policy, especially on the roles of economic integration and transition.

Fitoussi has regularly contributed to economic policy debates. He is a member of the Prime Minister's Council for Economic Analysis, of the *Commission Economique de la Nation*, expert consultant to the Economic and Monetary Committee of the European Parliament and has been secretary of the International Economic Association (1984-2008). Prior to that, he was Chairman of the Economic Council of the European Bank for Reconstruction and Development (1990-1993). Fitoussi has been director of Telecom Italia since 2004.

Fitoussi has received various awards and honours, including the *Association Francais de Sciences Economiques* Award, the Rossi Award from the *Academie des Sciences Morales et Politiques* and the decorations of *Officier de l'Ordre National du Merite* and *Chevalier de la Legion d'Honneur*. In 2008, The International Economic Association created a 'Jean-Paul Fitoussi' Lecture.

Recent working papers include *Europe in 2040: Three Scenarios* (with Eloi Laurent, 2009) and *The Ways Out of the Crisis and the Building of a More Cohesive World* (with Joseph Stiglitz, 2009). He has published a number of books, such as *La nouvelle écologie politique, Economie et développement humain* (2008) and *The Slump in Europe: Reconstructing Open Macro-economic Theory* (with Edmund S. Phelps, 1988).

ANTHONY GIDDENS

Lord Anthony Giddens is currently an emeritus professor at the London School of Economics. Giddens was director of the LSE from 1997 to 2003, before which he taught at Cambridge University, where he co-founded the Social and Political Sciences Committee. Besides teaching, Giddens served as a member of the Advisory Council for the Institute for Public Policy Research, launched *Polity Press* and contributed to the think-tank Policy Network.

Throughout his academic career, Giddens has introduced some of the most innovative and influential theories in sociology pertaining to methodology, structure, and the modern state of global, political and private dynamics.

Known as a vocal proponent of the Third Way, Giddens has been consulted by Tony Blair and Bill Clinton, among others, and continues to advise the British Labour Party, now from the bench of the House of Lords.

Some recent publications include *The Politics of Climate Change* (2009), *Runaway World: How Globalisation Is Reshaping Our Lives* (2000), and *The Third Way: The Renewal of Social Democracy* (1999).

PAUL DE GRAUWE

Paul de Grauwe is professor of International Economics at the University of Louvain, Belgium. After obtaining his PhD from Johns Hopkins University, he worked as a trainee at the European Economic Community before embarking on a teaching career, starting at his alma mater, followed by visiting professorships at, among others, the University of Michigan, the Wharton School of Business and the Freie Universität Berlin. De Grauwe is also *Doctor Honoris Causa* at the universities of Sankt Gallen and Genoa, as well as the Turku School of Economics and Business Administration in Finland.

De Grauwe has served as a consultant to the Centre for European Policy Studies and the European Central Bank. He currently sits on the economic advisory panel to José Manuel Barroso, the current president of the European Commission. From 1991 to 1995 and from 1999 to 2003, he served as senator for the Belgian Liberal and Democratic Party. He has held a seat in the Belgian parliament for the same party.

De Grauwe's research focuses primarily on international monetary relations, monetary integration, analyses of foreign exchange markets and open-economy macro-economics. He contributes to a wide selection of academic journals and writes regularly for the *Financial Times*.

His various books are not only praised for their insight but also their accessibility. They include *The Economics of Monetary Union* (2007), *The Exchange Rate in a Behavioural Finance Framework* (with Marianna Grimaldi – 2006), 'Gains for All: A Proposal for a Common Euro Bond' in *Intereconomics* (with Wim Moesen – 2009), and 'The impact of FX central bank intervention in a noise Trading Framework' in the *Journal of Banking and Finance* (with Michel Beine & Miranna Grimaldi – 2009).

PETER A. HALL

Peter A. Hall is Krupp Foundation Professor of European Studies and was formerly the director of the Minda de Gunzburg Centre for European Studies, both at Harvard. Hall has also been Associate Dean of the Faculty of Arts and Sciences, chair of the ACLS-SSRC Committee on Western Europe, and president of the Comparative Politics section of the American Political Science Association. He is co-director of the Successful Societies' Program of the Canadian Institute for Advanced Research, and a member of the advisory boards of the European Research Institute in Birmingham, at the Free University in Berlin, and until recently the Max Planck Institute for the Study of Societies in Cologne. Hall has been a Fellow for the Center for Advanced Study in the Behavioral Sciences at Stanford University, and of the *Wissenschaftskollege zu Berlin*, as well as a visiting scholar at the London School of Economics, the *Centre de Sociologie des Organisations* in Paris, the *Instituto Juan March* in Madrid and the *Wissenschaftszentrum*, Berlin.

Hall's research, focusing on the methods of social science, political responses to economic challenges in post-war Europe and the institutional context for public policymaking, has appeared in numerous academic journals and books. His work has garnered several awards, including the Woodrow Wilson award for the best book published in political science in 1986, the Luebbert award for the best article in comparative politics, the Alexander George award for studies in methodology, and the Aaron Wildavsky and Burton Gordon Feldman awards for contributions to the study of public policy.

His recent works include *Successful Societies: How Institutions and Culture Affect Health*, edited with M. Lamont (2009), *Changing France: The Politics that Markets Make*, edited with P. Culpepper and B. Palier (2004), and *Varieties of Capitalism: The Institutional Foundations of Comparative Advantage*, edited with D. Soskice (2001).

CHARLES MAIER

Charles S. Maier is Leverett Saltonstall Professor of History at Harvard University. Previously, he served as director of the Minda de Gunzburg Center for European Studies, as chair of the Committee on Degrees in Social Studies, and as Krupp Foundation Professor of European Studies, all at Harvard. In 2008 he was a visiting *Directeur de Recherche* at the *Ecole des Hautes Etudes en Sciences Sociales.* He was previously a professor of history at Duke University and visiting professor at the University of Bielefeld.

Maier has held an Alexander von Humboldt Research Prize, a John Simon Guggenheim Memorial Fellowship and a National Endowment of the Humanities fellowship. In 1999, he was awarded the Commander's Cross of the German Federal Republic (*Grosse Bundesverdienstkreuz*). He has chaired selection committees for the American Academy in Berlin and the American Academy in Rome, and is currently a member of the Council on Foreign Relations and the American Academy of Arts and Sciences.

Maier is best known for comparative studies of 20th-century Europe which focus on the political, economic and social history as well as historical analyses of the Cold War and trans-Atlantic relations. His most recent book is *Among Empires: American Ascendancy and its Predecessors* (2006).

DOMINIQUE MOÏSI

Dominique Moïsi is the Pierre Keller visiting professor at Harvard University's Department of Government, a professor at the College of Europe in Natolin, Warsaw, as well as a professor at the Institute d'Études Politiques in Paris. Moïsi is also the founder and Senior Advisor at the French Institute for International Relations.

Feeling equally at home in Europe, America, and Asia, Moïsi is a popular geostrategic thinker who also contributes regularly to journals and newspapers, including exclusive monthly commentaries to *Project Syndicate.*

In 2009, his latest book, *Geopolitics of Emotions*, was released in Europe and the United States.

STEPHEN ROACH

Stephen Roach holds a PhD in economics from New York University and is currently the chairman of Morgan Stanley Asia, a leading global financial services firm. He has held this position since April 2007, prior to which he had been Managing Director and Chief Economist of Morgan Stanley for 16 years. He is recognised as one of Wall Street's most influential economists and has been named the most widely read analyst in the world by First Call, the largest electronic distributor of Wall Street research.

Prior to joining Morgan Stanley in 1982, he worked as a research fellow at the Brookings Institution in Washington DC, on the research staff of the Federal Reserve Board in Washington DC, and was the Vice President for Economic Analysis for the Morgan Guaranty Trust Company in New York.

His recent research has focused on globalisation, the emergence of China, corporate restructuring, productivity, and the macro paybacks of information technology. His work has appeared in academic journals, books, congressional testimony and on the op-ed pages of the *Financial Times*, the *New York Times*, the *Washington Post* and the *Wall Street Journal*. His books include *On the Next Asia: Opportunities and Challenges for a New Globalisation* (2009) and *Debt Capital Markets in China* (with Gao – 2007).

MARIA JOÃO RODRIGUES

Maria João Rodrigues is currently the Special Advisor on the Lisbon Agenda for the European Union and a professor of European Economic Policies at the Institute for European Studies at the *Université Libre de Bruxelles* and at the Lisbon University Institute (ISCTE). She is also a member of the Governing Board of the European Policy Centre in Brussels, a member of the Board of Notre Europe in Paris, and member of the Council of the Institute for Strategic and International Studies in Lisbon.

Rodrigues has been deeply involved with the Lisbon agenda, acting as coordinator of the Lisbon European Council and of the action line of the Portuguese Presidency of the European Union in 2000, and as president of the Interministerial Commission on the Follow-up to the Lisbon Strategy for the Council of Ministers' Presidency in Portugal from 2001-2003, and again from 2003-2004. She has also held a variety of positions in the European Commission and other European Union bodies, as well as having worked in different capacities for the United Nations.

She is the author of over one hundred publications, mainly on Portuguese and European affairs, including *European Policies for a Knowledge Economy* (2003) and *Europe, Globalisation and the Lisbon Agenda* (2009).

DANI RODRIK

Dani Rodrik is a professor of International Political Economy at the John F. Kennedy School of Government at Harvard University. He has published widely in the areas of international economics, economic development, and political economy. His research focuses on what constitutes good economic policy and why some governments are better than others at adopting it. His most recent research is concerned with the determinants of economic growth and the consequences of international economic integration.

He is affiliated with the National Bureau of Economic Research, Centre for Economic Policy Research in London, Center for Global Development, Peterson Institute for International Economics, and Council on Foreign Relations. He was awarded the inaugural Albert O. Hirschman Prize of the Social Science Research Council in 2007. He has also received the Leontief Award for Advancing the Frontiers of Economic Thought, an honorary doctorate from the University of Antwerp, and research grants from the Carnegie Corporation, Ford Foundation, and Rockefeller Foundation. He is editor of *Review of Economics and Statistics*, and associate editor of the *Journal of Economic Literature*.

His most recent book is *One Economics, Many Recipes: Globalisation, Institutions, and Economic Growth* (2007) and he is also the author of *In Search of Prosperity: Analytic Narratives on Economic Growth* (2003).

ANDRÉ SAPIR

André Sapir is a professor of Economics at the *Université Libre de Bruxelles,* where he holds a chair in International Economics and European Integration. He is also a Senior Fellow at the Brussels European and Global Economic Laboratory (BRUEGEL) think tank, and a research fellow at the Centre for Economic Policy Research (CEPR). He holds a PhD from Johns Hopkins University.

He is a member of European Commission President Jose Manuel Barroso's Economic Advisory Group and worked for the European Commission for 12 years prior to 2005. From 2001 until 2004 he was Economic Advisor to President Romano Prodi. During this time, he was the Chairman of the High-Level Study Group that produced the 2003 report 'An Agenda for a Growing Europe', also known as the 'Sapir Report'.

Book titles include *Fragmented Power: Europe and the Global Economy* (editor and co-author – 2007), *Market Integration, Regionalism and the Global* (co-editor with Richard Baldwin, Daniel Cohen & Anthony Venables – 1999), while articles include 'A European Recovery Programme', in the *Bruegel Policy Brief* (with Jean Pisani-Ferry and Jakob von Weizsäcker – 2008) and 'What Economic and Social Model for Europe? A Debate with Philippe Herzog' (*Centre d'Analyse et de Prévision*, Paris, 2008).

FRITZ SCHARPF

Fritz Scharpf is the Director Emeritus of the Max Planck Institute for the Study of Societies in Cologne, Germany. Previously, he was the director and a research professor at the International Institute of Management and Administration of the *Wissenschaftszentrum* in Berlin.

He studied law and political science at the Universities of Tubingen, Freiburg, and Yale, obtaining his LLM Masters degree in law from Yale, and his doctorate from the University of Freiburg. He has taught at Yale Law School and the University of Konstanz.

His research interests include organisational problems and decision processes in government, multi-level governance in Germany and the European Union, applications of game theory, and comparative political economy of welfare states. He sits on the editorial board of the *Journal of European Public Policy* and the *European Law Journal.*

His work has been widely published and includes *Games Real Actors Play, Actor-Centered Institutionalism in Policy Research* (1997) and *Governing in Europe: Effective and Democratic?* (1999).

HELMUT SCHMIDT

Helmut Schmidt was elected the fifth Chancellor of the Federal Republic of Germany in 1974, and he held this position until 1982.

He studied Economics and Political Science at Hamburg University. During this period he became a committed Social Democrat and was elected chairman of the Socialist German Students' League in 1947. In 1949 he began work for Hamburg's Department of Economics and Transportation. He was elected to the Bundestag in 1953, and held a variety of positions before he became defence minister in 1969, economy and finance minister in 1972, and finally was elected Federal Chancellor in 1974.

As Chancellor, he established plans, together with the French President Giscard d'Estaing, to form the European Monetary Union. In 1979 he participated in the 'Summit of the Four' with Giscard d'Estaing, US President Jimmy Carter, and British Prime Minister Robert Callaghan.

Since resigning from the Bundestag in 1986, Schmidt's economic and foreign policy opinions have been widely published, and he is co-publisher of *Die Zeit.*

RICHARD SENNETT

In his own words, for better or for worse, Richard Sennett embarked on an academic career after his successful musical career under the stewardship of Pierre Monteux was waylaid by a hand injury.

Sennett attended the University of Chicago and Harvard University, receiving his PhD in 1969. He then moved to New York where, in the 1970s, he founded The New York Institute for the Humanities at New York University, with Susan Sontag and Joseph Brodsky. In the 1980s, he served as an advisor to UNESCO and as president of the American Council on Work; he also taught occasionally at Harvard. In the mid-1990s, Sennett began to divide his time between New York University and the London School of Economics. In addition to these academic homes, he maintains informal connections to MIT and to Trinity College, Cambridge University.

Some of his key works include *The Corrosion of Character: The Personal Consequences of Work in the New Capitalism* (1998) and *The Culture of the New Capitalism* (2005). His latest book is *The Craftsman* (2008).

DAVID SOSKICE

David Soskice is currently a research professor of Political Economy at Oxford University and Senior Research Fellow at Oxford's Nuffield College. He is also a research professor in the Political Science Department at Duke University, as well as being a research professor at the *Wissenscharftszentrum für Sozialforschung Berlin* (WZB). Previously, he held the position of School Centennial Professor at the London School of Economics and has held visiting positions at Harvard, Yale, the *Scuolo Superiore di St. Anna* in Pisa, and the University of Wisconsin at Madison, among others.

He has served on the *Conseil Scientifique* (CEREQ) since 2006 and is a member of the Max Planck Institute for the Study of Societies in Cologne. In addition, he has been a member of the editorial board for the *European Journal of Industrial Relations* since 1995 and for *Labour: Review of Labour Economics and Industrial Relations* since 1987.

His research focuses on varieties of capitalism, comparative political economy, macro-economics, and labour markets. His most recent books include *Varieties of Capitalism and Macro-economic Institutions* (2005) and *Macro-economics: Imperfections, Institutions and Policies* (2006), written with Wendy Carlin.

LOUKAS TSOUKALIS

Loukas Tsoukalis has been a special adviser to the President of the European Commission since April 2005. He is also the Jean Monnet Professor of European Economic Organisation at the University of Athens, the president of the Hellenic Foundation for European and Foreign Policy (ELIAMEP), and a visiting professor in the European General Studies Department at the College of Europe.

He was born in Athens, Greece, and studied economics and international relations at the University of Manchester and the College of Europe in Bruges, obtaining his doctoral degree at the University of Oxford.

His previous appointments include: visiting professor at Sciences Po, Paris; professorial fellow, Robert Schuman Centre, European University Institute, Florence; professor at the European Institute of the London School of Economics and Political Science; director of European Economic Studies, College of Europe, Bruges; president of the Administrative Council and Direct of the Hellenic

Centre for European Studies (EKEM), Athens; university lecturer and fellow of St. Antony's College, Oxford; ambassador and special adviser for EC affairs to the Prime Minister of Greece.

He is the author of many books and articles on European and international affairs, including *The New European Economy* (1997) and *What Kind of Europe?* (2005).

Biographies of the Editors

ANTON HEMERIJCK

Anton Hemerijck was employed at the Scientific Council for Government Policy from 2001 to August 2009, first as deputy director, and from 2003 on as director. Presently, he is Dean of the Faculty of Social Sciences of the Free University, Amsterdam. Anton Hemerijck has held teaching and research positions at, amongst others, MIT, the Max Planck Institute for the Study of Societies in Cologne, Leiden University, Antwerp University, and Lisbon University. Before joining the Free University, he was professor of Comparative Analysis of the European Welfare State at the Erasmus University, Rotterdam.

Anton Hemerijck studied Economics in Tilburg, the Netherlands. In 1992, he obtained his doctorate in political science at Oxford for his dissertation, supervised by Colin Crouch, entitled *The Historical Contingencies of Dutch Corporatism.* His key publications include *The Dutch Miracle* (with Jelle Visser) and *Recasting Europe in Welfare States* (with Martin Rhodes and Maurizio Ferrera – 2000). In 2010, Oxford University Press will publish his latest monograph, *In Search of a New Welfare State.* In addition to his academic career, Anton Hemerijck has advised the European Commission and various national governments on issues of European social policy.

BEN KNAPEN

Ben Knapen is a historian and a Council Member of the Scientific Council for Government Policy. He also holds a chair as Professor of Media Quality and Ethics at Radboud University, Nijmegen. Previously, he was a foreign correspondent in Germany, the United States and southeast Asia. He has held the positions of editor-in-chief of the Dutch national newspaper *NRC Handelsblad,* Senior Director of Corporate Communication, Marketing and Institutional Affairs at Philips and, until 2006, a member of the Board of Management of PCM publishers.

ELLEN VAN DOORNE

Ellen van Doorne studied Political Science and International Political Economy at the Universities of Amsterdam and Sussex and graduated in 1995. Afterwards, she entered the Dutch diplomatic service. Her first assignment was at the China desk of the Dutch Ministry of Foreign Affairs. She then served in the economic department of the Dutch Embassy in Berlin. In 2001, she entered the Dutch Ministry of General Affairs, first as deputy-secretary of the Cabinet and assistant foreign policy advisor, and later as advisor for the Dutch EU Presidency in 2004. Since March 2005, she has been strategy advisor at the same ministry.

The editors were assisted by the following team at the Scientific Council for Government Policy:

KATHERINE TENNIS

Katherine Tennis is a research fellow at the Scientific Council for Government Policy. She is also a Master's student at Leiden University, where she is studying International Relations and Diplomacy. Prior to this, she attended McGill University in Canada, where she received a Bachelor's degree in International Development Studies.

JESSICA SERRARIS

Jessica Serraris is a research fellow at the Scientific Council for Government Policy. She holds a degree in European Studies and American Studies from the University of Amsterdam. She won the International School for Humanities and Social Studies (ISHSS) prize for her Bachelor's dissertation, and was a finalist for the Faculty prize for European Studies with her Master's dissertation.

CASPER THOMAS

Casper Thomas is a research fellow at the Scientific Council for Government Policy. He holds a Masters degree in European History from University College London. He is also a freelance contributor to the *De Groene Amsterdammer*, a weekly magazine on arts and current affairs.